Ethnicity and Democratisation in the New Europe

Edited by Karl Cordell

London and New York

First published 1999
by Routledge
11 New Fetter Lane, London EC4P 4EE

Simultaneously published in the USA and Canada
by Routledge
29 West 35th Street, New York, NY 10001

Typeset in Baskerville by Routledge
Printed and bound in Great Britain by Creative Print and Design (Wales)
Ebbw Vale

British Library Cataloguing in Publication Data
A catalogue record for this book is available from the British Library

Library of Congress Cataloguing in Publication Data
Ethnicity and Democratisation in the New Europe/edited by Karl Cordell.
Includes bibliographical references and index.
1. Democracy – Europe. 2. Democratization – Europe. 3. Ethnicity –
Europe. 4. Europe – Politics and government – 1989 – . I.
Cordell, Karl.
JN12.E75 1998   98–27618
323. 1'4'09049–dc21   CIP

ISBN 0–415–17311–6 (hbk)
ISBN 0–415–17312–4 (pbk)

For Tadek

Contents

PART II
Contemporary case studies

Contributors

Agneza Bozic has studied in both Yugoslavia and the United States. She is currently completing her doctoral programme on the nature of the Yugoslav crisis, and has published a variety of articles and papers on aspects of the Yugoslav wars of succession.

Adam Burgess teaches in the Department of Sociology at the University of Kent. He is the author of *Divided Europe: The New Domination of the East*, and is currently writing a critique of the process of democratisation in Eastern Europe since 1989.

David Chandler is currently completing PhD research on democratisation in Bosnia at the International Social Policy Research Unit in Leeds and teaches Post-war East European Development at the University of Northumbria.

Karl Cordell is Senior Lecturer in Political Science at the University of Plymouth. He has written a variety of academic texts on topics which include inter-state relations in Germany, the nature of *Die Wende* of 1989–90, the role of the Evangelical Church in Germany, the nature of German national consciousness today, and the German minority in contemporary Poland. In 1995 he founded the Political Studies Specialist Group on Ethnic Minority Politics, of which he was convenor until 1997. He is currently engaged in long-term research on Poland's entry into the European Union.

Chris Gilligan is a doctoral student at the Department of Politics and Contemporary History at the University of Salford. He is a regular contributor to *Political Studies* on the politics of Northern Ireland, and together with Jon Tongue edited *Peace or War? Understanding the Peace Process in Northern Ireland*, which was published by Ashgate in 1997.

Montserrat Guibernau is Senior Research Fellow at the Centre for Research in Ethnic Relations at the University of Warwick and has also taught at the Universidad Autonoma of Barcelona. Her numerous publications in the area of nations and nationalism include: *Nationalisms: The Nation-State and Nationalism in the Twentieth Century* (Polity Press), and *The Ethnicity Reader* (Polity Press) which was written together with John Rex.

Stuart Horsman is based at the University of Sheffield and is currently researching into minorities, security and Islam in Kazakhstan and Uzbekistan, and has published on the Tajik civil war.

Boris Jesih was born in Maribor in 1956 and gained his Master's degree in 1992. Since 1982, he has been engaged in research at the Institute for Ethnic Studies, Ljubljana. His areas of interest include ethnic minority issues in Austria. He has authored a number of texts in this field, and is editor of the Institute's journal *Razprave*.

Tomasz Kamusella combines teaching duties at the University of Opole in Poland with his post at the provincial administration in Opole, where he is particularly concerned with Poland's entry into the European Union. He has studied in Poland, the Czech Republic and South Africa, and has published on the German minority in Poland in both English and Polish.

Martin Kovats is currently completing a PhD on the 'Development of Roma Politics in Hungary' at the University of Portsmouth. He has recently won a Wingate Scholarship with which he will conduct the first comprehensive research into the minority self-government system in Hungary.

Hugh Miall lectures in the Department of International Relations and Politics at the University of Lancaster. In addition to his consultancy work, he is the author of numerous texts on a variety of topics in the field of European politics. His most recent works include: *Albania in Transition: Development and Conflict*, and *Minority Rights in Europe: The Scope for a Transnational Regime*.

Alexander Ossipov gained his doctoral degree in ethnology from the Institute of Ethnology of the Russian Academy of Sciences in 1993. He is currently a programme officer with the Memorial Human Rights Centre, and the International Institute for Humanities and Political Studies in Moscow. He has also published in the area of inter-ethnic relations in post-Soviet Russia.

Philip Payton is a Reader in Cornish Studies at the University of Exeter and Director of the Institute of Cornish Studies in Truro, Cornwall. He has written extensively on the culture, history and politics of modern Cornwall, and has also published widely on comparative issues of ethnicity and territorial identity. He is the author of *Cornwall* (Fowey: Alexander Associates, 1996).

Jeff Richards is a freelance academic writer and consultant. Until September 1997 he was Dean of the Social Science Faculty at Southampton Institute. Prior to that appointment he lectured in Politics and Government at De Montfort University, Leicester. His research interests include the relationship between identity, community and nationality in plocal politics during the English civil war. He has authored a number of texts in all of these fields.

Robert Schaeffer is a professor of Global Sociology at San Jose State University. His most recent publications include: *Warpaths: The Politics of Partition, Power to the People: Democratization Around the World*, and *Understanding*

Globalization: The Social Consequences of Political, Economic and Environmental Change.

Sandra Schmidt is a research student at the University of Southampton. She has worked for Statewatch, and is currently completing her doctoral thesis on immigration and nationality policy in Germany.

Terry Sullivan is currently completing doctoral research at the University of Plymouth into the role of the German minority in contemporary Poland.

Part I

Setting the scene

1 Introduction: aims and objectives

Karl Cordell

The rise of ethnicity

In recent years the themes of nationality and ethnicity have come to assume increasing importance and interest to students of political science. This is especially true for those who study European politics. Since the coming to power of Mikhail Gorbachev in 1985 Europe has witnessed some truly startling events. Not only has the Soviet Union dissolved, but other avowedly multi-national states, namely Czechoslovakia and Yugoslavia, have taken the path of disintegration. Many of the successors to the three aforementioned multi-ethnic states have been created in accordance with a view of nationality which seeks to equate it with membership of a particular ethnicity, and which sees national self-determination as being coterminous with a sometimes ill-defined notion of democracy.

Such events in formerly communist countries of Europe must not be viewed in isolation from developments in the rest of Europe. Indeed, they have re-enforced a trend of ethnic revival which first became apparent in Western Europe during the 1960s, the results and objectives of which have varied according to circumstance and country. Despite the differing demands of such movements, their varying degrees of salience and indeed their different rates of success, we can point to common processes and themes which indicate a trend which is of increasing relevance for the whole of the continent. The first is that a specific feature of the idea of nationhood is being challenged; namely that nation-states created by either the *de facto* or *de jure* triumph of the political values and traditions of one ethnic group are no longer seen as being legitimate in their present form (Watson 1990). This demand for official recognition of the political salience of cultural difference indicates the appearance of a second phenomenon: that of ethnicity itself becoming politicised. For large numbers of people, it is no longer sufficient that their ethnic identity be recognised solely or primarily through the recognition of folkloric customs and the preservation of arcane symbols. Rather, there is a demand that the identity of allegedly subordinate nations within multi-national nation-states be recognised as being co-equal with that of the titular nation; and that in turn involves the articulation of political demands.

This indicates that for ethnic revivalists, the version of the nation-state to which we have become habituated in some way possesses a democratic deficit, precisely because such ethnic entrepreneurs view it as having stifled diversity, and as a vehicle for the pursual of unwelcome policies of homogenisation. To put it another way, from this perspective certain forms of the nation-state are in effect the product of some kind of original sin. Having affirmed that there is in effect an ethnic revival in Europe, and having acknowledged a major factor in the broadening of its scope, namely the Gorbachev reform process, we must now identify other perhaps longer-established reasons behind the appearance of this phenomenon.

Causes and effects

Many authors conclude that the ethnic revival is in some way linked to the appearance of globalisation. It is argued that globalisation not only brings advantages in terms of the dissemination of, for example, technologies and information, but that the process undermines a whole raft of structures and values which underpin the individual and collective existence of many millions of people. In the case of Europe, the globalisation of economic production has been a factor in the renewed attempt to breathe life into the European idea. Apart from anything else, it is argued that in Europe free-standing nation-states are simply no longer equipped to meet the challenges posed by the increasingly globalised nature of production. However, as is patently obvious to even the most casual observer, the renewed move towards European integration has precipitated a political reaction (Hutchinson 1994: 134ff.). There has in some countries, notably the UK, been a marked reaction to the process of European integration, precisely because it threatens the traditional nation-state in two ways. First, there is the advocacy of the transfer of sovereignty to common European institutions, in order to enable member states of the European Union better to meet the challenges of economic globalisation. Second, this position is itself complemented by the advocacy of the transfer of power to the regions, as a means of bringing government closer to the people, and of reducing the democratic deficit that necessarily exists in modern nation-states. Globalisation, and its political consequences, have as a result become factors in the destabilisation of the classical nation-state.

We have now identified a total of three factors which have in some way contributed towards the ethnic revival. However, their appearance does not in itself explain why ethnicity and not some other agency of identity has increasingly become both an individual and collective point of reference. Before attempting to answer that particular question we must first establish what is meant by ethnicity, and the circumstances under which ethnicity may differ from nationality. The definitions of ethnicity are legion, just as they are for nationality (Kedourie 1966). My definition of ethnicity which admits of no novelty characterises ethnicity as being constituted through those characteristics which a group of people defines as being unique to themselves, giving such group a common character and sense of belonging, and which they use in order to differentiate themselves from 'The Other'. Such characteristics may include a common mythology, a shared history, a shared religion, a shared everyday culture, a common language, and importantly an aspiration for sovereignty over a desired territory. Above all, it requires the belief on the part of such a group of people that all of the above are actually true, and if not actually true, then at the very least meaningful to them.

What then is the difference between ethnicity and nationality? Although, as we shall see, the two may be coterminous, there are circumstances under which they may differ. First, the definition of ethnicity I have offered parallels those definitions of nationality founded upon the doctrine of *jus sanguinis*, where nationality is accorded above all else according to cultural criteria as identified in the previous paragraph. In effect and sometimes in law, as in Poland prior to the Second World War, it is seen as being distinct from citizenship. Yet, in those countries which employ the doctrine of *jus soli*, nationality is seen as being coterminous with citizenship, and both may be accorded through an act of administrative fiat to an individual irrespective of that person's origins, or perception of who they are.[1] Countries such as the UK and France which have by tradition adhered to *jus soli* have as a consequence in effect pursued assimilationist policies towards both immigrant groups and indigenous minorities such as the Scots, Bretons, Welsh and Alsatians. Up until the 1970s such policies appeared to be working well, in so far as prior identities based around ethnicity were seemingly inexorably becoming exchanged for a folkloric regional identity within a common national framework, e.g. of Britishness. However, in recent years countries such as those mentioned above have faced increasing problems in convincing immigrant groups of the efficacy of assimilationist policies, and have also faced an increasing challenge from the regions.

The mobilisation of ethnicity

Why ethnicity should have emerged as a dominant mobilisational tool is a slightly different matter. The collective realisation of a common ethnicity is often connected with the process of political transition. It may affect a community of people living within a single state, or, as with ethnic Albanians, it may relate to a diaspora. This does not necessarily mean that a call for recognition equates with either a demand for independence or for unification with another state. It does, however, mean that recognition of diversity, and at the very least the acknowledgement of alleged previous wrongs, is seen as being integral to a process of renewal. In northern and western Europe, where the path of nation-building was smoother than elsewhere in the continent, and where episodes of violence connected with the process of nation- and state-building by and large play less of a role in shaping contemporary politics, such attitudes may appear archaic. On the other hand, East-Central Europe and the Balkans both have a much more recent experience of colonial and neo-colonial forms of rule, domestic dictatorship, policies of forcible assimilation of minorities and outright attempts at genocide (Kohn 1965: 44ff.). It should therefore come as no surprise that for many in these areas, democratisation and all that entails is often seen as being coterminous with national self-determination.

Such painful memories and indeed unsophisticated constituents are indeed a Godsend to both opportunists and ethnic entrepreneurs. Such circumstances enable both to utilise ethnicity as a political tool, and, as we have witnessed most recently in Bosnia, may facilitate the growth of a culture of carnage. However, the descent into barbarity is by no means a universal law. As we noted earlier, the mobilisation of ethnicity itself creates two related issues. Some groups, such as the Serbs and Frisians in Germany, although laying a claim for recognition, stake no claim for independence. The question then becomes through which mechanisms claims for recognition may be accommodated. The routes are varied, but invariably they will involve national governments signing and ratifying the various international agreements that deal with the protection of ethnic minorities, and in complementing such agreements with the requisite domestic legislation. At a very minimum such steps will involve measures which are aimed at maintaining the cultural and linguistic identity of such groups (Brass 1991: 50ff.). They may also involve a measure of administrative deconcentration as in the UK, the granting of meaningful autonomy as in Spain, federalism as in Belgium, or even the involvement of a third party as is the case between Austria and Italy with respect to South Tyrol. However, recognition is by no means universal, as was the case for the Germans of Upper Silesia in Poland between 1945 and 1989. Indeed, it may be almost entirely notional, as with the Roma almost everywhere. Inevitably in such situations, mutual estrangement and alienation are normally the results.

What then of those who demand the right of secession on the basis of ethnicity? If the demand for secession is recognised, as in the case of Czechoslovakia in early 1992, then the appearance of ethnic nationalism and the recognition of its validity can actually play a part in the wider process of democratisation. Indeed the case of Spain, with the partial exception of the Basque country, illustrates how ethnic mobilisation can in fact contribute to the process of democratisation, and transition from dictatorship.

The Spanish example shows that in fact the endeavour to create civil society in the face of an incipient threat against nascent democrats is not inimical to the recognition of ethnic diversity. The idea of civil society itself is constructed around the idea of tolerance and respect of difference. It is also built around the idea that the politics of accommodation is not only possible, it is desirable. In such societies politics is not viewed as being a zero-sum game. In Spain during the mid-1970s, liberal Castilian centrists together with Catalan separatists and others were forced to recognise this basic fact. They were encouraged to adopt a culture of compromise by the presence of a shared enemy, the Francoist political-military elite, which saw itself as the guarantor of the integrity of the Spanish state and nation, and viewed attempts to reconstruct either as being a mortal threat to such integrity. Yet, through the exercise of judicious diplomacy, both internal and external, and a realisation that the recognition of diversity did not in fact amount to a death warrant, Spain has changed almost beyond recognition.

Alternatively, as the case of Yugoslavia demonstrates, previously entrenched authoritarian modes of thinking can be affirmed and re-invent themselves, as has been shown through the phenomenon of the communist turned nationalist as in the cases of Slobodan Milosevic and Franjo Tudjman. In turn, as events in Croatia indicate, although national self-determination may be achieved, there remains a large question mark over the extent to which civil society as is commonly understood in Western Europe is actually under construction. The consequences of such complexities may result in such newly emergent states seeking to deal with the problem of indigenous minorities either by in effect denying them any practical means of expression, or by pursuing policies of forcible assimilation, ethnic cleansing, or worse.

In response to real, perceived and alleged cases of such discrimination, in recent years 'the international community' has sought to strengthen the collective rights of ethnic minorities. No matter how well intentioned such endeavours, they actually raise questions as well as (hopefully) solve problems. These issues revolve around three main questions: To what extent does the allegedly humanitarian concern for the rights of ethnic minorities mask a strategy of *realpolitik*? Can a minority rights regime actually deepen a crisis by re-enforcing societal division? Are group rights fully compatible with individual civil rights? As we shall see, the issues are rarely as clear-cut as they seem at first sight.

The question still remains of why it is ethnicity, and not that other great reference point of collective and individual identification, class, which has proven to be such a powerful mobilisational force. As we mentioned at the beginning of the chapter, in part the answer is contained within the wreckage of the failed experiment of Marxism–Leninism, and the inability of non-Marxist forms of socialism to forge cross-national identities (Gellner 1994: 1ff.). The other part of the explanation, which we referred to earlier in the narrative, seemingly lies in the inability of the liberal nation-state, which in itself is the product of an earlier political (Kedourie 1966: 19) and industrial revolution, to address the problems of the late twentieth century and a new type of industrial revolution. In the absence of any other meaningful frame of reference, ethnicity for many then becomes a fallback point precisely because nothing else is available. In recent years this has been particularly so in Eastern Europe (Brass 1991: 41ff.). The states of Czechoslovakia and Yugoslavia were tainted with failure on two counts. First, they failed to provide full social integration and economic prosperity both prior and subsequent to the Marxist ascent to power. Second, as became all too painfully aware in the case of Yugoslavia, over forty years of one-party rule had done nothing to depoliticise prior ethnic differences and render them incapable of being manipulated in a gruesomely exploitative manner. Both examples illustrate, as does the fate of some of the successor states to the Soviet Union, how ethnicity can be utilised to exploit grievance, to pursue semi-covert political agendas and to unleash forces of nationalism which are both violent and exclusionary.

Reconstruction or destruction

The examples of Yugoslavia and post-Soviet states such as Tajikistan illustrate how such mobilisation may easily become a force for destruction. However, it would be a mistake to assume that political mobilisation of ethnicity is an intrinsically negative or violent phenomenon. As should by now be apparent, the circumstances under which the fall of the old order leads to the commencement of either a process of democratisation or the release of ethnic tensions, or indeed both, are difficult but not impossible to identify. The factors which need to be considered are the immediate domestic situation of a given country and its residents, the political and cultural predispositions of a country, and indeed, the wider international environment. Given the increasing lack of fully functional alternatives, the liberal democratic path is an obvious one to follow. However, as has already been noted, although there may be circumstances under which the politics of ethnicity may become paramount, they are not necessarily matched by any corresponding move towards democratisation.

Nevertheless, there is clearly a link between nation building and democratisation. However, as has been demonstrated here and elsewhere, that link is not fixed (Hinsley 1973: 43). In certain circumstances the desire for national self-determination may be emancipatory in that it is harnessed to a trend towards the construction of civil society. In less favourable circumstances it may in fact underscore pre-existing authoritarian trends or serve to facilitate their mutation into new forms of authoritarian or quasi-authoritarian rule. The question remains of under what circumstances civil society as opposed to authoritarianism is likely to emerge. The factors already highlighted include history, political cultural practices, the existing mechanisms for conflict resolution, the balance of forces within a given country, and the disposition of international actors. Where the past is of itself no great burden, where there is a current of intellectual and social liberalism, and where cross-ethnic currents of co-operation exist, then the task of constructing and maintaining civil society in nation-states, whether they be new or old, multi- or mono-ethnic, becomes all the easier.

Yet there is one factor which we still have to consider. The decisive ingredient with regard to the mobilisation of people around the banner of ethnicity is perhaps that which has deliberately been left to last, that of the economy. Probably the greatest factor in the rise and fall of the political systems, and the erosion or maintenance of legitimacy, is the question of the economy. Where an economy is performing well, social, cultural, and religious differences may be all but eroded, and the task of assimilation proceeded with all the easier. Indeed, it may be argued that economic prosperity is the very motor of assimilation. However, when the economy begins to malfunction or where there exists the perception that the economic product of society is not being distributed equally, the possibility for disturbance arises. In a state beset by such problems, the full integration of its citizens becomes increasingly problematic. Where citizens are potentially divided from one another in terms of ethnicity, there is, as we have already noted, obvious potential for such differences to create the basis for mass political mobilisation. Economic recession may then provide the spark which finally allows ethnic mobilisation to occur, and which allows a continuous challenge to be mounted to the existing symbols of nationhood. The rationale for the continued existence of an extant common state thereby increasingly comes into question.

In such circumstances, nationalists come to reject existing political structures, and may increasingly seek solutions posited upon independence as opposed to autonomy. In extreme circumstances the need for adaptation and change may be fuelled by references to a mythologised golden age during which time the ancestors of the historic people Y of the extinct country of X lived lives blessed with abundance, and free from the oppressive rule of people W with whom they now share country of Z. The solution then posited is exclusionist and very often reactionary, with all that is entailed by the adoption of such postures. If, however, a state is long-established and if a process of assimilation or integration has been all but completed, then in times of economic crisis the potential for mass mobilisation around the banner of ethnicity is correspondingly weak. Yet, the less established a state is, and where the processes of assimilation and integration have yet to be completed, then the potential for secessionist movements and the possibility of success for such movements is all the more greater. In other words, in the event of economic malaise, older established states, whether they be liberal democracies or not, are much better equipped to deal with and accommodate diversity, than are newer states in which the nature of identity itself is open to question. This is particularly so when there is also an uncertain international environment, and lastly where no mechanisms for internal peaceful conflict resolution exist.

Concluding remarks

The observations made in the preceding paragraphs may be considered in two ways. First, they offer an assessment of the causes and nature of the ethnic revival. Second, they may be considered as constituting a framework around which this volume is constructed. All of the contributors to this collection address each or some of these themes according to the dictates of the subject-matter under review, and indeed their own perspectives. In so doing they offer valuable observations concerning the nature of the politics of ethnicity in Europe, with regard to a number of specific and important themes. These include the conceptual formulation of ethnicity; the role of the state as a political entity in the light of the ethnic revival; the international environment and the role of international organisations in achieving conflict resolution; and lastly by reference to case studies of the politics of ethnicity within individual states and communities. The results and conclusions drawn are designed to be of dual benefit to the discipline and students of political science. The first of these benefits relates directly to the study of European politics, and more especially to those who are studying the themes and issues highlighted in this volume. The second lies with the broader field of comparative politics. It is self-evident that the themes of democratisation and ethnicity are by no means confined to Europe. A carefully crafted study of such issues as they relate to Europe has the added benefit of facilitating points of comparison and contrast with parallel phenomena in other parts of the world. Areas of similarity as well as points of comparison and contrast are thereby made available to the judicious scholar. The objectives of facilitating understanding of the twin themes of ethnicity and democratisation, and of demonstrating their salience within Europe together with their relevance to an extra-European audience, are central to the enterprise of this volume.

Note

1   It must be borne in mind that these two concepts rarely operate as ideal types, and that most governments employ an admixture of the two.

References

Brass, P. (1991) *Ethnicity and Nationalism*, London: Sage Publications.
Gellner, E. (1994) *Encounters with Nationalism*, Oxford: Blackwell.
Hinsley, F. (1973) *Nationalism and the International System*, London: Hodder & Stoughton.
Hutchinson, J. (1994) *Modern Nationalism*, London: Fontana Press.
Kedourie, E. (1966) *Nationalism*, London: Hutchinson & Co.
Kohn, H. (1965) *Nationalism, Its Meaning and History*, London: D. Van Nostrand.
Layton-Henry, Z. (ed.) (1990) *The Political Rights of Migrant Workers in Western Europe*, London: Sage Publications.
Stack, Jr., J. (ed.) (1981) *Ethnic Identities in a Transnational World*, London: Greenwood Press.
Thompson, D. and Ronen, D. (eds) (1986) *Ethnicity, Politics, and Development*, Boulder, CO: Lynne Rienner Publishers.
Watson, M. (ed.) (1990) *Contemporary Minority Nationalism*, London: Routledge.

2 Ethnicity and democracy – complementary or incompatible concepts?

Jeff Richards

Introduction

This chapter examines the concepts of ethnicity and democracy in relation to ideas of identity, community, and nationality in the context of change in post-war Europe. Above all, it seeks to examine just how 'democratic' is the ethnicity factor in modern European politics.

Some hope that by the end of the twentieth century the European Union (EU) will have become a political and economic union in reality as well as in name through both enlargement and deepening. Yet parallel to this integrative process there has been a marked increase in decentralisation or devolution in most European (unitary) states and, since the disappearance of the 'Iron Curtain' and the disintegration of the former Soviet bloc, many new and former polities have emerged onto the map. How then is this paradox of greater economic and political convergence at the same time as the increased splintering into a greater number of states to be explained? Why, in particular, is nationalist sentiment resurgent again in Europe? Is the ethnic factor compatible with democracy? Some clues to the answers to these questions may lie in the very nature of ethnicity and nationalism under examination here. The notions of 'identity', 'community', and 'nation' will be explored in relation to ideas of ethnicity and democracy.

It is argued that the impact of globalisation and its concomitant threat to identity has generated a transmodernity debate and fuelled the ethnic revival of recent years. What is important about the ethnic dimension within the context of the contemporary global society is its ability to provide a source of identity. Yet the relationship between participation in a community or state and between ethnicity and democracy is by no means clear. Ethnic solidarity can lead to such phenomena as ethnic cleansing. Liberal democracy and nationalism were seen as complementary for much of the nineteenth century. For much of the twentieth century, however, they have been regarded as less compatible. Having established the parameters of the debate, we now need to ask how does the revival of ethnicity challenge the essential pluralistic nature of modern (Western) democracy or does it revitalise our understanding of what it means to belong to a self-conscious community?

Identity, community and nation

The notion of identity has received considerable attention in recent years, not least in political science and international relations literature. It may refer to the individual and his or her sense of belonging and points of reference to the world in which he/she finds himself or herself. It tends to be linked to familiarity and a sense of shared orientations in a community of the similar. There are echoes here of Ferdinand Tönnies' notion of *Gemeinschaft*.

The need for identification with a community in order to achieve individual identity or self-respect is in part a function of socialisation experiences. The group constituting the community may vary historically and geographically from family, extended family, through kith and kin to clan and tribe and on to a larger community. In this sense it relates mainly to a community based on a shared history and culture. In a historic culture-community the modes and goals of identification are given by the group and its past experiences as they coalesce into a collective tradition which distinguishes a particular ethnic identity.

Similarly, the word nation has had a variety of uses before its modern version. In the past it has been used in the same sense as such related terms as race, political class exercising power, people, community, tribe, state, clan, and society. Lack of space prohibits full illustration of this except to mention that, for example, in the Middle Ages the University of Aberdeen contained the four 'nations' of Mar, Buchan, Murray, and Angus whilst the University of Paris was composed of the 'nations' of France, Picardie, Normandy, and Germany. Anthony Smith, who has written widely on the ethnic origins of nations, suggests that 'the "modern nation" in practice incorporates several features of pre-modern ethnic community and owes much to the general model of ethnicity which has survived in many areas until the dawn of the "modern era"' (Smith 1989: 18).

He also suggests that

> It is fashionable for modern Western observers, securely ensconced in their own national identities forged in toil and blood several centuries ago, to pour scorn on the rhetorical excesses and misguided scholarship of nationalist intellectuals in nineteenth-century Europe or twentieth-century Africa and Asia. Those whose identities are rarely questioned and who have never known exile or subjugation of land and culture, have little need to trace their 'roots' in order to establish a unique and recognisable identity. Yet theirs is only an implicit and unarticulated form of what elsewhere must be shouted from the roof-tops: 'We belong, we have a unique identity, we know it by our ancestry and history'. It matters nothing that these are so many 'myths' and 'memories' full of deceptions and distortions. The 'self-evident' nature of English or French national identity is made up of such myths and memories; with them, the English and French are 'nations', without them, just so many populations bounded in political space.
>
> (Smith 1989: 2)

Ethnic nationalism in Europe has a long tradition. Recent events in the 'New Europe' have caused many to reassess their attitudes, not least in the academic community. Today it is a commonplace among social scientists that ethnic cleavages can affect politics and political stability. Indeed, the rehabilitation of the study of nationalism has progressed to such an extent that Tom Nairn recently observed:

> The whole subject of nationalism used to be regarded as more or less taboo in academic circles....It is no counter-culture or side eddy, interfering with the majestic mainstream of Progress. Nationalism is the mainstream, and it's time we recognised the fact.
>
> (Nairn 1995: 76)

We also need to recognise that the traditional discrete boundaries between academic disciplines in studies of ethnicity and nationalism are becoming increasingly redundant. In order to better consider the relationship between ethnicity, nationalism, and democracy the origins of these terms and their subsequent interpretations will now be examined.

The concept of 'ethnicity' and its origins

Although the use of the term ethnicity is recent, the sense of kinship, group solidarity and common culture to which it refers is as old as historical records, and probably older still. Ethnic communities have been present in every period and continent and have played an important role in all societies. Though their salience and impact have varied considerably, they have always constituted one of the basic modes of human association and community. The same is true of the sense of ethnic identity.

The word ethnicity first appeared in the English language in the 1950s. 'Ethnicity seems to be a new term', observed Nathan Glazer and Daniel Moynihan in 1975 when they pointed to its first appearance in the *Oxford English Dictionary* in 1972 (Glazer and Moynihan 1975: 1). It is a derivative of the much older term and more commonly used adjective ethnic, which in the English language goes back to the Middle Ages. This in turn derived from the Ancient Greek term *ethnos* and was used as a synonym of gentile, that is, non-Christian and non-Jewish pagan in New Testament Greek. In French, for example, the Greek noun survives as 'ethnie', with an associated adjective 'ethnique'. English has the adjective 'ethnic' but not a real noun equivalent. As Tonkin *et al.* observe, 'One of the problems for English speakers is that the concrete noun from which it [i.e. ethnicity] is derived does not exist in our own language. We have no "ethnos", no "ethnie"' (Tonkin, *et al.* 1989: 11).

The Ancient Greeks originally used the term *ethnos* in a variety of ways. What these various usages have in common is the idea of a number or group of people or animals who share some cultural or biological characteristics and who live and act in concert. Yet these usages refer to 'other' people who, like animals, belong to some group different from one's own. Hence the tendency to characterise non-Greeks, peripheral, foreign, barbarians, as *ethnikos* or *ethnea*. Greeks tended to refer to themselves as *genos Hellenon*. This dichotomy between a non-ethnic 'us' and ethnic 'others' has continued to be associated with the concepts in the fields of ethnicity and nationalism. We find it reproduced in the ways in which the Latin *natio* was applied to distant, barbarian peoples, whereas the Roman term for themselves was *populus*. We find it also in the English and American (White Anglo-Saxon Protestant) tendency to reserve the term nation for themselves and ethnic for immigrant peoples, as in the frequently used term ethnic minorities.

Ethnicity is not to be confused with race. The former relates essentially to shared cultural identification whilst the latter relates to physical appearance and often spurious, biologically distinct origins. Indeed, the core of ethnicity itself resides in myths, memories, values and symbols, rather than in any idea of race. This is an important point. It is not unusual for social work or social service agencies to refer to 'black and ethnic communities' as if they are one and the same. This is demonstrated by the following extract from a letter from Hampshire County Council Social Services Department under the heading 'Ethnic Monitoring – Service Users'.

> As you will know, Hampshire Social Services Department has adopted a race policy. The policy identifies the need to *record and monitor the ethnic background of people using our services*. This recording will enable us to monitor the service requests and usage by people from the black and ethnic communities in order to assist this department in the planning and development of appropriate services…. Identification of ethnic origin will be by the service user themselves and will not be required of third party referrer…. I am sure that you will wish to support us in this important step in improving our service to people from the black and ethnic communities.
>
> (Hampshire Social Services Department 1993)

It can be argued that the above usage of the term ethnic is incorrect. 'Ethnic' should not just mean non-white or minority group, nor should it be used to refer to colourful, peasant-style clothing!

From about the middle of the nineteenth century, scholarship shifted the sense of the term 'ethnic' from its use in English in its Greek New Testament sense of gentile or pagan to meaning something like 'a group of people having shared characteristics'. Despite this the adjective 'ethnic', as can be seen in the example given above, has not been generally applied to an indigenous population or populations. It has been, however, readily applied to groups of relatively recent immigrants who are perceived to be sufficiently different. Indeed, one measure of perceived difference would be the ease with which the adjective 'ethnic' could be employed.

It might well be obvious that if 'ethnicity' exists it is something that inheres in every group that is self-identifying – whether minority or majority. As Everett C.

Hughes observed, 'We are all ethnic' (Hughes and Hughes 1952). Ethnicity, however, has so far refused to be socially neutral in this way. As should now be apparent, the issue of the usage of the term 'ethnic' is an interesting one. As far as its implications for the relationship between ethnicity and democracy is concerned, it bears closer examination.

The concept of democracy and its origins

Democracy which is derived from the ancient Greek word *demos* is traditionally described as government by the people as a whole, rather than by any one section, class or interest within it. 'The people' referred to in this original sense are more accurately those belonging to the city-state, the *polis*, who are legally entitled to participate in political activity and government, i.e. the citizens. In classical Athens, which was the model for this early democracy, it excluded women, slaves, and resident foreigners (*metics*). This mixture of the exclusivity and inclusivity relating to democracy in the ancient past, more recent past, and the present has considerable significance for the purposes of this chapter and will be returned to later.

Citizenship in the Athenian democracy was a privilege normally attained by birth, for a Greek remained a citizen of the city-state to which his parents belonged. It entitled a free-born native man of the city-state of Athens to membership of the body-politic. In other words he was expected to participate in public business and political activity as a citizen of the state. The whole body of male citizens formed the Assembly, or Ecclesia, a town meeting which every Athenian was entitled to attend after he had reached the age of twenty years. However, the two bodies which were the keys to popular control of government were the Council of the Five Hundred and the law courts with their large popular juries (Sabine 1937).

For purposes of local government the Athenians were divided into about a hundred *demes* or wards/parishes. Membership was hereditary and even though an Athenian might move from one locality to another he remained a member of the same *deme*. Accordingly, although the 'deme' was a locality, the system was not purely one of local representation. The 'demes' were the door by which the Athenian entered into citizenship. They kept a register of members and every freeborn Athenian boy was enrolled at the age of eighteen. But their most important function was the presentation of candidates to fill the various bodies by which the overall government of Athens was carried on. The system was a combination of election and lot. The *demes* elected candidates, roughly in proportion to their size, and the actual holders of office, such as magistrates, were chosen by lot from the panel thus formed by election. For ancient Greeks this mode of filling office was the distinctively democratic form of rule, since it equalised everyone's chance to share in the exercise of power. This reflected the importance to the 'democrat' of both civic responsibility and civic participation.

It was the proudest boast of Pericles that Athens, better than any other state, had found the secret of enabling her citizens to combine the care of their private affairs with a share of public life. But the freedom of the Athenian democrat also implied respect for law. The law had been framed through the participation of all citizens and was administered by them in the manner outlined above. In such a free state the law, rather than an individual ruler, is sovereign, and the law deserves the citizen's respect, even though in a particular case it might work against him. Freedom and the rule of law are two foundation stones of good government – the secret of the city-state democracy and its modern-day successors. The Athenian ideal may be summed up as the conception of free citizenship in a free state. To Pericles and his fellow Athenian democrats, however, it was the prerogative of their city-state and only possible amongst the Greeks alone amongst the peoples of the world. The citizen's freedom depended upon his rational capacity and the democratic city-state alone of all classical forms of government gave free play to this. As for the 'barbarians' (the *ethnos* or non-Hellenes), according to Aristotle they were slaves by nature. Democracy thus allowed for government by citizens according to the rule of law; but did it mean respect for minority rights if such minorities had no civic rights? As we shall see, this dilemma has continued to face more modern versions of democracy.

Nationalism and democracy

The relationship between nationalism and democracy is not a simple one; it has definitional, conceptual and historical aspects. Liberal democracy and nationalism were seen as complementary for much of the nineteenth century. For much of the twentieth century, however, they have been regarded as less compatible.

Both modern democracy and modern nationalism may be traced to the revolutionary legacy of the 1789 French Revolution which saw the establishment of the idea of 'popular sovereignty'. What Tom Nairn has described as 'the Janus-faced bequest' of this period produced both universalist and inclusive 'civic' ideas of liberal and 'democratic' nationalism and also romantic, reactionary, particularist and exclusive 'ethnic' nationalism.

Indeed, the link between nationalism and the nation-state lies in the concept of 'national sovereignty' rather than the sovereignty of a single ruler or oligarchy within a state. The idea of national sovereignty comes to us via Jean-Jacques Rousseau and his doctrine of 'popular sovereignty' which influenced the French Revolutionaries. The French Revolution, in turn, sparked off many nationalist movements elsewhere in Europe. Some were in emulation of it and were usually movements aimed at overthrowing domestic or foreign dynasties. Others (including the German version) constituted a reaction to the values and perceived threat of the Revolution.

As a result, a new collective subject of political action – the nation – had emerged. Yet it contained dynamic tensions. It could be both universalistic and exclusive. Each nation was held to have its own characteristics. Even the French Revolutionaries, who stressed a new common 'civic' identity and promised to liberate the rest of Europe, embraced the concept of the nation. Citizens of the Republic should be prepared to give their lives to defend the nation.

Assumptions of basic homogeneity and the existence of no basic ethnic divisions within the state were made. Historically the attempt to export the Revolution sparked off reaction against it. French armies helped to create the linguistic and reactionary sense of German nationalism based on the idea of *Volk* which was little concerned with accountability and control of political leaders.

Stemming from this common historical heritage, both nationalism and democracy are modern, popular and/or populist. Particularly in the twentieth century, nationalism has been able to serve as an alternative to democracy because it has resembled it in its populist, mass mobilisation aspects. Democracy has, however, generally emphasised in addition the importance of a common citizenship and the accountability of elected political leaders. Nationalism, by contrast, gave first priority to the idea of the nation, national identity and cohesion. It provides a set of more exclusive criteria to determine who may be counted as a member of the political community. Membership of the nation becomes synonymous with membership of the state and gives a sense of identity, bonding, and meaning; there is an emphasis on particularity and difference from 'others'. Thus, both democracy and nationalism are about collective entities – in either case usually characterised as 'the people'. Democracy emphasises the accountability and control of elected leaders to and by 'the people'.

There are four main views on the nature of the relationship between nationalism and democracy. The first is that they are complementary and stem from the same roots as outlined above. The nation is the basis for the democratic community through national self-determination in a nation-state. The second is that nationalism and democracy are inimical; that right-wing radical nationalism leads to fascism which is explicitly anti-democratic and hostile to the key values of democracy. It has often sought to create a *Volksgemeinschaft* of the national-culture-community and used 'ethnic cleansing' to achieve this. The third view is that nationalism and democracy, both invoking 'the people', appear to be similar but mean different things – as outlined above – and centre on different priorities. The fourth view depends on a differentiation between ethnic nationalism and civic nationalism, the latter being seen as more tolerant and as compatible with democracy. This can be an attractive notion; but is this dichotomy between ethnic 'bad' and civic 'good' versions of nationalism too simplistic and overstated? Can it be affected by the way in which a nation achieves statehood and sovereignty?

The road to the nation-state and national self-determination

It has been claimed by traditional writers on nationalism such as Hans Kohn (1961) and Eli Kedourie (1960) that there have been two distinctive routes to the establishment of nation-states in Europe – one followed mainly in Western Europe and the other followed mainly in Central and Eastern Europe. This approach has been given a new exposition in more recent years by Anthony Smith (1989).

According to this view the 'Western' European path leads from state to nation. It is that experienced by 'territorial' nations occupying fairly well-defined areas and it manifests early 'bureaucratic–rational' state forms. The process of nation formation via this path includes three revolutions: the transition from feudalism to capitalism, the centralisation of state administration, and cultural and educational revolution – with the consequent spread of standardisation. These contributed over varying periods to the centralised and culturally relatively homogenous states of late-nineteenth- and early-twentieth-century Europe. The classic examples here are Great Britain and France where state unity came early and assisted in the process of nation-building.

The 'Eastern' European path, on the other hand, leads from nation to state. It is that experienced by 'ethnic' nations where cultural awareness is strong whilst existing state forms with which to identify are not. In this case the three revolutions mentioned above came later. This path transformed ethnic ties and sentiments into a national identity, and then into a state, through mobilisation, territorialisation and politicisation. This route emphasised genealogy, customs, 'folkish' elements, etc., more, and much less the civic rational-legal emphasis than in the western case. The eastern and central route also placed a stronger emphasis on ethnic homogeneity and 'purification'.

What happens when the nation has achieved its statehood? Much seems to depend upon the twentieth-century view of the state as a nation-state – a product of the nationality/national self-determination principles so firmly embraced in the early years of the century. Yet the question remains – is, in principle, the nation-state a good or a bad thing? In 1861 John Stuart Mill set out the essence of the case in favour of the nation-state: 'Where the sentiment of nationality exists in any force, there is a prima facie case for uniting all members of the nationality under the same government, and a government to themselves apart'.

Indeed, he went further in the same work claiming that 'free institutions are next to impossible in a country made up of different nationalities' (Mill 1961).

In the following year Lord Acton (of 'absolute power corrupts absolutely' fame) gave the essence of the counter argument.

> The co-existence of several nations under the same State is a test, as well as the best security of its freedom. It is also one of the chief instruments of civilisation; and as such, it is in the natural and providential order, and indicates a state of greater advancement than the national unity which is the ideal of modern liberalism.
>
> (1907)

In complete contrast to Mill, Acton went on to claim that 'if we take the establishment of liberty...to be the end of civil society, we must conclude that those states are substantially the most perfect which, like the British and Austrian Empires, include various distinct nationalities without oppressing them' (Acton 1907). With the benefit of hindsight and subsequent evidence we can see that Mill's view is closer to the truth than Acton's optimism.

The Treaties of Versailles, St Germain and Trianon recreated the map of Europe after 1918 with redrawn boundaries and new nation-states on the basis of national self-determination; but not as far as the defeated combatants were concerned. This legacy caused accelerated strife which led to the Second World War.

Indeed, the two World Wars of the twentieth century were caused in large part by ethnic conflicts and nationalist considerations. The first was sparked off in Sarajevo in Bosnia with the assassination of Archduke Franz Ferdinand in 1914 by Serbians opposed to the Austro-Hungarian presence. The second was caused over the Sudetenland, Danzig and the Polish Corridor with Hitler seeking to add 'lost' territory and ethnic *Volksdeutsch* to the German Reich to form a *Gross Deutschland* which would incorporate territory from virtually all of its neighbours. Some commentators have come to refer to them as two *European Civil Wars*.

Democracy, ethnicity and the use of violence

It follows, therefore, that modern states have often legitimised themselves in terms of, and waged political and military campaigns in the name of, 'the people' or 'the nation'. Whilst identitive elements of state power derive most strongly from the ethnic and national backgrounds of the state, the coercive elements tend to be under-rated in relation to their importance in underpinning its authority. Indeed, the use of force in politics is often under-rated in advanced western political systems where constitutional theory emphasises the importance of consent between government and governed. Yet, it is difficult to think of a state which has not been founded through or by the use of violence.

In the area of international affairs it is more usual to acknowledge the use of force at times; war being regarded, according to von Clausewitz, as '*the continuation of politics by other means*'. Even so there is a tendency to be selective in our acknowledgement of this.

There is a story from the period before the Second World War which illustrates this. At a diplomatic reception held in London during the Italian invasion of Ethiopia a British lady cornered the Italian ambassador and berated him for the 'uncivilised' way in which aeroplanes, tanks, and machine guns were being used against 'natives' armed with little more than spears. This, she informed him, was decidedly unsporting and was not the British way. In response the ambassador politely but pointedly observed: 'Madam, I am a Roman Catholic and as such I subscribe to the doctrine of the Immaculate Conception; but I believe that it refers to the birth of Our Lord rather than to the birth of the British Empire'.

It has been suggested that in certain circumstances popular sovereignty has been used to legitimise the removal of minority groups, often ethnic minorities, in the name of 'the people'. This may be done in various ways, for example by expulsion, forced assimilation, deportation, genocide or what has come to be known as 'ethnic cleansing'. Contemporary ethnic cleansing has been described as 'the sustained suppression by all means possible of an ethnically or religiously different group with the ultimate aim to expel or eliminate it altogether' (Ahmed 1995: 73).

Michael Mann argues that this is part of what he terms the 'flip-side' of democracy and that historically there is a strong relationship, at times of mass mobilisation, between democratic struggles and genocide (Mann 1997). Part of the distrust of classical democracy felt by Plato and Aristotle was based on the fear of the tendency of 'the people' (as a mob) to attack unpopular minorities and to create a tyranny of the majority. Both liberal democracy and ethnic or organic democracy have been prone to this, although with the latter, which is closer to ethnic nationalism, it has been more common. 'The people' are usually held to be synonymous with 'the nation', especially in the nation-state. When the Founding Fathers met in Philadelphia in 1787, however (thirty-five white middle-aged and middle-class gentlemen), to establish a Federal Constitution for the United States of America in the name of 'We, the People...', they excluded slaves, native Americans, and women (shades of Athenian democracy again). Their British contemporaries would have differentiated also between 'the people' (i.e. those having 'interests' and entitled legally to participate in the body politic) and 'the populace' (i.e. the rest of the inhabitants of the country, or the crowd, the rude unenfranchised multitude). 'The people' were traditionally defined by property and/or social class. Such a society and system of government could still be described as a liberal (i.e. plural) democracy because it rested on various interests. Class and gender stratify a society but do not necessarily always separate or segregate it. There is usually an interdependence between social classes and inevitably between the sexes. This tends to place limits on the levels of disagreement and, in extreme cases, the violence between these groups. Extensions of the franchise have led to all social classes and both genders in modern democracies being admitted to the body-politic or 'the people'. Stratification has remained as a central core of liberal or pluralist democracy as opposed to the reduction to the major overriding factor of ethnic or national identity in organic democracy. In the former type of democracy, class or gender exploitation may have been common but genocide has been rare.

This has not always been the case in the history of such states. Until the latter half of the seventeenth century, religious differences in Europe were amongst the most salient and religious minorities often suffered from genocidal attacks. In the colonies of the major European powers there was often also a racial division of labour. Where, in such cases, there were distinct competing communities, rather than the stratification of society as in the colonial homeland, this could lead to genocidal attacks on the natives by the settler population. Indeed, the freer (i.e. the more 'democratic') the settlers then often the greater the tendency for the 'ethnic cleansing' of the native population, for example as in North America and Australia. Democracy, like 'the rights of Freeborn Englishmen', was for 'the people' and not for the native population or ethnics. This is an interesting and important paradox. Often the native populations were safer under strong imperialist regimes who had an interest in stability and regulating the excesses of the settlers who wanted more 'independence'.

Back in Europe itself the earlier-established states of Western Europe tended to institutionalise differences and to recognise stratification by gradually admitting more and more groups within the populace to the 'body-politic'. Thus the 'democracy' was extended to make the populace synonymous with 'the people' on the basis of civic rights and participation. In central and south-eastern Europe, however, there existed a different set of circumstances. Parliamentary and constitutional rights were far more limited in development, restricted and fragile. Often the populace were in opposition to autocratic and/or alien oppressors. They were often mobilised against these hegemonic states, elites, or minorities on the national issue or through the assertion of ethnic identity. Thus, much more suddenly than in the west, the populace or the masses became the sovereign group led by nationalist leaders at the end of the nineteenth or the beginning of the twentieth century. In as far as they espoused democracy it tended to be of the organic or ethnic variety which was usually advocated as being of a higher form, representing the whole national culture community or 'the people'. Conflicts of interest between strata of society could be transcended. This form of democracy placed few controls on its leaders, tending to exclude ethnic minorities and those who sympathised with them. It became associated with authoritarianism and a one-party state. Through its nationalist imperative it sought first to identify the national essence, then to create a strong state to defend it, and then finally to exclude 'others' from that state. Sometimes national majority–minority relations were reversed between neighbouring states as in the period between 1914 and 1946. Where there was no strong protector for the minority in the form of a neighbouring state of the same ethnic origin, they suffered far more, e.g. the Jews, Gypsies, and Armenians, as alien enemies of 'the people's' nation-state. Many fascists who rejected liberal democracy at first espoused such 'organic democracy' as represented by the leader, the party, the people, and the state.

Thus, though most easily recognised in the case of 'organic democracy', genocide has frequently been a concomitant to a rapid mobilisation in the name of democracy. This approach can now be seen most clearly in the 'Third World', for example recently in Rwanda, Burundi, and Zaire (now the Democratic Republic of Congo). Yet it was also witnessed in the former Yugoslavia in recent years, most notably in Bosnia and Croatia. It was a danger that Aristotle saw in the democracy of his time. Although it is now, thankfully, almost entirely absent from modern liberal democracy it is important that we realise that only a firm adherence to the Rule of Law and respect for Minority Rights will prevent abuses in the name of 'the people' again.

Conclusion

The historical role of the state in Europe in homogenising populations and stimulating their cultures and sentiments has been considerable. It could not have achieved its results, however, without building upon ethnic roots and feelings of national identity for mobilising popular aspirations and feelings of shared interests and community. Without ethnic bases there could not be the starting points for nations or nationalisms. Failure to appreciate this can only prevent us from understanding the antagonisms that so often plague relations between states, within states, and between states and individual citizens so often in the New Europe and elsewhere in the world.

There is, however, a third route to statehood in addition to the two outlined earlier. This is the pluralist approach which places an emphasis on civic nationalism rather than on territorial or ethnic nationalism. Membership depends on attaining citizenship and is rational-legal based rather than on being born within the territory of the state or within the ethnic core of a nation. Examples of civic nationalisms are those of the USA, Canada and Australia. In each case there is a dominant ethnic group which has provided the dominant language and legal system, but it is as a result of the interaction between the dominant group and later immigrant groups that a new civic nationalism is developed. Both Tom Nairn and Michael Ignatieff, the latter in his six-part television series *Blood and Belonging* (Ignatieff 1994), expound the view that such civic nationalism is the only effective antidote to the antagonisms of ethnic nationalism. Civic nationalism is not, however, a model native to Europe, as we have seen in recent years. The emotional sources of European nationalisms, based on their ethnic roots, should not be under-estimated.

Most modern democratic societies in reality have a mixture of ethnic and civic nationalisms within them. The real danger for, and from, democracy is when ethnic identity is used to deny minorities in a state civic rights. The question of who is to be a citizen then becomes central. It is the citizens who, as 'the People' in a democracy, can legitimately employ the power of the state. These issues are as real today as they were in the times of Ancient Greece. Recent examples include the case of Fiji in 1987 when, following the coming to power following a general election of a coalition government dominated by ethnic Indians, the army intervened and installed a constitution that would make this impossible in future in order to safeguard the identity and interests of the 'real' (i.e. 'ethnic') Fijians. Thus citizenship became related to ethnicity. Nearer to home the United Kingdom government is resisting pressure from its partners within the EU to open Britain's frontiers and to relax passport and immigration controls. More starkly the German government continues to restrict citizenship rights of immigrant children born in Germany. Indeed, Germany is the only major western industrial nation to maintain the principle that nationality is passed down through the blood line. Some commentators claim that this has echoes of the Nazi stress on *Blut und Boden* ('Blood and Soil'). The German authorities do not distinguish between the concept of citizenship as the criterion of nationality and the ethnic background of individuals. Historically, Germany has absorbed a multitude of ethnically distinct groups, reflecting the country's position at the cross-roads of Europe. They now form the German nation. The 'guest-workers' and other immigrants have made a substantial contribution to Germany's post-war economic miracle. They retain, however, the equivalent status to the 'metics' of classical Athenian democracy. The non-Germans are seen as the 'ethnics'. What price a common European civic citizenship, given the above examples?

The attempt to make a rigid distinction between 'good' civic nationalism which is liberal democratic and 'bad' ethnic nationalism which is organic democratic is neither accurate nor helpful. One must synthesise rather than dichotomise between civic and ethnic/organic democracy. Ultimately the test of democracy is respect and toleration for individual choice and rights. In considering the relationship between citizenship and national identity the cognate concepts of ethnicity, nationality and citizenship must not be fused together. The tendency to do so, given the underlying assumptions of nationalism and the rationale of the nation-state, is very strong. The dynamic tension between the concepts of ethnicity and democracy is best seen over the issue of citizenship. As this chapter demonstrates, these issues are not new and they are not easily resolved.

References

Acton, Lord John (1907) 'Nationality', in J.N. Figgis and V. Lawrence (eds) *The History of Freedom and Other Essays*, London: Macmillan.

Ahmed, A.S. (1995) 'Ethnic Cleansing: A Metaphor For Our Time?', *Ethnic and Racial Studies* 18 (1).

Glazer, N. and Moynihan, D.A. (eds) (1975) *Ethnicity: Theory and Experience*, Cambridge, MA: Harvard University Press.

Hampshire Social Services Department (January 1993) Letter on Ethnic Monitoring – Service Users.

Hughes, E.C. and Hughes, H.M. (1952) *Where Peoples Meet: Racial and Ethnic Frontiers*, Glencoe, IL: The Free Press.

Ignatieff, M. (1994) *Blood and Belonging*, BBC television series.

Kedourie, E. (1960) *Nationalism*, London: Hutchinson.

Kohn, H. (1961) *The Idea of Nationalism*, New York: Macmillan.

Mann, M. (1997) 'The Flip-Side of Democracy: In What Circumstances Has Popular Sovereignty Legitimated Murder?', paper presented to the Seventh Annual Conference of the Association for the Study of Ethnicity and Nationalism, London School of Economics, 18 April.

Mill, J.S. (1961) *Considerations of Representative Government*, Everyman's Library, London: Dent.

Nairn, T. (1995) 'The Worth of Nations', *Times Higher Education Supplement*, 11 August 1995.

Sabine, G.H. (1937) *A History of Political Thought*, New York: Harrap & Co.

Smith, A. (1989) *Ethnic Origins of Nations*, Oxford: Blackwell.

Tonkin, E., McDonald, M. and Chapman, M. (1989) *History and Ethnicity*, London: Routledge.

3   Ethnicity in Western Europe today

Philip Payton

Constructing Western Europe

For many years after the Second World War, discussions of ethnicity were moulded largely by the contributions of writers such as Karl Marx and Emile Durkheim who had argued that the influence of ethnicity in political behaviour would inevitably disappear in the process of economic and political modernisation (Newman 1996: 3). Certainly, in the immediate aftermath of the War, observers saw in the 'final defeat' of fascism the demise of ethnicity as a major determinant of political and social behaviour in Europe, and stressed instead the inherently liberal-democratic characteristics of the new Western Europe that had arisen from the debris and destruction of intra-continental conflict. This new Western Europe was a 'triumph of ideals' (Jay 1996: 281) in which American-led notions of social, economic and political liberty had (despite the hesitations of European, especially French, elites) established an ideological coherence from which the new institutions of Western European coalescence would emerge.

The economic impetus of the 1948 Marshall Plan was an important, practical aspect of this coalescence, and so too was the Soviet reaction – the falling of an 'Iron Curtain' and the creation of an all-encompassing division between the western and eastern halves of the continent. The birth of NATO in 1949 confirmed and reinforced this new reality, and the establishment in 1952 of the European Coal and Steel Community gave further meaning to the emerging sense of Western European coalescence. The creation in 1958 of the European Economic Community by 'The Six' (the Benelux countries, together with France, West Germany and Italy) established a common market in Western Europe, an institution which almost every Western European state – including post-Imperial Britain – sought sooner or later to join.

The new liberal-democratic Western Europe thus defined was seen as part of a wider pattern of consolidating 'civic cultures' (which also included North America and the so-called 'White Commonwealth') in which ethnic consciousness was seen as irrelevant (even distasteful) and destined to disappear. Within these 'civic cultures', the popular legitimacy of institutions and the emergence of consensus politics, together with improved political participation, enhanced socio-economic and geographical mobility, universal education, universal welfare and health care, and ever-more sophisticated communications, made for increasingly homogeneous states in which democratic institutions were secure and where any residual ethno-territorial diversity would quietly evaporate. The resultant political culture was one in which the 'management of cleavage is accomplished by subordinating conflicts on the political level to some higher arching attitudes of solidarity' (Almond and Verba 1965: 492). As Hughes and Dowse put it, 'civic culture' encompassed

> the notion of participation in structures widely regarded as legitimate but in which, for most people at least, life offers a range of opportunities for commitment to parochial and a-political institutions, a commitment which helps to develop both a sense of potential personal competence and a sense of trusting other people. The sense of competence *and* trust allows the citizen to feel at ease with the government.
>
> (Hughes and Dowse 1972: 231)

For commentators such as Almond and Verba, the United Kingdom was seen as the most advanced example of a 'civic culture' within Western Europe, and in 1963 Jean Blondel could add that 'Britain is probably the most homogeneous of all industrial countries' (Blondel 1963: 20). Although, as Blondel admitted, there were geographical variations in voting and other socio-political behaviour – so that Wales tended to be Labour, South East England Conservative, and so on – this 'geographic' factor was but one strand of a broader explanation of the influence of 'tradition and environment', which was itself of less importance than considerations such as class and trade union membership. 'Civic culture' and homogeneity went hand-in-hand, producing a participatory but largely content political society in which there was little variation from one locality to another and where the essential *raison d' être* of the state was not in doubt or dispute.

Upsetting the textbooks

However, even as this orthodoxy was being articulated, so new tensions were becoming apparent in the supposedly homogeneous, consensual, democratic 'civic cultures' of Western Europe. As Michael Keating put it, a 'wave of "peripheral nationalist" movements...confounding most orthodox wisdom, swept through advanced western countries in the 1960s and 1970s', upsetting 'many of the textbook theories of politics in Western nations' (Keating 1988: 1).

In the United Kingdom – that apparently textbook example of a consolidating 'civic culture' – the sudden re-emergence of the Northern Ireland problem in the late 1960s reminded observers that the boundaries (both territorial and cultural) of 'Britishness' remained contested and unresolved (McBride 1996: 1–18). What was presented initially as a struggle for 'civil rights' by a disadvantaged Catholic community demanding full access to the fruits of a wider 'civic culture', was seen later as 'a deeply entrenched ethnic conflict' between two distinct ethnic groups – Catholic and Protestant – in which it was important for those 'thinking about Northern Ireland…to appreciate the strength of ethnic identification, the power of ethnic divisions' (Bruce 1994: vi).

Although the Northern Ireland conflict was often presented as something quite outside the bounds of normal political behaviour within the modern British state, the concomitant rise of nationalist sentiment in Scotland and Wales indicated that the contested boundaries of Britishness were not restricted to the far-flung Irish edge of the Union. Although, with the exception of isolated outbreaks of hostility towards English in-migrants or holiday-home owners, neither Scotland nor Wales exhibited sustained ethnic conflict, there was a significant heightening of ethnic consciousness in both countries in the years after 1945. Its expressions were varied and complex, ranging from growing concern for the future of the Welsh language to the popular desire to assert both Welshness and Scottishness on the sports field – particularly in contests with England! However, despite the long-standing 'Home Rule All Round' item on the British constitutional agenda, this growing consciousness did not translate easily into political nationalism, although both the Scottish National Party and Plaid Cymru (Party of Wales) had established themselves as credible political actors by the 1970s. It was not until 1997 – with the emphatic 'Yes, Yes' vote in Scotland and more cautious 'Yes' vote in Wales – that Welsh and Scottish nationalism combined with a more general sense of anti-metropolitanism to demand a level of self-government for both countries.

This blend of heightened ethnicity and growing anti-metropolitanism was also observable in Cornwall, ostensibly an integral part of England but also an increasingly vocal component of Britain's 'Celtic fringe' (Payton 1992, 1993). A nationalist movement, Mebyon Kernow (Sons of Cornwall), was formed in 1951 to fight for Cornish self-government but (with the exception of a handful of local government victories and a credible showing in the 1979 Euro-elections when it achieved almost 10 per cent of the Cornish vote) it was not successful in penetrating the electoral system. However, it was highly successful in creating an 'anti-metropolitan debate' within Cornwall. The main beneficiaries of this, paradoxically, were the Liberal Democrats who in the 1997 general election won all but one of the Cornish seats at Westminster, their local manifesto demanding the creation of a Cornish Development Agency and at least one of their MPs calling for a Cornish Assembly. Intriguingly, regionalism as it emerged in the north east of England consciously adopted the language of ethnic assertion deployed elsewhere in the United Kingdom, implying that the north east was a peripheral appendage of the 'real' England of the south. Thus 'Even in historical terms, England is a bit of a myth' (Temperton 1978: 19).

The United Kingdom's experience was replicated elsewhere in Western Europe. The radical restructuring of post-Franco Spain (to take account of Catalan, Basque, Galician and other aspirations) revealed a complex pattern of ethnic sensibilities and rivalries, and led to the explicit recognition in the 1978

Constitution of *Espana de Las Autonomias* (Williams 1994). Indeed, the early years of transition to democracy were characterised by the fear that failure to accommodate regionalist and ethno-nationalist demands might threaten the durability of fledgling democratic institutions. In Spain, rather nervously, and not without contradiction, Article 2 of the new Constitution declared that 'the Constitution is based on the indissoluble unity of the Spanish nation, the common and indivisible motherland of all Spaniards, and recognises and guarantees the right to autonomy of the nationalities and regions of which it is composed...' (Williams 1994: 90). The resultant accommodation, however, was by no means a panacea. To begin with, the aspirations of different regions were by no means identical, which led to complex arrangements in which some regions (such as Catalonia and Galicia) were given substantial levels of autonomy, while others (such as Andalusia and the Canaries) were allowed to bid for higher levels of autonomy than those earmarked for them initially. Still others were offered a trial period of more modest devolution. However, inter-regional jealousies remained, as did a persisting suspicion in several autonomous regions of central government designs, while the problem of separatist terrorism in the Basque Country was by no means resolved.

In neighbouring France, Basque nationalism was far less a challenge to the authority of the state, although Corsican separatism – with its not infrequent recourse to violence and terrorist outrage – was a substantial threat to the *République indivisible*. In Brittany, a Celtic revivalist movement that in the early years of this century had exhibited a cultural ethno-nationalism akin to that of Wales, Scotland and Cornwall turned in the 1970s and 1980s into a more focused critique of French centralism. This was part of a 'Regional rebellion' (Wagstaff 1994b: 28) that had gripped France by the 1970s, a widespread protest in peripheral regions which led, amongst other things, to the 're-emergence' or at least attempted reassertion of an Occitan nationality in the southern part of the *Hexagon*. Even Normandy spawned its own regionalist movement, in the process constructing something like an ethnic identity which claimed that present-day Normans were a distinctive people descended in part from medieval Scandinavian settlers. These new demands for regional accommodation emerged at a time of wide-ranging economic change in France, and were met in the early 1980s by attempts by the new Mitterrand government to match governmental administration to the requirements of contemporary socio-economic conditions in the regions. This established the relative responsibilities and competencies of *communes*, *départements* and *régions* as levels of territorial administration, as well as awarding Corsica (and the major cities of Paris, Lyons and Marseilles) a particular kind of regional status (*statut particulier*).

In Belgium, the accommodation of ethno-nationalist and regionalist demands went further, leading to what was claimed by some commentators as nothing less than a *de facto* partition of the state (Wagstaff 1994c: 46). In contrast to the United Kingdom, Spain and France, Belgium is a relatively recent construct, owing its origins to the post-Napoleonic Congress of Vienna which aimed to produce a buffer state to contain France. Within this highly 'artificial' creation, there was a fundamental cleavage between the French-speaking Walloons and Dutch-speaking Flemings, with the further complication of a substantial German-speaking minority. In the period after the Second World War, Walloon–Flemish dissension was exacerbated by a growth in Flemish economic power and influence and a corresponding decline in Walloon interests. The 'linguistic laws' enacted by the Belgium parliament in the early 1960s devolved cultural autonomy to the two major communities, in the process enshrining linguistic differences as a basic territorial division within the state. By the 1970s this had led to the formation of three (Walloon-, Fleming-, and German-speaking) *Communautés* or territorially based cultural entities, and to the establishment of socio-economically autonomous *régions*. In 1993 these developments were rationalised in a constitutional revision which effectively created a federal state.

If the Belgian state seemed a recent and possibly 'artificial' construct, then so too did Italy. A product of nineteenth-century Romantic nationalism, the Italian state emerged from the Second World War with its hitherto centralist assumptions in tatters. Centralism, it was thought, had facilitated the rise of fascism, and new democratic structures were sought which would ensure a more pluralistic balance of power (Bull 1994: 71). The Socialist and Communist parties, however, were suspicious of proposals to devolve power to potentially reactionary regions, and the new Constitution of 1948 was something of a compromise. Regions were established as essentially administrative units with limited legislative capacities, although five of these twenty regions were given additional autonomous responsibilities – Sicily, Sardinia, Valle d'Aosta and Trentino Alto Adige in 1948, and Friuli-Venezi Giulia in 1963. Sicily and Sardinia had already exhibited separatist tendencies, while the northern regions contained German-speaking and other ethnic minorities. In practice, only the five 'special' regions received early administrative devolution, the others having to wait until the 1970s when the government was persuaded to act in the face of increasing regional disquiet. Although this accommodated a variety of regional demands, it did not prevent the rise of the Northern League – a party whose aspirations seemed to vacillate between federalism and separatism, and which by the 1990s had established real electoral credibility in Lombardy and other parts of northern Italy. Significantly, the Northern League couched its regionalist demands in the language of ethno-nationalism – asserting or even inventing an array of ethno-cultural differences to differentiate northerners from southerners.

Although the experience of the United Kingdom, France, Spain and elsewhere had much in common, the pattern was by no means uniform. Some nation-states appeared inherently more resilient than others (often, but not always, a reflection of their historical longevity), while the constituent parts of some states appeared more restive than those of others. For example, despite the loss of the greater part of Ireland earlier this century, the United Kingdom appeared a relatively old and durable construct, and yet was troubled not only by unresolved aspects of the Irish problem but by an increasingly restive Scotland. West Germany, on the other hand, had been comprehensively (re)-invented by the Allied powers after the Second World War. The creation of a federal system of *Länder* had been an integral part of a strategy to ensure the construction of a diffused, pluralistic democracy, and had the additional effect of helping to create the post-war 'economic miracle'. Within this West German construct, Bavaria, with its historic particularism and potential separatist sentiment, settled down as a distinctive but enthusiastic element of the new democracy.

In other respects, however, the West German experience offered distinctive examples of the new manifestations of ethnicity in Western Europe. Although having apparently avoided the ethno-territorial pressures that had characterised other states, West German conceptions of citizenship created two areas of potential difficulty – the status of foreign (largely Turkish) 'guest workers' and the rights of German minorities beyond the borders of the state. For the former, access to German citizenship was extremely difficult, leading critics to observe that West Germany had created *de facto* 'second-class' citizens, as well as encouraging the anti-immigrant outbursts of Neo-Nazi fringe groups. Meanwhile, the process of rapid change in Eastern Europe in the late 1980s and early 1990s had not only precipitated the absorption of the former German Democratic Republic by West Germany, but had highlighted the existence of hitherto invisible German minorities in Poland, Romania, Hungary, Ukraine, and elsewhere (Payton and Syme 1992: 99–100). The ideological commitment to ethnic Germans beyond the state meant that these newly discovered Germans were able to claim German passports and the right to emigrate to Germany. In 1990, for example, Germany indicated that it was willing to accommodate the aspirations of the German community in post-Ceausescu Romania (some 210,000 souls), including economic assistance for those who chose to remain in Romania and political pressure on the Romanian government to ensure cultural freedom for its ethnic minorities.

Although these issues were distinctively German, they were echoed elsewhere in Western Europe as states sought to come to terms with their post-colonial legacies (Cohen 1994). Varying conceptions of citizenship meant that the United Kingdom, France, Belgium and the Netherlands were the recipients of millions of immigrants from former colonial territories. Afro-Caribbean and Asian communities became familiar elements of British urban life, while France received large numbers of immigrants from Algeria. In the United Kingdom the benign assimilationism of the 1960s and 1970s had moved towards a more proactive policy of multicultural accommodation by the 1980s and 1990s, but this did not prevent the continued articulation of anti-immigrant, racist sentiments by groups such as the National Front, nor did it discourage some immigrant Islamic groups from demanding what would be effectively constitutional and legal autonomy – a state within a state. In Britain, the National Front did not establish itself as a credible electoral force, but in France – more resistant as it was to notions of multiculturalism – Le Pen's right-wing National Front was able to mobilise significant political support on anti-immigrant themes.

Whereas the issues surrounding non-indigenous ethnic groups appeared at first glance to be quite distinct from the indigenous, territorially based assertions of ethno-nationalism, in fact both raised similar questions about the existence (or otherwise) of 'civic cultures', the assumptions of homogeneous convergence in modern Western European states, and indeed the ability of those states to respond effectively to the often conflicting demands of ethnic diversity. Across the board, conventional wisdoms had been shattered, and the search was on for explanations to account for these new phenomena.

Searching for answers

Inevitably, answers were sought in the societal structures and cultural history of Western Europe. What one might term 'pessimistic' explanations took the view that the underlying political culture of Western Europe was inherently undemocratic, even anti-democratic. Such perspectives insisted that, far from being an entrenched norm fundamentally characteristic of modern Western societies, the democratic 'civic culture' was a recent 'Anglo-Saxon' invention which had been 'forced' upon other Western states in war (Germany, Italy) or through political/diplomatic pressure (Spain, Portugal, Greece). In the aftermath of the Second World War, it was American military and economic might that had created the illusion of Western European coalescence, and it was continuing American hegemony in the continent (facilitated in part by British complicity) that had underwritten the establishment of democracy in Spain, Portugal and Greece and their participation in NATO. A more enduring influence upon Western European political behaviour, it was argued, was that of 'handed-down values' (Cortada and Cortada 1996: 1–22), a varying mix of authoritarianism, individualism and nationalism in which ethnicity was both a significant causal factor and an inherent threat to the 'newly-imposed' democratic structures. Such a view saw ethnicity as a primordial factor in human behaviour, one which could in certain circumstances transcend more transient factors such as class or nation-state membership/allegiance.

Although such analyses are routinely dismissed as simplistic, there is nonetheless a more general assumption that recent assertions of ethnicity threaten not only state structures but democracy itself. David Held, for example, has asked: 'with forces such as nationalist and social movements seeking to redraw the boundaries of political life, how legitimate and sustainable is liberal democracy?' (Held 1992: 7). Wagstaff, in his survey of European regionalism, fretted over 'The prospect of imminent institutional collapse in Italy…' and regretted that 'The goal of [Western European] political union remains no more than a hazy outline in the distance…', all the while looking over his shoulder to the existence 'Further afield, but well within the bounds of what Mikhail Gorbachev called "the common European house", [of] the dystopian fantasies of ethnic nationalism [which] magnify minor difference into tribal conflict' (Wagstaff 1994a: 1). Schulze, another Euro-enthusiast, saw the recent upsurge in ethno-nationalism in Western Europe as not only surprising but also (in a sort of 'Euro-Whig' interpretation of history) as an unwelcome and untimely threat to the orderly movement towards democratic European integration and homogeneity. It is 'an irksome phenomenon that apparently resists all our efforts to establish a more or less uniform society...based on a radical foundation of liberal and democratic values' (Schulze 1996: ix).

Others, however, have called for a more detached analysis, one which avoids simplistic or mono-causal explanations (such as the 'primordial') and which resists the assumption that ethnicity is somehow a perverse interloper which threatens the 'natural progress' of Western European development. Rokkan and Urwin, for example, warned against the then prevalent mono-causal explanations of peripheral protest or regional restiveness in Western European states, demanding 'a broader approach which stresses the dichotomy between centre and periphery, seeking to place ethnic variations in a general framework of geopolitical location, economic strength and access to the loci of decision-making' (Rokkan and Urwin 1982: 2).

For observers such as Rokkan and Urwin, recent assertions of ethnicity in Western Europe could only be understood within the context of an analysis of state structures themselves, investigating the territorial origins and development of these structures, not least with regard to the relationships between 'centres' and 'peripheries'. For Rokkan and Urwin, the success (or otherwise) of modern Western European states in accommodating their ethno-territorial components was largely a function of the centre-periphery relationship. Thus Bavaria had been accommodated successfully within the balanced structure of a federal West Germany, whereas Scotland had been less well accommodated within a 'top-heavy' United Kingdom.

The emphasis in this largely structural explanation upon the significance of a historical perspective (which asked fundamental questions about how states were constructed over time in Western Europe) has been echoed in more recent discussions of state formation and identity, notably Linda Colley's *Britons* (1992). In this seminal work Colley has argued that 'Britishness' was a post-1707 construct conditional upon the link between commerce, industry and empire, forged in war and underpinned by Protestantism, an identity which reflected the state structure of Great Britain and was imposed upon an array of internal differences but did not imply the integration or homogenisation of disparate cultures within these islands. As Colley herself admits, this view of the Union as a conditional construct begs questions about its durability or even desirability in the post-Imperial age. This is a theme which has been picked up by James Mitchell (Mitchell 1997), who argues that the last great attempt to re-invent a 'Britishness' with which Scots (and perhaps other constituent peoples) could identify was the creation after the Second World War of the 'British' welfare state and a 'British' nationalised economy. The progressive dismantling of this particular 'British project' during the Thatcher years, argues Mitchell, accounts for increasing Scottish political differentiation, and poses long-term questions about the ability of the British state to avoid fragmentation.

Scots ethnicity, then, is not merely a primordial quality that has somehow burst through as Britain (or the United Kingdom) has reached its 'sell-by date' but is rather one device (amongst others) that has been mobilised in the search for alternative political futures in the face of an existing political structure that is perceived to be failing the people of Scotland. This is a phenomenon that is observable elsewhere in Western Europe. At its most extreme, it can be seen in Northern Ireland where the 'failure' of the British state has fostered alienation and despair. As one Catholic put it, 'I mean, lots of people vote Sinn Fein because they don't see any other option. A lot of people see the IRA as their protectors if it came to a civil war...' (Clare 1990: 36). In Italy, too, the re-assertion (or invention, depending upon one's point of view) of a Lombardian and wider 'northern' ethnic identity as a political force is, according to Anna Bull, a function of the 'failure' of the Italian state.

In other words, ethnicity was the vehicle rather than the causal factor in a political movement that was motivated by the 'failure' of the state, an ethnicity that was enhanced through and by the articulation of regional discontent. In addition, as Bull explains, socio-economic development in Italy has remained uneven, state policies designed to improve the condition of the south having proved largely unsuccessful, with the north – in an echo of the complaints of neighbouring Slovenia and Croatia in the erstwhile Yugloslav state – increasingly impatient with what it sees as its draining subsidy of the inherently inefficient south. This disparity has further heightened the perception of state 'failure', a feature that is also recognisable in the new Spain. Williams notes that 'Massively uneven development in the 1950s and the 1960s also contributed to the revival of nationalism and regionalism' (Williams 1994: 87) but he adds, crucially, that the post-Franco restructuring has also failed to fully address this problem:

> The process of inter-regional transfers is critical for the future of Spain which remains a country with deep regional economic differentials. Despite the dynamism of the Spanish economy in the 1980s, some of the poorest regions in the EC are to be found in Spain....At the other extreme are Barcelona and Madrid which have claims to be considered world cities.
>
> (Williams 1994: 93)

To this growing perception of state 'failure' in Western Europe was added the general inability or unwillingness of those 'failing' states to react quickly, positively or decisively to the felt need for change. Even though, as Kofman and Williams have noted, 'In general the advanced industrial state has demonstrated its ability to devise strategies by which the divergent and conflicting cultural and economic issues may be contained...', in fact these state responses – such as those which partitioned Ireland in 1922 or institutionalised the ethno-territorial divides in Belgium or Spain – 'may well resolve one set of issues for the moment...[but] may often engender quite a different set of issues which serve to perpetuate conflict' (Kofman and Williams 1989: 20–1). Such pragmatic responses are indicative of state structures grudgingly (and often belatedly) reacting to demands for change, rather than an intrinsic desire within those structures to proactively initiate change.

These contemporary accounts of the 'failure' of modern western states and their relative inability to develop were anticipated at least in part in the more theoretical analysis offered by Anthony D. Smith in his *Theories of Nationalism* (1971). Smith focused on the emergence of the 'scientific state' in modern Europe. This 'scientific state' had grown out of the old 'possessive state' (for example, the Tudors in England, the Bourbons in France) which, to serve the 'political-personal ends' of its ruler, pursued policies designed to expand and secure the territorial dimension of the state. Thus, for example, Brittany had to be incorporated into the French state, while England expanded progressively in its 'Celtic fringe'. The 'possessive state' was developed gradually into the more modern 'scientific state', characterised by its drive for administrative efficiency (and thus intolerance of regional diversity) and its demand for a high degree of loyalty from its citizens in the implementation of its 'welfare' policies. This state was highly centralised, the culture of the metropolis becoming the standard for the state as a whole, and within this structure ethno-territorial minorities found themselves 'doubly socialised' into both their indigenous cultures and the culture of the state. This was successful (as in the case of Scotland) so long as the 'scientific state' could deliver the fruits of its interventionist, centralising, 'welfare' project. Yet when it appeared that the 'scientific state' could not in fact deliver what it had promised (or indeed had retreated from those promises), then those who had been 'doubly socialised' were presented with a crisis of acute proportions – the result of which was the emergence of ethno-nationalism.

'Democratic deficit' and 'democratic renewal'

As the recent collections of Hutchinson and Smith attest (Hutchinson and Smith 1994, 1996), Smith's analysis has been followed with an array of explanations and perspectives, but the discussions offered by Rokkan and Urwin, Colley, Mitchell, Bull, Smith and many others converge in their apparently common identification of contemporary state 'failure'. Significantly, this academic consensus is mirrored in the more practical discussions of 'democratic deficit' in modern Western European states routinely offered by journalists and politicians. Will Hutton's *The State We're In* (1995) and Andrew Marr's *Ruling Britannia: the Failure and Future of British Democracy* (1995) are exemplars of a wider concern expressed throughout Western Europe by many commentators about the alleged failure of democratic institutions. For some, such as the French writer Alain Minc, the future promises only 'decaying Western systems', a pessimism bordering on cynicism which has led Marr to object that 'The dominant Western thinkers today are a gloomy lot' (Marr 1995: 316–17). However, Marr epitomises a more optimistic stand in Western European writing when he calls for 'democratic renewal', a recognition that the state is 'failing' but with an insistence that it is not beyond redemption (Marr 1995: 349).

Politicians such as Paddy Ashdown have echoed such calls for 'democratic renewal' in Britain and Western Europe and, alleging a fundamental breakdown in the 'contract' between people and state, have demanded new, decentralised institutions as a prerequisite for perpetuating and re-invigorating democracy (Ashdown 1994: 206–7).

Calvert has argued that both 'democratic deficit' and the need for 'democratic renewal' are most keenly felt in the United Kingdom, particularly laying the blame at the feet of the Thatcher years: 'After 1979 Britain undermined the liberal consensus that had prevailed in Europe since the end of the Second World War' (Calvert 1994: 66). As an academic, Calvert was claiming common cause with politicians such as Ashdown and journalists like Marr. In so doing, he was further evidencing the convergence between concern for 'democratic deficit' and those analyses of Western Europe that had identified state 'failure' as the root cause of contemporary ethno-nationalism. Put another way, the emergence of ethno-nationalism as a result of state 'failure' in Western Europe was best understood as a function of the wider 'democratic deficit' that afflicted those states.

A significant consequence of such a perspective was the negation of the 'pessimistic' assessments of ethnic assertion (which saw a destructive ethno-nationalism as the inevitable and recurring function of the tyranny of history), and their replacement by an alternative view which argued that the deployment of ethnicity might in fact be one device to enable Western Europe to confront and resolve issues of 'democratic deficit'. The appeal to a 'Europe of the Regions' may have a role to play in this process (Loughlin 1997), encouraging a more democratic decentralisation of powers within states while allowing both existing and new regional constructs to bypass central governments in dealing with each other or with European institutions such as the European Union or the Council of Europe. Indeed, for some observers there is evidence that such processes are already in hand. Not only have the German *Länder* set a model for regional participation in Europe but, as Newman notes, in Belgium ethnic politics 'succeeded in peacefully dismantling the centralised state without riding roughshod over democratic rights and may even have expanded avenues for political participation' (Newman 1996: 2). Additionally, one might speculate that the success of the 'Yes, Yes' and 'Yes' campaigns in Scotland and Wales may signal not so much the beginning of the collapse of the post-War 'British project' but rather (as Tony Blair has argued) its re-invention as part of a wider process of 'democratic renewal'.

Conclusion

If the latter is the case, then this gives force to Keating's recently articulated view that, in Western Europe at least, nationalist movements have shifted from demands for exclusive autonomy to concern for preserving social cohesion in a world of weakened states, a shift which, paradoxically, increasingly stresses the 'civic' over the 'ethnic'. Here the effective deployment of national institutions is increasingly more important than, for example, the insistence on cultural exclusivity. As Keating notes:

> The civic dimension has strengthened over the years. It is strongest in Scotland, where the nation was built by institutions from diverse ethnic components. It is strong in Catalonia, where nation-building elites have

consciously adopted a civic formula. Nationalism focuses more on the building of a territorial society than in the past, and nationalist elites boast of their openness to incomers.

(Keating 1996: 217)

Paradoxically, then, the assertions of ethnicity that we have witnessed in Western European states may not after all have been a repudiation of 'civic culture' but rather a plea for the creation of new 'civic' entities to replace or repair failing structures. Far from the shedding of an externally imposed and culturally alien value-system (as Cortada and Cortada contended), the deployment of ethno-nationalism may be both a symptom of state 'failure' and a means of seeking state 'renewal' within a democratic ideology which is indeed characteristic of late-twentieth-century Western Europe.

References

Almond, G. and Verba, S. (1965) *The Civic Culture*, Boston, MA: Little, Brown.

Ashdown, P. (1994) 'Democratic Renewal', in M. Foley (ed.) *Ideas That Shape Politics*, Manchester: Manchester University Press.

Blondel, J. (1963) *Voters, Parties and Leaders*, London: Penguin.

Bruce, S. (1994) *The Edge of the Union: The Ulster Loyalist Political Vision*, Oxford: Oxford University Press.

Bull, A. (1994) 'Regionalism in Italy', in P. Wagstaff (ed.) *Regionalism in Europe*, Oxford: Intellect Books.

—— (1997) 'Italian Regionalism and the Northern League', unpublished paper presented at the European Centre for Traditional and Regional Cultures conference on 'Regional Autonomy in Europe', Llangollen.

Calvert, P. (1994) 'Authoritarianism', in M. Foley (ed.) *Ideas That Shape Politics*, Manchester: Manchester University Press.

Clare, P.K. (1990) 'Subcultural Obstacles to the Control of Racketeering in Northern Ireland', *Conflict Quarterly* X (4).

Cohen, R. (1994) *Frontiers of Identity: The British and the Others*, London: Longman.

Colley, L. (1992) *Britons*, New Haven, CT: Yale University Press.

Cortada, J.N. and Cortada, J.W. (1989) 'National and Regional Pluralism in Contemporary Spain', in R. Herr and J.H.R. Polt (eds) *Iberian Identity: Essays on the Nature of Identity in Portugal and Spain*, Berkeley: Institute of International Studies.

—— (1996) *Can Democracy Survive in Western Europe?*, London: Praeger.

Held, D. (ed.) (1992) *Prospects for Democracy*, Oxford: Blackwell.

Hughes, R.E. and Dowse, J.A. (1972) *Political Sociology*, London: John Wiley.

Hutchinson, J. and Smith, A.D. (eds) (1994) *Nationalism*, Oxford: Oxford University Press.

—— (eds) (1996) *Ethnicity*, Oxford: Oxford University Press.

Hutton, W. (1995) *The State We're In*, London: Penguin.

Jay, M. (1996) 'From Modernism to Post-Modernism', in T.C.W. Blanning (ed.) *The Oxford Illustrated History of Modern Europe*, Oxford: Oxford University Press.

Keating, M. (1988) *State and Regional Nationalism: Territorial Politics and the European State*, London: Wheatsheaf.

—— (1996) *Nations Against the State: The New Politics of Nationalism in Quebec, Catalonia and Scotland*, Basingstoke: Macmillan.

Kofman, E. and Williams, C.H. (1989) 'Culture, Community and Conflict', in C.H. Williams and E. Kofman (eds) *Community Conflict, Partition and Nationalism*, London: Routledge.

Loughlin, J. (1997) ' "Europe of the Regions" and the Federalization of Europe: Fact or Fiction?', unpublished paper presented at the European Centre for Traditional and Regional Cultures conference on 'Regional Autonomy in Europe', Llangollen.

Marr, A. (1995) *Ruling Britannia: the Failure and Future of British Democracy*, London: Penguin.

McBride, I. (1996) 'Ulster and the British Problem', in R. English and G. Walker (eds) *Unionism in Modern Ireland*, London: Macmillan.

Mitchell, J. (1997) 'Scotland – The Next Step Forward?', unpublished paper presented at the European Centre for Traditional and Regional Cultures conference on 'Regional Autonomy in Europe', Llangollen.

Newman, S. (1996) *Ethnoregional Conflict in Democracies: Mostly Ballots, Rarely Bullets*, London: Greenwood.

Payton, P. (1992) *The Making of Modern Cornwall: Historical Experience and the Persistence of 'Difference'*, Redruth: Dyllansow Truran.

—— (ed.) (1993) *Cornwall Since the War: the Contemporary History of a European Region*, Redruth: Dyllansow Truran/Institute of Cornish Studies.

—— (1994) 'Ethnicity', in M. Foley (ed.) *Ideas That Shape Politics*, Manchester: Manchester University Press.

Payton, P. and Syme, V. (1992) 'Eastern Europe: Economic Transition and Ethnic Tension', in M. Pugh (ed.) *European Security: Towards 2000*, Manchester: Manchester University Press.

Rokkan, S. and Urwin, D.W. (1982) *The Politics of Territorial Identity: Studies in European Regionalism*, London: Sage.

Schulze, H. (1996) *States, Nations and Nationalism: From the Middle Ages to the Present*, Oxford: Blackwell.

Smith, A.D. (1971) *Theories of Nationalism*, London: Duckworth.

Temperton, P. (1978) *Up North! How to Unshackle a Forgotten People*, Hebden Bridge: Campaign for the North.

Urwin, D.W. (1985) 'The Price of a Kingdom: Territory, Identity and the Centre–Periphery Dimension in Western Europe', in Y. Meny and V. Wright (eds) *Centre–Periphery Relations in Western Europe*, London: George Allen & Unwin.

Wagstaff, P. (ed.) (1994a) *Regionalism in Europe*, Oxford: Intellect Books.

—— (1994b) 'Regionalism in France', in P. Wagstaff (ed.) *Regionalism in Europe*, Oxford: Intellect Books.

—— (1994c) 'Regionalism in Belgium', in P. Wagstaff (ed.) *Regionalism in Europe*, Oxford: Intellect Books.

Williams, A. (1994) 'Regionalism in Iberia', in P. Wagstaff (ed.) *Regionalism in Europe*, Oxford: Intellect Books.

4 Citizenship, ethnicity and democratisation after the collapse of left and right

Chris Gilligan

Introduction

Democratisation consists of more than simply introducing polling booths and the freedom to organise parties into states where these did not previously exist. It is also a broader question of how the state relates to the people who exist within the boundaries of its jurisdiction. Can a state's citizens expect fair and equal treatment under the law? Do they have freedom of speech, thought and faith? Or the freedom to own property? In the absence of these guarantees of individual freedom the right to vote or to participate in political institutions can easily become a token right. In addition to these rights there is the question of the provision which the state makes for the many who are excluded from full participation in society through no fault of their own. Does the state provide affordable health care, financial assistance for the unemployed and the elderly? A state, which does not value its citizens, is likely to be treated with suspicion by those within its jurisdiction. Democracy, rule by and for the people, must care about the people.

This wider conception of democratisation is generally accepted today. It is contained, for example, in the criteria of the Democratic Audit of the United Kingdom (UK). The Audit examined the workings of parliament but also asked questions about the broader rights which the electorate enjoys. The Audit was concerned with how far political institutions in the United Kingdom reflect the diversity of the political culture existing in the country (Livingstone and Morison 1995: 3). This modern conception of democratisation has been popularised through the discussions about the democratic deficit and the need for constitutional reform (Hennessy 1995; Jenkins 1995; Marr 1995).

This chapter explores the changing relationship between the state and its citizens through an examination of the issue of citizenship. In recent years there has been a rapid growth in the literature on citizenship. A number of developments in contemporary western society – the crisis of class politics, the increasing heterogeneity of western society, and the process of globalisation – have stimulated this growth. The need to re-integrate the citizenry into society is a constantly recurring theme. The means by which this is to be achieved differ; suggested measures vary from the promotion of greater popular participation in political life to the adoption by the state of measures which encourage social inclusion.

Miller notes that 'a climate of enthusiasm for citizenship as a political concept' derives from a coincidence of interest from both the left and the right (Miller 1995: 433). One of the assumptions underlying this chapter is that it is no longer useful to conceive of politics in terms of left and right. The coincidence of interest which Miller notes has become a convergence of ideas. The clash of competing ideals is no longer a defining feature of contemporary politics. Confrontation is eschewed in favour of conciliation. Aspiration is tempered with pragmatism. Ideals are brought down to earth by cynicism.

This climate of conciliation and cynicism provides the context within which democratisation is being discussed today. These prevailing sentiments will leave their mark on the institutional structures and practices which are developed in the process of democratisation. Many radicals are enthusiastic about the utilisation of citizenship as a political concept. For Mouffe the idea of citizenship is important for rallying 'radical democratic forces in the attempt to defeat [New Right] neo-liberalism' (Mouffe 1992b: 3). In this chapter I argue that Mouffe fails to appreciate the significance of what has changed in contemporary politics. Far from promoting radical democracy, the institutionalising of the new citizenship actually threatens to undermine the radical ideals of liberty and equality which were the foundation blocks of democracy.

Equality, ethnicity and citizenship

> [Citizenship] postulates that there is a kind of basic human equality associated with the concept of full membership of a community…which is not inconsistent with the inequalities which distinguish the various economic levels in the society. In other words, the inequality of the social class system may be acceptable provided the equality of citizenship is recognised.
>
> (Marshall 1950/1992: 6)

> The concept of race emerged…as a means of reconciling the conflict between the ideology of equality and the reality of the persistence of inequality.
>
> (Malik 1996: 6)

The concept of race, or ethnicity, and that of citizenship share a common feature in that they both aim to reconcile the tension between the ideology of inequality and the reality of a society based on inequality. The concept of race seeks to provide an explanation for inequality in biology. The concept of ethnicity seeks an explanation in the sphere of culture (Malik 1996: 174–7). The concept of citizenship attempts to provide a means by which disadvantaged citizens can be reconciled to their lower position in society. The argument presented here is that citizenship is an appropriate concept for contemporary politics because of its use as a concept which reconciles citizens to inequality.

This argument is illustrated through a re-examination of what T.H. Marshall has described as the core components of citizenship (Marshall 1950/1992). The trinity of civil, political and social rights is examined in order to point out their historical significance and thus to highlight the significance of recent changes in western society. We examine each of these rights in turn and add a further set of rights, which we call empowerment rights. This historical dimension is designed to highlight the significance of the changes in contemporary society. The largest section of the chapter is a more detailed exploration of empowerment rights.

The question of race, or ethnicity, is used in each section to help illustrate the changing relationship of the state to its citizens. Some readers may find the interchangeable use of the concepts of race and ethnicity confusing. The reason for the lack of differentiation between the two concepts is outlined at the end of the section on social rights.

Civil rights

Civil rights date from the late eighteenth century and are concerned with the liberty of the individual in society. Civil rights developed in the context of the struggle of the emerging bourgeoisie against the old feudal aristocracy. The freedom to own and sell property was important as this was the key to producing and holding onto wealth. Under feudal law the right to own and sell property was restricted by a series of local customs. The bourgeoisie strove to break down these constraints on their ability to accumulate wealth. From the point of view of the bourgeoisie, the state, as it was constituted under feudalism, was a barrier to the accumulation of capital. They were opposed to state regulation of society and believed that its role should be confined to administering justice internally and defending the state from external threats (Bottomore 1992: 55–6).

Civil rights may be an expression of the interests of the emerging bourgeoisie but they go beyond the immediate interests of the emerging capitalist class. The development of civil rights can be viewed as the values of the Enlightenment being put into practice. They are not articulated as the interest of a particular section of society, but as the universal values of 'liberty, equality and fraternity' which should be enjoyed by all citizens (Hobsbawm 1975: 53–76). The assumption that humans are rational and infinitely perfectible underpins the writings of figures such as Thomas Paine. This belief in humanity is underlined by the emphasis on rights rather than on duties. It is a belief which found its inverse in Edmund Burke's emphasis on the importance of tradition and obligation for the maintenance of social order. The left/right divide in politics, epitomised by Paine and Burke, originates in this period.

During this period of history the majority of the population had little or no relationship with the state. The state itself had a minimal existence and parliamentary representatives were elected by an electorate that constituted a tiny proportion of the population. There have been many critics of civil rights. Criticism of the Rights of Man has not only come from the right. Radicals have pointed to the limitations of the ideas of freedom and equality. Marx quipped that workers were free in two senses, free to sell their labour-power and free to starve (Marx 1974: 166), and feminists have pointed out that it was the Rights of *Man* which were championed (Vogel 1994: 81–5). Anti-racists have pointed to the contradiction between the ownership of slaves and the commitment to the principles of human equality and freedom. This contradiction is often taken as proof that those who fought for civil rights were racist, and their commitment to equality and freedom was rhetorical (Fryer 1984).

There were certainly limits to the application of the ideals of 'liberty, equality and fraternity'. Robin Blackburn has noted that the Scottish Enlightenment philosopher Francis Hutcheson had a difficulty taking a clear stance on the issue of slavery. Hutcheson wanted to uphold the idea of human liberty and equality, a position which logically meant attacking slavery, but this contradicted his desire 'not to infringe legally acquired property rights or question long-term indenture...such as still survived in the coal mines of eighteenth century Scotland' (Malik 1996: 64). According to Malik this led Hutcheson to the peculiar compromise of attacking the slave trade while not attacking slavery itself. Many of those who were formally committed to equality and liberty were prepared to put up some defence of slavery, but it was motivated by a defence of private property and not in the belief that black people are inferior.

It is important to recognise that the commitment to equality and freedom was not simply rhetorical. If the commitment were simply rhetorical it is difficult to understand how slavery came to be abolished at all. Critics may point to the limitations of the Enlightenment commitment to equality and freedom, but there were two ways in which the ideals of freedom and equality helped to undermine the institution of slavery. The changes in the law which derived from the promotion of these ideas helped to create a sphere of freedom in which citizens could challenge the limitations of elites' commitment to equality and liberty. The primacy of common law over local custom gave a universal character to the law. The establishing of *habeas corpus* placed the burden of proof on the state to justify the incarceration of any of its citizens; and the right to free speech provided the freedom to criticise the existing order.

Political rights

The development of political rights is the term used to refer to the universal extension of the franchise and the opening up of parliament and local government to influence from the citizenry. This development began across most of Europe at the turn of the century. The bourgeoisie which had emerged in Europe during the course of the eighteenth century had by the middle of the nineteenth century established a dominant position in society. By the latter quarter of the nineteenth century they experienced a challenge to their dominance from two different directions. The rise of an organised and militant workers' movement challenged them domestically and in the international arena they found themselves coming increasingly into competition with the capitalist classes of other European nation-states. These are the two most significant factors that provide the context for the development of political rights.

The development of capitalism also entailed the creation and growth of the working class – the class of property-less labourers who were free to sell their labour-power or free to starve. This class was highly heterogeneous, they worked in different branches of the economy, they worked under different conditions and for much of the nineteenth century they were regionally segregated. In many instances the workforces in different branches of industry were ethnically distinct, a consequence of the coincidence of new waves of immigration with the development of new branches of industry. It was the development of the political ideology of socialism that fused these disparate groups into a collective organisation. Socialism as a political ideology acted to prevent ethnic differentiation taking on a social significance.

The development of political rights was a logical extension of civil rights. Government forms legislation for the whole of the nation. Socialist parties agitated to have an input into this process through extra-parliamentary means. They pressurised government for laws, such as for an eight-hour week, which would be of benefit to the whole of the working class. More obviously they agitated for universal suffrage in order that the working class could have a direct avenue to influence the legislative process (Hobsbawm 1987: 112–29).

The other side of the process of extending the franchise was the incorporation of the working class into the political life of the nation-state. The 'social question' troubled political elites. Elite figures, like Joseph Chamberlain in Britain, argued that reforms were necessary to head off social revolution. His suggested remedy for this situation was expansion into new territories. For political elites the benefit of imperialism was that it could tackle the twin perils of socialism and foreign competition. Through the ideology of Social Darwinism this was presented as a progressive mission. The history of capitalism was the history of the progress of civilisation. Through imperialism the working class would benefit from advancing prosperity and the colonial peoples would be 'civilised' by the white man.

The triumph of nationalism over socialism within the working class appears to be obvious in the level of support which workers gave to their own nation-state in the First World War. But the reality is more complex. Support for the nation-state was an indication of how nationalism had merged with socialism in the minds of the working class. For many workers the two were seen as compatible rather than in opposition to each other. Popular support for the nation in the First World War was not mobilised on the basis of an aggressive superiority, but defensively 'as a threat from abroad to civic advantages peculiar' to a worker's own nation. This is how the working class could support the war effort while also taking militant action against their employers. Or, as in the case of the rent strikes in Glasgow, against co-nationals of a different class (Hobsbawm 1992: 88–9, 123–30). The extent to which there was a conflict between nationalism and socialism depended on two, inter-related, factors. The extent to which the nation-state was viable and the extent of the individual worker's idealism.

Hobsbawm notes that in the European states which were defeated in the First World War, Russia, Germany, German Austria and Hungary, 'collapse led to social revolution' (Hobsbawm 1992: 130). Yet even in these states, where socialism posed a serious threat to nationalism, there were some who fought wholeheartedly for emancipation from capitalism and others who had more modest goals.

The ambivalence towards nationalism found in the working class was also apparent in their attitude to imperialism. Where workers saw common cause with colonial peoples they campaigned in their support, for example in the public denunciations of 'Chinese slavery' in the South African mines. Where they saw their immediate interests as being threatened by colonial people they took sides with their employers, for example the unions in the Lancashire cotton industry joined with their employers to oppose the industrialisation of India (Hobsbawm 1987: 72). The development of political rights was one side of the process of incorporating the working class into the political life of the nation-state. The other side was the development of social rights.

Social rights

Social rights are those elements, such as education and welfare, which allow citizens to enjoy a standard of living and a level of understanding which allows them to participate in society. The development of social rights initially accompanied the extension of political rights in the latter decades of the nineteenth century. However, they eventually developed beyond political rights to take a distinct institutional form in the shape of the welfare state. The reason we are dealing with social rights separately from political rights is not simply because their development chronologically extended beyond the establishment of the universal franchise, but because they are logically distinct.

Political rights do not advocate any particular role for the state, but merely recognise that all citizens should, through their elected representatives, be able to have an input into the legislative process. In Isaiah Berlin's terms they are a negative freedom. Social rights, by contrast, advocate an active role for the state. They assume that the state has a responsibility to intervene in society and manage the problems created by the market. Viewed as a relationship between the state and its citizens, political rights are a means for the citizens to have an input into the state, social rights are a means for the state to have an input into its citizens. Under social rights it is the state which exercises the rights for its citizens; in this sense it is misleading to refer to social rights as rights, it is more useful to refer to them as entitlements.

The extension of social rights was relatively unproblematic in the sphere of education. In an era of technological development the economy increasingly required a literate workforce. The other benefit of universal primary education was that it could be used as a means to inculcate civilised values into the working class (Hobsbawm 1987: 149–50). Measures such as the extension of pension rights and assistance for the infirm were designed both to ameliorate the ravages of the market and to promote the state as an instrument through which the conditions of the working class could be improved. This met with more resistance from business and political elites, especially in Britain. State intervention ran counter to the doctrine of *laissez-faire* which dominated liberal thinking in the nineteenth century. (*Laissez-faire* was seen as the economic equivalent of civil rights.) Hostility to social insurance also found an expression in the working class. The proud tradition of workers' independence meant that there was often a stigma surrounding state assistance. But even in Britain by 1906 the necessity for social rights had been almost universally accepted (Marshall 1975: 35–7).

The working class were the main direct beneficiaries of the initial development of social rights. This development took the form of state-established social insurance. It provided the working class with a cushion from the negative effects of the market. Some European states, notably the newly united Germany, went further and intervened in the economy to cushion industrialists from the negative effects of the market. This move was strongly resisted in Britain. But during the Great Depression of the 1930s even British industrialists could not stay immune from the charms of state intervention in the economy. Across Europe in the 1930s and 1940s there was practically no-one who would put up a defence of the market: and those who did were often defensive in their advocacy. After the Second World War state intervention in society became institutionalised through the welfare state (Furedi 1992: 172–7).

There are a number of 'ethnicity issues' which were raised in this period. We have seen that nationalism became a dominant ideology at the end of the nineteenth century, and as such helped to divide peoples according to their national origin and which has continued into the twentieth century. The twentieth century has also been a century of immigration controls. In Britain the Aliens Act (1905), which was specifically targeted at East European Jews, was passed in parliament. We may note that the significance of the Act was not in its effect on immigrants or on immigration, the Act was limited in scope and not vigorously enforced. Rather, the historical significance of the Act was that the long-standing principle, that entry to Britain should be open to all, was breached for the first time (Mason 1995: 26–7).

We have already seen that Social Darwinist thinking developed alongside the extension of social rights. The brutal and inhuman consequences of state action based on ideas of racial superiority were illustrated to the world by the Nazi Holocaust. The experience of the Holocaust discredited notions of racial superiority, but it did not end the practice of categorising humanity into distinct ethnic or national groups. Malik (1996) notes that in the post-war period ethnicity developed as a concept through which people could 'divide humanity into discrete groups without feeling the taint of racial ideology' (Malik 1996: 175). (It is in order to draw attention to the close affinity between the concepts of race and ethnicity that the two terms are used interchangeably in the text.)

The immigration controls enacted in Britain and in France in the 1960s and 1970s were justified primarily on economic grounds. It was argued that the economy could not support an increase in population. But the principal concern of political elites was that immigration would cause social disruption. Government developed a two-pronged approach to the 'problems' posed by immigrants. The flow of black immigrants was arrested through further restrictions on immigration and a series of measures were instituted which were designed to integrate ethnic minorities into the political life of the nation-state (Deakin 1969). This two-pronged approach was to become important for what we refer to as empowerment rights.

Empowerment rights

Empowerment rights is the term used to describe the contemporary measures which help citizens to participate more fully in the smooth running of society. They include measures such as children's rights, Aids awareness education, and multiculturalism. The concept of empowerment rights is proposed here as a useful theoretical tool with which to understand the contours of contemporary citizenship. There is a tendency in the literature on citizenship to argue for the adaptation of social rights in the absence of Keynesian state planning (Cahill 1995). We believe that this can lead to confusion over what is distinct about contemporary citizenship. At a superficial level the proposed new social rights share features with the rights enjoyed under the welfare state. Both rely on the state to deal with the negative effects of the market. Yet there have been dramatic changes on both sides of the relationship between the state and the citizenry.

We noted previously that political and social rights developed in an attempt to incorporate a working class that had been given coherence by the political programme of socialism. This political programme has collapsed and with it the working class has lost its organisational coherence. The influence of trade unions has been increasingly weakened throughout the course of the economic crisis of the 1970s and 1980s. In the process of the unravelling of the welfare compromise the working class became disaggregated. In the space which opened up alternative sources of identification emerged. For example it was in the 1970s in Western Europe that the first wave of contemporary movements for regional autonomy emerged.

The other side of the assault on the institutions of the welfare state was their impact on the state. When Margaret Thatcher came to power in 1979 she declared that she would 'roll back the state'. This declaration, like many of Thatcher's other utterances, was rhetorical. Under Thatcher public spending increased year-on-year throughout the 1980s. Thatcher did not succeed in cutting public spending, but her government did succeed in reorganising the institutional framework of the state.

The single most significant achievement of the New Right in the 1980s was their gaining universal acceptance for the idea that 'there is no alternative' to the market. The universal acceptance of this principle finally came with the collapse of the Soviet bloc in 1989. Paradoxically the triumph of the market was quickly followed by the collapse of the New Right. The foremost ideologue of the free market, Margaret Thatcher, was ousted as leader of her party a year after the collapse of the Berlin Wall. There may be universal acceptance that 'there is no alternative' to the market, but it co-exists with a profound unease about market forces. The role of the state has become more modest, it is no longer to plan society or regulate the economy but simply to deal with the negative impact of the market. One of the consequences of the shift in focus from the economy has been to focus attention on people's behaviour as a means to minimise the negative impact of the market.

The 1980s are routinely referred to as the 'greedy eighties'. The problems of the 1990s are considered to be a consequence of rampant individualism. Communitarians propose that 'we put a new emphasis on "we", on the values that we share, on the spirit of the community' as a means to reconstitute society (Etzioni 1993: 25). This idea converges with the 1990s' conservative argument that society needs 'a re-assertion of moral values and social responsibility' (Miller 1995: 433). It is worth challenging this myth that the New Right promoted individualism. Neo-liberalism did not represent a return to the era of civil rights, to the promotion of liberty and the strong individual. Strong individuals like Arthur Scargill were people who Thatcher bitterly opposed. Indeed, the miners found that taking a stance could lead to the loss of livelihood and liberty. The problem afflicting West European societies in the 1990s is not one of strong individuals but of weak ones. Thatcher succeeded in undermining the power of the trade unions and of destroying other forms of social solidarity, but she did not succeed in developing any replacement. One effect of this was to leave individuals isolated and vulnerable (Furedi 1997: 139–42).

The obverse of accepting that there is no alternative to the market is the acceptance that there is a limit to what human action can achieve. Society is now considered to be governed by forces that are beyond human control. Many of the popular concepts in social sciences today, for example globalisation and environmentalism, highlight processes which are largely outside of human control. Empowerment rights represent the integrative edge of this acceptance of the limits of human capabilities.

The co-existence of a generalised acceptance that there is no alternative to the market with a generalised fear of the consequences of the market displays other paradoxical features. Despite fear of its effects the market is more pervasive than at any time in human history. Market relations are being extended into areas where they never previously existed. Through fund holders' budgets the market has been introduced into the health service. Through the use of measures such as league tables, market relations now exert an influence on the education system. The influence of market forces is further enhanced by initiatives, like the Citizen's Charter, which grants rights to citizens as consumers of public services. The elevation of citizens' rights for people as consumers has been accompanied by a shift from democratic accountability to the promotion of market efficiency (Jenkins 1995).

The powerful appeal of empowerment rights is that they appear to provide some protection for people who feel vulnerable in a society that has become unpredictable. It is difficult to outline in a coherent manner what we mean by empowerment rights. They are not yet clearly formulated as a set of practices or policies. The process has gone furthest in the United States and Britain. In the last section we will briefly present some of the emerging themes of empowerment rights.

Six themes in empowerment rights

The first theme we want to draw attention to is the importance attached to attitudes. The Conservative government is often associated with racism and racist attitudes. Thatcher's 'swamp speech' in 1978 is often cited as an example. As with much else about Thatcher there was a gap between the ideological bluster and the pragmatic approach taken to the day-to-day administration of society. Contrary to what might be popularly believed, one of the early reports which had an influence on the development of multicultural education, *Education for Equality* (1981), was produced by the Conservative-controlled Berkshire Education Committee. The approach adopted in the report, and in the government-sponsored Rampton Inquiry, was that racism was a result of prejudice and stereotyping which may affect individuals' 'attitude and behaviour towards members of [ethnic minority] groups' (Tompson 1988: 115). If the problem was prejudice then the answer was to adopt measures which overcame this prejudice. This entailed the promotion of positive images of ethnic minorities in conjunction with educating the prejudiced attitudes out of the mind of the racist citizen. The role of the state in influencing racial ideas, for example through racist immigration policies, is downplayed and the attitudes of individuals are focused on. The state can then play an important role in educating the individual to think correctly.

A second theme, the importance of inclusion, is related to the first. It is pointed out that prejudice can prevent ethnic minorities from playing a full role in society (Mason 1995: 114–19). This is undoubtedly true, but the problem with the discussion of inclusion is that inclusion is seen as an end in itself. In the absence of any ideals to aspire to in society, social inclusion can easily become social conformity.

A third theme is the need for pluralism. Malik notes that equality has been 'redefined from "the right to be the same" to mean "the right to be different"' (Malik 1996: 261). In the 1960s and 1970s anti-racists campaigned for an end to immigration controls or for an end to segregation. They argued that black people should have access to the same material opportunities as whites. In the 1990s anti-racism has come to mean campaigns for separate schools, or for the right to maintain particular cultural practices. He also points out that 'proclaiming difference requires us to accept society as it is, to accept as given the divisions and inequalities that characterise our social world' (Malik 1996: 262).

A fourth theme is an emphasis on individuals as victims. The dangers latent in this theme can be seen in the British Labour government's proposals that there should be a special penalty for crimes which have a racial motive. At the time of writing it is unclear whether this will reach the statute books, but even the fact that it can be proposed at the annual party conference is significant. If this special provision is to become law it will undermine the important principle of civil rights that all are equal before the eyes of the law. Ironically it also reinforces the idea that black people are not the same as whites, that they are a special case.

A fifth theme is that of limits. The idea that immigration should be severely restricted has been almost universally accepted, even among black people themselves. This is another example of how people are restricting the horizons of what they believe to be possible.

The sixth theme is the promotion of morality as the route to winning an argument. In the case of immigration the only arguments put forward today are around asylum, that it is morally wrong to exclude people who are victims of human rights abuses abroad. Ironically there are echoes here of the idea that 'we' are civilised and people 'out there' are not. The use of moral or emotional argument is not in-and-of-itself dangerous. But in the absence of any supporting rational argument it can easily feed into wider trends towards irrationality.

Conclusion

The criticisms put forward in the last section may appear to be excessively harsh. If that is so it is partly because the implications of the trend towards empowerment rights are extremely worrying. The new rights threaten to undermine all of our previously existing rights. Liberty is becoming conditional, and is also coming to mean freedom from other people. Equality has come to mean difference. And our political rights are threatened by the trend towards representing people on the basis of their identities rather than their ideals. Theoretically, the idea of Group Rights may have universal application. There is a danger, however, that the blanket application of such rights carries the threat of catering for people on the basis of collective identity rather than according to individual ideals. In that way individual political and civil rights may come to be undermined, and barriers may be erected where none previously existed. Another problem with the current fashion for emphasising difference is that the fashion itself is barely questioned, which in itself is a worrying trend.

The reader would be justified in asking me what alternative I propose. Unfortunately I cannot propose a grand solution (these are not times for 'grand narratives', let alone grand solutions), but there are a few points that I would make. One is that it is important to take a critical stance towards these new 'rights'. A second is that collective action cannot be counterposed to these trends towards individuation. Any displays of collectivity today are latched onto as evidence of a re-creation of community and as such only help to exasperate the trend. The funeral of Diana, Princess of Wales, provides a good example of this phenomenon, the mass demonstrations against paedophiles in Belgium provide another example more specific to continental Europe. One way in which people can challenge the development of empowerment rights is through emphasising what we have in common with other people, not as communitarians but out of individual self-interest.

References

Bottomore, T. (1992) *Citizenship and Social Class: Forty Years On*, London: Macmillan.

Burke, E. (1969) *Reflections on the Revolution in France*, London: Penguin.

Cahill, M. (1995) *New Social Policy*, Oxford: Blackwell.

Deakin, J. *Citizenship and Colour*, London: Penguin.

Etzioni, A. (1993) *The Spirit of Community*, London: Fontana.

Fryer, P. (1984) *Staying Power: the History of Black People in Britain*, London: Pluto.

Furedi, F. (1992) *Mythical Past, Elusive Future: History and Society in an Anxious Age*, London: Pluto.

—— (1997) *Culture of Fear: Risk-taking and the Morality of Low Expectation*, London: Cassell.

Hennessy, P. (1995) *The Hidden Wiring: Unearthing the British Constitution*, London: Gollancz.

Hobsbawm, E.J. (1975) *The Age of Revolution*, London: Weidenfeld & Nicolson.

—— (1987) *The Age of Empire*, London: Weidenfeld & Nicolson.

—— (1992) *Nations and Nationalism Since 1780*, Cambridge: Cambridge University Press.

Hoggart, R. (1990) *The Uses of Literacy*, London: Penguin.

Jenkins, S. (1995) *Accountable to None: the Tory Nationalisation of Britain*, London: Penguin.

Kymlicka, W. (1995) *Multicultural Citizenship*, Oxford: Oxford University Press.

Livingstone, S. and Morison, J. (1995) *An Audit of Democracy in Northern Ireland*, Belfast: Fortnight Educational Trust.

Malik, K. (1996) *The Meaning of Race*, London: Macmillan.

Marr, A. (1995) *Ruling Britannia: the Failure and the Future of British Democracy*, London: Michael Joseph.

Marshall, T.H. (1950/1992) *Citizenship and Social Class*, London: Pluto.

—— (1975) *Social Policy*, London: Hutchinson.

Marx, K. (1974) *Capital*, vol. 1, London: Lawrence & Wishart.

Mason, D. (1995) *Race and Ethnicity in Modern Britain*, Oxford: Oxford University Press.

Miller, D. (1995) 'Citizenship and Pluralism', in *Political Studies* 43 (3): 432–51.

Mouffe, C. (1992a) 'Preface', in C. Mouffe (ed.) *Dimensions of Radical Democracy*, London: Verso.

—— (1992b) 'Democratic Citizenship and the Political Community', in C. Mouffe (ed.) *Dimensions of Radical Democracy*, London: Verso.

Paine, T. (1985) *The Rights of Man*, London: Penguin.

Preuss, U.K. (1996) 'Two Challenges to European Citizenship', in *Political Studies* 44 (3): 534–52.

Tompson, K. (1988) *Under Siege*, London: Penguin.

Turner, B. (1992) 'Outline of a Theory of Citizenship', in C. Mouffe (ed.) *Dimensions of Radical Democracy*, London: Verso.

Vogel, U. (1994) 'Marriage and the Boundaries of Citizenship', in B. van Steenbergen (ed.) *The Condition of Citizenship*, London: Sage.

5 Critical reflections on the return of national minority rights regulation to East/West European affairs[1]

Adam Burgess

New focus on national minority rights

The Vienna Concluding Document of the Human Dimension of the Conference on Security and Co-operation in Europe (CSCE), now the Organisation for Security and Co-operation in Europe (OSCE), produced in 1989, marked a new centrality accorded the issue of national minority rights in Europe. In November of 1991, the CSCE's Paris Charter pledged its determination to improve the lot of minorities, and for the first time in its history used the term 'minority' in its own right (dropping the usual rider 'where they exist'). December of 1991 saw the European Community (EC) declare that, along with observance of the rule of law, democracy, and respect for human rights in general, minority guarantees were a prerequisite for the recognition of new states in Europe. In line with these developments, the European Parliament has also adopted documents on minorities, in particular the Resolution on Linguistic and Cultural Minorities in the European Community of February 1994. Later that year, the Framework Convention for the Protection of National Minorities was passed by the Council of Europe. It obliges signatories to undertake extensive measures to positively promote minority concerns, rather than simply refrain from discrimination.

As a consequence of such measures, the question of national minority rights has become an issue in its own terms. No longer subsumed among concern about rights in general as had been the case since the Second World War, it was 'emancipated from human rights' (Christopulos 1994: 172). So elevated has this concern become that Catherine Lalumiere, then General Secretary of the Council of Europe, felt confident to declare that 'Europe will be judged on how it solves its minority problems' (Christopulos 1994: 173). The minority issue is no longer simply concerned with the actual treatment and status of the minority in question, but has become a measure of moral progress for European nations, and the continent as a whole.

States are obliged by the Council of Europe, among others, to promote minority culture through measures such as ensuring minority access to the media, and encouraging the use of minority languages. Far from being viewed as potentially problematic for state authority, encouraging minorities in this fashion

is seen to 'enrich' the diversity of pluralistic democracy. More practically, international minority protection is a central component of 'conflict prevention' – a
burgeoning academic and policy sector within contemporary Europe. Attempts at
the assimilation of minority cultures, on the other hand, are widely seen as undesirable – part of an anachronistically monolithic political culture which Europe
is leaving behind. This is the measure by which Lalumiere among others wishes to
see Europe judged, and of which minority protection, even encouragement, is such
a central component. Somewhat curiously perhaps, the maturity of (majoritarian)
democracy is now to be gauged by the extent of such measures: 'treatment of
minorities is the touchstone of democratic progress' (Liebich 1996: 84).

It is not the whole of Europe that is the subject of concern. In the European
context, it is largely the new democracies of Central and Eastern Europe which
are the focus. Indeed, the recent rehabilitation of national minority rights has
developed largely as a consequence of concern for the fate of non-dominant
groups in a region considered ripe for a revival of nationalist intolerance
following the collapse of communism. There, non-dominant groups are invariably classified as indigenous 'national minorities' in order to differentiate them
from such 'immigrant' groups as, for example, the Arabs of France, or Turks of
Germany. These are also the countries which find themselves outside the principal European institutions. Insistence on respect for the rights of minorities can
therefore be utilised as an important carrot and stick through which 'Europe
proper' is to steer societies, seen to be disfigured by half a century of communism, into the European fold. The opportunity to make such demands is
stimulated by the desperation of these new democracies to escape marginalisation. As one historian put it recently:

> Since all these states are looking Westward, towards greater integration with
> the European Union, it is, as in the 1920s, possible for the West to require
> some evidence of minority rights...as part of the price for accepting the
> Eastern European states into a wider European community.
>
> (Cornwall 1996)

There has been little comment upon, let alone criticism of, the issue of
national minority rights returning to the centre stage of European relations with
its 'East'. Few have even asked why national minority rights were removed from
the historical agenda, requiring their return in the 1990s. Given the troubled
history of when a 'minority rights regime' last ruled Europe – in the interwar
years – this is surprising. The demand that Central and Eastern Europe conform
to externally imposed standards regarding the treatment of its citizens is historically bound up with great power politics, and the subjugation of these societies
which benefited neither their minority not majority. The only beneficiaries were
the principal world powers – exempt from such scrutiny, and able to reap moral
dividends from their elevated status as European policemen on behalf of the
oppressed. There is reason to believe that the same arrogant mistake is being
made again.

The rise, fall and return of national minority rights supervision

There is a significant history to extra-national intervention 'in support of' East European minority nationalities. Napoleon Bonaparte pioneered the approach through adopting the Poles (against Russia), and later sponsorship of the South Slav 'Illyrian' state to counter the Habsburgs. The Russians imitated Napoleon with support for Serbian independence and (together with Britain) the cause of Greece. The sponsorship of particular minorities and their right to self-determination was intimately bound up with the 'Eastern question' which dominated nineteenth-century European diplomacy. While a measure of great power co-operation was established towards the end of the century, naked state patronage of national minorities returned with a vengeance in the inter-war years. This was clearest among those 'revisionist' powers which suffered most from the post-First World War settlement, and they deliberately set out to undermine the Versailles system through encouraging the aspirations of aggrieved minorities. The victorious powers also politicised the issue by institutionalising a system of minority rights regulation for the new states of Eastern Europe. Its crucial consequence was a codification of their subordinate, and ultimately utilitarian, status in a new European order organised around the containment of Bolshevik Russia and an unstable Germany.

In a clear parallel of today's Europe where it is 'part of the price' to be paid in order to even merit consideration for admittance to European institutions, the new states of Eastern Europe 'were all persuaded, cajoled or intimidated into signing Minorities Treaties as a condition of their diplomatic legitimation by the Allies' (Pearson 1983: 142). A Minorities Section was created within the League of Nations to deal with any breach of obligations reported by non-dominant groups. This state of affairs was fiercely resented by the regimes themselves. Hannah Arendt pointed out in *The Origins of Totalitarianism* that they 'regarded the Minority Treaties as an open breach of promise and discrimination because only new states, and not even defeated Germany [Upper Silesia excepted], were bound to them' (Arendt 1973: 270–1). It was not so much the practical impact of the committee's recommendations which rankled – after all, only fourteen cases were ever sent by the Minorities Section for examination by the Council of the League. It was the institutionalisation of inequality between east and west which was at the heart of East European objections to the new system of minority regulation.

Despite the rhetoric of rights, the driving force behind this new form of regulation was power. As Pearson explains: 'The Great Powers set themselves up as custodians of international justice not on grounds of proven competence or unimpeachable probity, but through their political and military clout' (Pearson 1983: 138). While the new regimes of Eastern Europe remained effectively on probation, key members of the League, including Germany, were largely exempt from any scrutiny. This double standard had a clear ideological thrust. As one expert noted, there was one proposition put forward with 'particular eagerness'.

This was 'the idea that although justice would require identical obligations from everyone, in practice some countries, enjoying a higher standard of civilisation "had already grown out of" the period of intolerance, and thus did not deserve to be under any limitations' (Sierpowski 1991: 28). The Council was not receptive to the Polish suggestion that Britain, France, and the United States sign similar undertakings with respect to the Irish, Algerians, black Americans and other colonial subjects.

On a practical level, the system was worse than useless. Such clear infringements of sovereignty led states openly to disregard obligations which they saw as being designed to undermine internal legitimacy. Minorities themselves were invariably hostile to institutions and mechanisms considered entirely ineffective. Despite being a supporter of the monitoring process, British historian C.A. Macartney, in perhaps the most authoritative survey of the inter-war experience, concluded that the experience was 'not very heartening' (Macartney 1934: 490). Where it was 'effective', it only provided legitimacy for great power manoeuvring: 'the chief cases where pressure has been put upon it by some power which would have championed the minority in question even without the League'. He went on to argue that 'experience surely justifies the thought that any interference by one or more states in the affairs of another is provocative of irritation and ill feeling, and should not be undertaken without good reason' (Macartney 1934: 491).

The system of inter-war minority rights monitoring was only 'effective' in codifying the inferior and conditional status of the new democracies. This sense of inequality endured regardless of the activities of the League's committee. Macartney considered it was only the 'special quality' (rather 'inequality') of Eastern Europe that justified such measures. At root, that 'special quality' was a moral deficiency which required their supervision by superiors. Not surprisingly, Germany was both amused and gratified by the way in which their new neighbours, supposedly friends of the Allies, were stamped second class by having to account to the League for their treatment of members of non-titular national groups. It was rightly interpreted by Germany as a signal (along with many others) that it was not a question of whether 'independent Eastern Europe' was to be regulated by others, only by whom. The spread of Nazi influence in the region from the mid-1930s was largely unopposed by their European rivals, and by that time seemed an almost natural and seamless development. Fittingly, perhaps the most decisive moment of that process was justified by the alleged discrimination of a minority, as the invasion and partition of Czechoslovakia was ostensibly concerned with above all the protection of the country's Sudeten German population.

However, it was precisely the association with Nazism which led to the discrediting of international minority rights enforcement. There was no reference to minority rights in the United Nations (UN) Charter of 1945, or in the Universal Declaration of Human Rights. As the British academic James Mayall argues, 'Moreover, the concept of minority rights fell into disrepute after Hitler had invoked it as a justification for his expansion into Central and Eastern

Europe' (Mayall 1994: 9). States were protected by the Charter from any interference in their internal affairs. The term 'minority' was omitted from the lists of
prohibited grounds of discrimination in both the Charter and Declaration of
Human Rights. As late as the 1980s, even defining a minority was still considered problematic. The study carried out by Francesco Capotorti for the UN,
which remained the leading study on discrimination against minorities, initially
foundered upon lack of consensus as to the definition of a minority.

Regardless of any lingering definitional difficulties, however, the issue has
now returned to the centre stage of European relations. The Convention for the
Protection of Minorities of 1991 proposed setting up a machinery to protect
minorities remarkably similar to that of the League of Nations. Under the terms
of the Convention, a committee receives petitions and tries to achieve a 'friendly
settlement' between minority and government. Yet while there are some clear
historical continuities between the inter-war and contemporary experience, the
current vogue for minority rights enforcement goes far beyond anything in the
past. The emphasis is not upon equal treatment, but rather the promotion of
minority identity. States are now obliged positively to help minorities, rather than
simply refrain from discrimination. Thus the UN General Assembly 1992 declaration, in paragraph 33, 'requires that states shall take measures to create
favourable conditions to enable persons belonging to minorities to express their
characteristics...' (Mullerson 1994: 109). The novelty of the Vienna Concluding
Document was that it

> extends the traditional clause of non-discrimination to positive affirmative
> action in favour of minorities...in other words, not only do the states have
> the obligation to abstain from policies which could harm minorities...they
> have to create conditions for the promotion of the minority identity.
>
> (Christopulos 1994: 164)

In the inter-war period by contrast, 'Although the minorities might be granted
certain basic rights, they were not to be encouraged to believe that they had a
privileged position within the new "national states"...' (Cornwall 1992).

The consequences of this development are considerable. The demanding test
of 'what have you done to promote minorities?' has developed hand in hand
with minority treatment becoming a measure of 'Eastern' democratic progress.
Yet the shift from 'mere' equal rights to an obligation to 'positively promote'
minority identity removes any clear measure by which 'progress' can be
measured.

The international isolation of Slovakia, for example, has come about to a
considerable extent through the perception of its backwardness with regard to
the protection of the country's sizeable Hungarian minority. Criticism concerns
the state's alleged reluctance to promote Hungarian minority identity – particularly with regard to language provision. Supranational institutions such as the
OSCE are demanding that the Slovak authorities devote special resources for the
encouragement of Hungarian identity among Slovakia's Hungarian population.

Until they are judged to have shown enough willing in this regard they are likely to remain marginalised. Perceived attentiveness to the wishes of minorities is deciding the fate of states and not simply that of non-titular national minorities.

Preventing 'Eurogeddon' and containing cultural legacies?

Why then this insistence upon minority rights regulation in contemporary Eastern Europe? The answer has to be located in a world far more favourably disposed towards the claims of culture and the potential victim. More specifically, the return of minority rights is based upon large assumptions about both east and West in Europe. 'The East' is assumed to be culturally predisposed towards intolerance of all varieties – most seriously towards other ethnic and racial groups. The west in this context, meanwhile, figures as a suitable tamer of such dangerous passions through its claim to have left intolerance behind on the domestic front, and to be no longer motivated internationally by the selfish power politics of old. Both of these assumptions are not borne out by reality.

Minority rights are no longer simply seen to be an internal matter for states themselves, but are considered international concerns because of their purported potential to involve wider conflict. For example, the Moscow meeting of the Conference on the Human Dimension in 1991 expressly referred to the minority issue from the perspective of the peaceful settlement of disputes. This perspective is based upon the alleged potential for the region to descend into 'Yugoslavia writ large'. Particularly in the early 1990s, as Liebich describes: 'At this point, Western policy makers, now prodded by a horde of recycled security specialists, began to give credence to the most alarmist pronouncements' (Liebich 1996). The worst case scenario mentality of the 'recycled security specialists' was reflected in the media coverage of the region (bizarrely, conflict was even anticipated in Slovakia – see Burgess 1997b).

Fears of 'Eurogeddon' have proven to be patently false. Francis Fukuyama, for example, noted: 'If we look carefully, what is striking is not the strength of intolerant nationalism but its weakness....There have been any number of conflicts that have so far failed to materialise in the former Soviet bloc' (quoted in Griffiths 1993: 1). Yugoslav disintegration, even if we were to interpret it as an internally driven 'tribal war', was evidently more an exception than rule.

It is difficult to avoid the conclusion that these fears were more an expression of western anxieties than eastern realities.

In any specific sense, it is by no means self-evident why East Europeans are considered to have a unique proclivity towards the oppression of minorities. It was the Yugoslavs, for example, who were actually at the forefront of returning minority rights to the international agenda. Their draft to the UN subcommittee on Prevention of Discrimination and Protection of Minorities in 1978 suggested a declaration of commitment to a wider definition of minority rights. More broadly, outside the context of historical great power intrigue in the region, and especially if we consider the relative absence of ethnic conflict since the Second World War, there is little specific evidence to substantiate any special predisposition towards ethnic intolerance.

The heightened western sense of eastern ethnic intolerance is based upon proposition more than evidence – principally the alleged power of cultural legacies from the past. Many commentators have drawn upon the supposedly enduring reaction to Ottoman and Habsburg influence in the nineteenth century. Even more popular is the argument that the experience of communism has moulded a people incapable of accepting difference, and disposed towards a return to the more familiar world of 'authoritarianism'. Ken Jowitt's influential *New World Disorder*, for example, diagnosed a population so crippled by the experience of 'Leninism', that they would find the 'Protestant liberal capitalist way of life boring, demeaning, and, in good part, unintelligible' (Jowitt 1992: 291). A wealth of other developments have been 'explained' through this same framework. There is insufficient space here systematically to challenge the 'cultural legacy' argument (see Holmes 1996; Burgess 1997a). Yet the promiscuous fashion in which alleged cultural legacies rather than the pressures of everyday existence are employed to explain all manner of (often quite contradictory) phenomena suggests that accounts which explain everything, equally explain nothing at all.

Innumerable 'cultural characteristics' can be extrapolated from the experience of living under communism. In Eastern Europe since 1956, we can identify a population indifferent to any form of political mobilisation and direct influence of the state ('Leninism' was a joke even for the elite) – in the name of proletariat, nation or race. More widely, 'communism' created an intensely privatised people concerned more with entrepreneurial opportunities in the shadow economy than scapegoating minorities. It is hardly surprising that even the appeals of anti-centralist 'nationalism', which were evident with the collapse of the old regimes, rapidly diminished.

Generalisations about East Europeans who led a life untouched by official ideology and political action are at least as credible as those of a backward 'Eastern' mentality derived from old theories of 'totalitarianism'. No wonder the apocalyptic anticipations of 'Eurogeddon', upon which the necessity for international supervision of minority treatment was based, proved to be false.

An end to *realpolitik*?

No less open to question in any examination of the assumptions behind the return of external minority rights supervision is that the naked self-interest which characterised great power enforcement in the past has been transcended. Internationalising national minority rights was rejected after the war to prevent revanchist ambitions on the part of defeated states and others such as Poland, which had been subject to arbitrary border changes, being pursued through a concern for the 'protection of minorities'. The return of minority rights to European relations presumes such dangers have passed. This is unjustified.

As in the inter-war period, Western Europe remains largely immune from such scrutiny by virtue of the continuing definition of their 'non-native' populations as 'immigrants' – even if, for example, the Arab inhabitants of France face considerably greater social barriers than the Hungarians of Slovakia. Where a possibility of the spotlight falling upon the more powerful players in European affairs remains, those in a position to influence the rules of the game remain at an advantage. For example, the OSCE High Commissioner on National Minorities was given a mandate to receive information from any source but 'will not acknowledge communications from any person or organisation which practices or publicly condones terrorism or violence' (Christopulos 1994: 173). According to Christopulos, the clause was inserted after pressure from Britain and Turkey. They did not relish the prospect of representatives of the Kurds or Irish Republicans causing embarrassment. Thus in order to escape the attentions of the OSCE, the Irish within the United Kingdom and Turkish Kurds are here redefined as putative 'terrorists'.

Even accepting that 'the East' should constitute the exclusive focus of minority attention, there remains a clear geopolitical rationale determining that some minorities are more equal in the eyes of the west than others. Until recently there has been little said in the West European media about the largest of the minorities of the former Eastern bloc – the Russians of the former Soviet republics. This blind spot in minority rights enforcement is peculiar not only because of the size of the minority, but because many Russians face open legal discrimination – not simply a lack of state resolve to encourage identity. Support for Estonian membership of pan-European organisations, despite the exclusion of the 'alien' Russian minority from Estonian citizenship, is but one example. Even after changes which left most Russians as non-citizens who could not stand for office, Estonia has been commended for its co-operation with European institutions, and praised for 'the attachment of Estonia to democratic principles and its commitment to dialogue and compromise and non-confrontation with its communities and its neighbouring countries' (Mullerson 1994: 183–4). Putting pressure upon a powerful Russia appears to have dictated a less than consistent European attitude towards this particular minority.

More common than such blind spots are the numerous instances where powers have used very particular minority issues in order to further diplomatic ends. Slovenia was forced to devise a system of minority protection by the OSCE in relation to its tiny Italian minority – under threat of exclusion from international organisations. Italy has now largely relented in its pressure upon the Slovenes, having determined 'who's boss' among these Adriatic neighbours by inventing a problem over Slovenia's minority policy. Austria's prominent and one-sided intervention in former Yugoslavia was especially ironic. So vociferous was the Austrian intervention in favour of the Croats and Slovenes that their delegation to the June 1991 CSCE meeting in Berlin included the Slovene Minister for External Affairs amongst its number. At the same time, Austria had been attempting to assimilate its own Slovene minority in the Klagenfurt basin and the Croats of Burgenland with little regard to its obligations towards minorities under the 1955 State Treaty.

Two of the key events in post-Cold War Eastern Europe have been marked, and indeed shaped, by a similarly duplicitous approach to the minority question. For all the talk of minority rights, the now discredited former President Berisha of Albania was supported by West European governments, on the basis that he wouldn't politicise the situation of ethnic Albanians in Kosovo and Macedonia. The implosion of Albania was intimately related to the continued international support enjoyed by the regime, which in turn was the product of its role in containing, rather than politicising, the minority question. More critical still was the highly selective approach to minorities taken by the principal international players in former Yugoslavia. The defining act of a revitalised German posture in the region, the recognition of Croatia, was carried out with no regard to the condition of the significant Serb minority in the Krajina (later 'ethnically cleansed' by Croatia in Operation Storm).

The European powers accepted German insistence on the recognition of Croatia in December 1991, just five weeks after the Community declared independence could only be envisaged in the context of an overall settlement. It was rubber stamped after a tokenistic, and allegedly now 'lost', letter from Croatian President Tudjman that he would respect the Serb minority in an independent Croatia. Despite the entirely accurate presentiment of violence that would follow the endorsement of Croatian nationalism, and to the fury of then chief EC negotiator Lord Carrington amongst others, the other powers went along with Germany. With the Maastricht summit looming, it would appear that the other European powers were reluctant to antagonise Germany over its espousal of Croatian self-determination, and the corresponding abandonment of Serbs inside and outside of Serbia. Recognition also coincided with pressure being put on Bulgaria to prevent, or at least postpone, their recognition of Macedonia. As Garton Ash suggested: 'Could it, just possibly, be a deal: Germany would not (yet) support the recognition of Macedonia if Greece did not oppose the recognition of Slovenia and Croatia? Oh, brave new world!' (Garton Ash 1994: 396). The same can be said for Germany's discouragement of independence for the Baltic states, an approach which again stood in stark contrast to support for Slovenian and Croatian secession from the Yugoslav federation.

Such examples cannot simply be dismissed as unfortunate inconsistencies from an otherwise worthy project of restoring national minority rights to the centre stage of European relations. There is a consistent pattern of greater interest in the pressure such an emphasis puts on selective non-western states, rather than abstract concern for minorities *per se*. 'International', in effect 'Western', supervision of the conduct of other states will inevitably reflect, and become bound up with, the real and unequal relations of power which persist within Europe and the wider world.

This is not to suggest that recent great power involvement in the region has simply followed a classical nineteenth-century pattern of 'Balkanisation', whereby one power backs one minority claim, while their rival backs another. Through the course of the Yugoslav war in particular, a remarkable degree of international consensus was established. All agreed upon the isolation of Serbia and the Serbs. Any competitive impulse was discernible predominantly through the rivalry over who could claim the most vociferously anti-Serb and pro-Bosnian Muslim orientation. Examples of purely individual self-interest, such as with the Italians and their disciplining of the Slovenes, are now relatively marginal to a wider trend of 'West versus the rest' on important issues.

It is also important to recall that such a state of affairs is not without precedent; indeed it is entirely consistent with earlier patterns of east/west domination. In a manner reminiscent of today's joint protectorate over Bosnia, towards the end of the nineteenth century, 'Increasingly, the Great Powers were implicitly down-grading self-interested promotions by individual states in favour of joint action over the Eastern question' (Pearson 1983: 128). A temporary international consensus, a 'concert' of the major powers, was constructed between 1878 and 1914. As the historian Andrew Janos describes, the regime sought to prevent conflagration among the powers themselves

> and, as a corollary, the encouragement of 'civilised' forms of government in territories in the newly independent states.... The main instruments of this international regime were ad hoc congresses that would assign special peacekeeping and civilising missions to one or more participants.
>
> (Janos 1994: 11)

The managing of world affairs was, at least for a time, carried out through a division of labour based upon a common agenda. It was no less self-interested, as only 'the West' was sufficiently confident in its domination to generalise specific self-interest into a wider moral mission to 'civilise'. Then, as now, policing the treatment of minorities was central to the agenda through which this objective was pursued.

One Europe or two?

There remain some serious causes for concern regarding the position of non-dominant groups within Eastern Europe. The predominantly Albanian province of Kosovo is entirely estranged from its nominal state, Serbia. There is no obvious solution to this problem in sight. The position of the Roma throughout the region is also problematic. Any improvement of their marginalised position within society is difficult to envisage short of a more general transformation of these societies. However, there is no evidence to suggest that such intractable problems as these, let alone less serious ones, can be solved through external intervention. Historical evidence suggests that the politicisation which follows external involvement is more likely to escalate domestic stand offs into wider conflicts, and local rivalries into broader questions of the international pecking order, than bring peace and harmony. No matter how difficult, internal problems can only be resolved by internal actors – without the 'disciplining' force of external powers looming over them.

Tellingly, perhaps, the claims of contemporary national minority enforcement do not stand principally on a claim to resolve confrontation. It is generally 'conflict prevention' not 'resolution' which is preached. The essential purpose of minority rights enforcement is a larger one. Returning to the claims of Lalumiere, regulating 'the East' through minority rights points towards a harmonisation of pluralistic European norms and values throughout the continent. Spreading the word of rights is a (potential) means of inclusion in a new Europe founded upon a rejection of xenophobia and intolerance. All of Europe will be judged on its treatment of minorities, and all those who meet the mark will merit inclusion.

The conditional inclusion of selected ('central' European) friends is indeed an aspect of the process of 'democratisation' of which minority treatment is such a crucial component. At least as important, however, is the corollary of this selective inclusion – the exclusion of those deemed 'not worthy'. How one escapes this marginalisation is unclear. The standards are themselves elusive and difficult to define. Who is to say, and how are 'we' to measure, when Slovakia, for example, has 'done enough' for their Hungarian minority to satisfy European institutions? It is revealing that the constant criticism of the country is rarely accompanied by a list of specific and attainable objectives, only that 'more must be done'. The moving goal posts of 'demonstrate democratic behaviour or be damned' for East Europeans are ultimately impossible to fulfil.

Who is to be included and excluded is in reality bound up with Western geopolitical concerns. Germany's close relationship with the Czech Republic, for example, appears to have determined their favoured treatment – despite Czech treatment of its Roma population which has denied them full formal equality. Attacks on the Roma in the Czech Republic have been frequent. On the other hand, Germany determined from the outset that the Slovak half of the former federation was a no-go area (Chancellor Kohl refuses to even speak with Slovak Premier Meciar), and endless complaints about a lack of democracy have followed.

The contemporary, as with the inter-war, moral division of those judged to have transcended 'intolerance', and those who remain in its clutches, is not yielding to facts, and certainly not to any comparative perspective. The little-noticed EU proposal to abolish the right of asylum within member states in June 1997 was proposed on the basis that there is no threat to refugees, since all member states are alleged fully fledged democracies which defend civil liberties.

If they were uniquely democratic beforehand, it is difficult to see how these states would remain so after abolishing the right of asylum. In reality, this action and the wider framework of 'civilising the East' would appear to be little more than self-flattery which distracts from anti-democratic behaviour in the west through elevating the congenitally anti-democratic 'culture' of 'the East'. In short, the contemporary revival of western monitoring of East European treatment of minorities is codifying an illegitimate moral division of Europe every bit as consolidated as the political division of Europe which marked the Cold War, and which it appears to have replaced.

Note

1 Part of this chapter is based upon my 'National Minority Rights and the "Civilizing" of Eastern Europe', *Contention*, Winter 1996, 5 (2).

References

Arendt, H. (1973) *The Origins of Totalitarianism*, 2nd edn, New York: Harvest.
Burgess, A. (1997a) *Divided Europe: the New Domination of the East*, London: Pluto Press.
—— (1997b) 'Writing Them Off to the East? British Quality Press Coverage of Slovakia', *Nationalities Papers*, Chicago, IL: Association for the Study of Nationalities.
Christopulos, D. (1994) 'Minority Protection: Towards a New European Approach', *Balkan Forum* 2 (1), March.
Cornwall, M. (1992) 'Eurogeddon?', editorial in *New Statesman and Society*, 19 June.
—— (1996) 'Minority Rights and Wrongs in Eastern Europe in the Twentieth Century', *The Historian* 50.
Garton Ash, T. (1994) *In Europe's Name*, London: Vintage.
Griffiths, S.I. (1993) *SIPRI Research Report No. 5: Nationalism and Ethnic Conflict*, Oxford: Oxford University Press.
Holmes, S. (1996) 'Cultural Legacies or State Collapse? Probing the Postcommunist Dilemma', in M. Mandelbaum (ed.) *Post-Communism: Four Perspectives*, New York: Council on Foreign Relations Press.
Janos, A.C. (1994) 'Continuity and Change in Eastern Europe: Strategies of Post-Communist Politics', *East European Politics and Society* 8 (1).
Jowitt, K. (1992) *New World Disorder: the Leninist Extinction*, Berkeley, CA: University of California Press.
Liebich, A. (1996) 'Getting Better, Getting Worse', *Dissent*, Summer.
Macartney, C.A. (1934) *National States and National Minorities*, London: Oxford University Press.
Mayall, J. (1994) 'Sovereignty and Self Determination in the New Europe', in H. Miall (ed.) *Minority Rights in Europe*, London: Pinter.
Mullerson, R. (1994) *International Law, Rights and Politics*, London: Routledge.
Pearson, R. (1983) *National Minorities in Eastern Europe 1848–1945*, London: Macmillan.
Sierpowski, S. (1991) 'Minorities in the System of the League of Nations', in P. Smith (ed.) *Ethnic Groups in International Relations*, Aldershot: European Science Foundation.

6 The OSCE and the internationalisation of national minority rights

David Chandler

Introduction

The Organisation for Security and Co-operation in Europe (OSCE) is the international institution generally acknowledged in recent years to have had most success in establishing new norms in the promotion of national minority rights. Between 1989 and 1991 this inter-governmental forum took qualitative steps forward with regard to normative standard setting and established the principle that national minority issues were a legitimate international concern, not merely an internal affair of the state concerned. At Helsinki in 1992, the OSCE's establishment of the post of High Commissioner on National Minorities was even more radical and unique in scope, as it established an early warning and international conflict resolution mechanism that could operate independently, without the consent of the OSCE member states. The framework of normative standards established by the OSCE has now become enshrined in international law with the Council of Europe's Framework Convention for the Protection of National Minorities, ratified in 1995.

This chapter seeks to consider how OSCE policy developed in both normative and regulative directions and the problems confronted in the process. It will be suggested that two related tensions were crucial to shaping policy. First, the drive to regulate possible tensions in the east whilst attempting to forestall the encouragement of minority group demands which may invite instability. Second, the desire to pose minority rights regulation in universal terms while facing reluctance from western democracies to open their minority policies to international scrutiny. Both these tensions were addressed through the OSCE narrowing the focus of policy to national minorities whose activities allegedly posed a security threat and shifting minority rights from being a human rights issue to a security concern.

The change in approach resulted in criticisms of the institution for reinforcing a negative view of national minorities as a problem, and establishing a selective and differential framework for international involvement in minority issues. This study ends with an assessment of the OSCE national minority rights framework in relation to its stated aims of improving the status of minorities, regulating potential conflict in the 'new' democracies and preparing the groundwork for a more unified Europe.

The OSCE before 1990

The OSCE is the institutionalised development of the Conference on Security and Co-operation in Europe (CSCE) established in 1975 by the signatories to the Helsinki Final Act. In December 1994, in recognition of its permanent nature, the title was changed to OSCE, which for the sake of consistency will be used to refer to the organisation throughout this chapter. The institution was originally an informal and *ad hoc* inter-governmental forum bridging both sides of Cold War Europe, involving the states of the former Soviet Bloc and of Western Europe, Canada and the United States. Its main focus of activity was achieving agreements in the areas of three 'baskets': political and security issues, economic co-operation and humanitarian and other questions.

Prior to 1990, although the protection of national minorities had been on the agenda of the OSCE, it had received only a low priority (Bloed 1993b: 4). However, the development of the organisation up to that point gave it the ability to transform the international regulation of minority rights issues in the early 1990s. A number of factors unique to the OSCE process were central.

First, the OSCE was the only international forum that defined respect for human rights as an essential factor for international security and not a purely domestic concern. The linking of the three baskets, and inclusion of human rights concerns in the Helsinki Act, clearly implied that human rights could no longer be defined as being exclusively an internal affair. Under the Helsinki Act supervision was organised through the 'thorough exchange of views on the implementation of the Final Act' held at the Follow-up Meetings (FUM) and at occasional expert meetings. At the Madrid FUM (1980–3) the US raised 65 cases, at the Vienna FUM (1986–9) Britain addressed 86 questions to the Soviet delegation (Brett 1993: 144–9).

At Vienna the European Community (EC) states pushed for the establishment of a permanent mechanism to monitor compliance with OSCE undertakings on human rights. As a consequence the Human Dimension Mechanism was established consisting of four 'stages' or points: (1) the provision of information upon request from another participating state; (2) the holding of bilateral meetings; (3) notification of other states about the use of the procedures; (4) the provision of information to the review conferences (Bloed 1993a: 60–1). The establishment of this mechanism was a further vital step in institutionalising human rights issues as a legitimate subject to be discussed between states (Zaagman and Zaal 1994: 101). It was only later that the mechanism was declared to be applicable to questions relating to national minorities.

The original EC proposal had been for stage four to include the convening of a special forum to resolve specific cases. This was adamantly opposed by East Europeans on the grounds that this would create supranational tribunals geared towards east–west confrontation. Even without this proposal it is clear that those concerns were well founded. Between January 1989 and April 1990, the Human Dimension Mechanism was used at least 103 times; 92 times against East European states. Of the 103 instances there is only one known instance of usage between countries of the same geo-political group: Hungary's use against Romania over disturbances in Transylvania. This exception clearly underlined the predominantly confrontational nature of the procedure (Bloed 1993a: 73; Brett 1993: 146–53).

Second, although not legally binding, not abiding by OSCE policy put states in an 'almost untenable position' (Heraclides 1993: 8). The East European states gained through the process through official recognition of the territorial status quo in Europe. Even more important in practical terms was the linkage with economic co-operation; the central lever used to force acceptance of the more sensitive human rights issues against the initial protests of the Soviet Union's allies who alleged this was an interference in their own internal affairs.

Third, what makes the OSCE process unique is the lack of any judicial or quasi-judicial institutions for establishing policy or for dealing with violations. Other traditional international human rights instruments have tended to proclaim a set of general principles, much as the Guiding Principles of the Helsinki Final Act that established the OSCE process. However, since the late 1980s the OSCE has not only expanded its catalogue of rights but introduced ever more detailed rules amplifying and clarifying their meaning and scope. This has established a novel interpretative rule-making procedure that escapes the ties of domestic legal and constitutional constraints (Buergenthal 1993: 11). In escaping the binds of domestic legislation and the slow process of drafting and voting on international treaties the OSCE was able 'to cover more ground and make bolder strides ahead' (Heraclides 1993: 8). The OSCE developed a great flexibility and dynamism in comparison with its regulation-laden international competitors. This applied as much to the creation of rules as their application, interpretation, amendment and suspension (Bloed 1993a: 52). In fact many OSCE commitments defied legal formulation as they actually questioned some sovereign state rights of control over territory (Heraclides 1993: 8).

Fourth, the OSCE, by evolving into a developmental process of state-level meetings, became 'ongoing and unidirectional', i.e. it had either to keep coming up with results in the form of implementation of commitments or of new normative commitments or bring the Helsinki process to an end. This meant that every new development went further in penetrating the sphere of internal affairs of states; this 'increasing intrusiveness' was particularly prominent in the Human Dimension (Zaagman 1994b: 233). One authoritative study points to four factors which together gave the OSCE process a dynamic which was not always a rational or calculated one. First, the sheer inertia of an institution whereby the call for further intervention was practically a reflex reaction at any gathering. Second, the fact that supporting any worthwhile ideas often meant accepting others as part of the overall negotiating process. Third, competition between the United States and European delegations over policy. Fourthly, the fact that any states accused of being slow to support international humanitarian measures could compensate by proposing commitments in a sphere in which they were unlikely to incur any costs. This process threatened to increase normative commitments to the point where the OSCE risked being seen as 'trivial or far-fetched...as if locked in an absurd exercise...of trying to constantly raise standards so as to proclaim more and more states as wrongdoers' (Heraclides 1993: 138–42).

1990 – national minority rights and the making of the OSCE

During the Cold War the OSCE showed little interest in national minority rights protection. Somewhat ironically (in the light of subsequent events) it was Titoist Yugoslavia which was keenest on developing proposals in this area, including the protection of ethnic, linguistic and religious minorities, but there was little enthusiasm from other states east or west (Brett 1993: 154). The Helsinki Final Act of August 1975, which established the OSCE framework, contained few precise provisions on national minorities, providing merely that participating states

> on whose territory national minorities exist will respect the right of persons belonging to such minorities to equality before the law, will afford them the full opportunity for the actual enjoyment of human rights and fundamental freedoms and will, in this manner, protect their legitimate interests in this sphere.
>
> (OSCE 1995: 3)

These obligations were reaffirmed at follow-up meetings including the Vienna Meeting which established the Conference on Human Dimension (CHD) of the OSCE to develop commitments in the sphere of human rights. At this point there was still little indication that minority rights issues would be central to the OSCE's development. The first CHD meeting was held in Paris in June 1989, before the transformations in Eastern Europe. At the Paris meeting no new agreements were made in relation to minority rights.

The collapse of Soviet domination in Eastern Europe was the catalyst for change within the OSCE. The second meeting of the CHD was held in Copenhagen in June 1990. The Copenhagen Document issued by that conference became a landmark in establishing normative standards of minority rights protection. Section Four of the Copenhagen Document went beyond previous measures against discrimination and for equal treatment to argue for positive rights. It marks the first reference to autonomous administrations (paragraph 35) and the use of mother tongue in dealing with authorities. States were now obliged to protect 'the ethnic, cultural, linguistic and religious identity of national minorities on their territory and to create conditions for the promotion of that identity' (paragraph 33) including provision of instruction in mother tongues and the use of mother tongues 'wherever possible or necessary' before public authorities (paragraph 34) (OSCE 1995: 9).

Before Copenhagen the very existence of the OSCE itself was under question. However, the development of an extensive national minority rights policy demonstrated its unique policy-making capacity and helped secure its position

(Heraclides 1993: 16; 1994: 287). The OSCE as a forum promoting democracy and human rights, where states met across the East/West divide, was uniquely placed to become 'the conscience of the continent', setting a 'moral and political tone for the new European political order' (Mastny 1992: 230, 253). In November of the same year, at the Paris Summit, permanent institutions were established.

1991 – the limits of national minority rights promotion

'Freedom', the by-word of the discussions on national minorities in 1989 and 1990, soon began to be replaced by 'danger'. Divisive international negotiations on the break-up of Yugoslavia made major powers think twice about encouraging national minority identities, rushing in to recognise the existence of new 'nations' and renegotiating the boundaries of the East European states (Guerra 1996: 20). Copenhagen marked the high tide of normative standard setting to promote national minority rights. The follow-up conference, initially proposed in order to take this process further, at Geneva, instead set out the framework of a new approach to minority rights, one which changed the emphasis from standard-setting to conflict regulation.

The CSCE Meeting of Experts on Minorities in Geneva in July 1991 insisted that the normative standards laid down in the Copenhagen Document constituted the utmost that could be achieved at the time. However, they did make changes which were crucial in two respects. First, and most importantly, Geneva formally institutionalised the developing conception of national minority issues as a legitimate international concern, strengthening the regulative authority of the international community and, in doing so, altering the domestic authority of the state *vis-à-vis* national minorities, stressing:

> Issues concerning national minorities, as well as compliance with international obligations and commitments concerning the rights of persons belonging to them, are matters of legitimate international concern and consequently do not constitute exclusively an internal affair of the respective state.
>
> (OSCE 1995: Section 2, 15)

Second, Geneva sought to rein in minority claims that questioned the geopolitical status quo. There were concerns that the Copenhagen suggestion of 'autonomous administrations' could have a destabilising impact on Eastern Europe. This was achieved through creating a 'shopping list' of possible forms of minority representation, stressing that 'no single approach is generally applicable' (OSCE 1995: Section 4, 17–18).

The Moscow CHD Meeting later in the year confirmed the policy direction established in Geneva. First, it reaffirmed the end of the standard-setting spiral, asserting that normative commitments had reached a limit beyond which it was difficult or even pointless to go (Heraclides 1993: 18). Second, it gave additional

powers to the international regulatory mechanisms of the OSCE after emphasising the security dangers of neglecting human rights issues. While the Vienna
Human Dimension Mechanism left state sovereignty untouched, Moscow
changed this radically. Four additional measures were introduced: (1) a member
state may invite in a mission of experts; (2) it may ask another state to invite in a
mission of experts; (3) if a state fails to accept a request from another state then
with the support of at least five other participating states a mission may be established against the will of the state concerned; (4) if a state considers there to exist
a particularly serious threat then the procedure in (3) may be established with the
support of at least nine other states without asking the permission of the state
concerned. This revolutionised the previously consensual procedural mechanism
of the OSCE, which could now be initiated by a minority of states against the
will of the state to be visited (Bloed 1993a: 64). For some western states this was
going dangerously far in restricting their sovereignty; the British delegation made
the most restrictive interpretative statement in order to circumscribe its reach on
the basis of public safety or national security (Zaagman and Zaal 1994: 102,
108).

These new regulative mechanisms developed through a concern with the
destabilising consequences of minority rights began to produce a second
problem for the OSCE. States in the west began to grow concerned about the
implications of pursuing a highly regulative, but at the same time universal,
policy.

1992 onwards – national minority rights as a security issue

Internationalising the question of minority rights was deemed useful as the
OSCE sought to establish its international profile as a leading post-Cold War
institution establishing the standards that the 'new democracies' would have to
meet to ensure the creation of a united and peaceful Europe. However, the shift
in importance of minority rights to the top of the international agenda, influencing western approaches to East European states, and the spiral of increasing
normative commitments, began to raise the question of double standards in the
treatment of minorities in the 'established democracies' in the west. The OSCE
was keen to draw a clear distinction between the promotion of minority rights
after the First World War and the situation of a united Europe in the early
1990s. In the First World War settlement the Minority Treaties were imposed on
the new eastern states but not in the west. This provoked hostility from many
states who felt that they were being treated as second class. For the OSCE, the
solution was to pose the minority rights policy in universal terms yet develop the
standards restrictively (Barcz 1992: 94).

The major western OSCE powers had no conception of how to apply such
policies in relation to their own minorities or of accepting such a level of international regulation in their affairs of state. Concerns were voiced by western
states at the possibility of their sovereignty being questioned. Indeed, the OSCE

had never provided a definition of what exactly constituted a 'national minority'. This had already caused problems at Copenhagen, Geneva and Moscow when Western states such as Britain, France and Switzerland appeared to weaken the momentum because they did not want OSCE intrusion in their own affairs. France and Switzerland, after fierce discussion, forced the Geneva Report to include the statement that 'not all ethnic, cultural, linguistic or religious differences necessarily lead to the creation of national minorities' (OSCE 1995: Section 2, 15). Switzerland did not want its model of cultural pluralism opened up to direct OSCE regulation (Brett 1993: 155; Heraclides 1992: 14). France took the opposite approach in refusing to recognise the existence of cultural pluralism within its own territory (Brett 1993: 158; Barcz 1992: 98). The discussion on minority issues revealed it was not just East European states that had sensitivities in this sphere: Germany forced the exclusion of 'new' minorities, such as migrant workers, to avoid the question of its treatment of the Turkish minority; the United States insisted that 'indigenous peoples' could not be classified as a national minority.

The different tensions, discussed above, attained their clearest organisational expression in the creation of the post of High Commissioner on National Minorities (HCNM) at the Helsinki Meeting, ending in July 1992. The perceived need to regulate minority rights in East Europe on the grounds of security concerns was given added impetus by the spreading conflict in former Yugoslavia, and at the same time, the war and the differing responses emerging in the European Union (EU) reinforced the dangers of encouraging minority secession. This resulted in a further institutionalisation of the shift to concerns of international security. This change in approach to national minorities was further reinforced by the reluctance of western states to risk having their sovereignty undermined through commitments to ethnic minorities.

At Helsinki, with greater international regulation being proposed, the appeals for exclusion from western states became more forceful. The United States, France and Greece stated that they did not recognise the existence of national minorities, arguing that all citizens had the same rights and duties regardless of ethnic group. Other states such as Turkey did not recognise certain groups as national minorities (Zaagman and Zaal 1994: 105–6). However, with the non-indigenous minorities, such as the Asians and African-Caribbeans in Britain, the Turkish and Kurdish communities in Germany and the Arab people of France, excluded from the remit of the proposed HCNM it was assumed that the focus of the OSCE's regulative powers could now be the East European states without any obvious double standards.

The Helsinki discussions were to make the OSCE claims to universal commitments on national minorities ring hollow. When OSCE influence in western states could not be negated through the denial of the existence of national minorities a second rider was proposed. The United Kingdom and Turkey, supported by Spain, insisted that the HCNM could not intervene in national minority issues where terrorism was involved, effectively taking the Irish, Kurdish and Basque questions off the international agenda. This provoked uproar due to the restrictive nature of the proposal, which meant that existing national minority conflicts (in the west) were excluded while only potential conflict (in the East) became a focus of concern (Chandler 1996: 111–12).

The second tension, that of potentially causing instability by focusing on minorities, was addressed by making the new post of High Commissioner part of the conflict-prevention machinery of the OSCE. In doing so the post was distinguished from the Human Dimension and the responsibility of safeguarding minority rights per se. The post was titled High Commissioner on National Minorities, not for National Minorities, to make it clear that it had not created an Ombudsman. The HCNM was explicitly excluded from considering 'violations of OSCE commitments with regard to an individual person belonging to a national minority' nor does he protect the rights of national minorities, either as individuals or as a group (OSCE 1995: 22). These limitations were imposed to meet concerns that the HCNM might underline differences between various national minorities or prompt national minorities to make more and greater demands and claim privileges that the state concerned could not afford to offer the rest of the population, thereby creating new inequalities or conflict (Bloed 1993b: 5; Zaagman and Zaal 1994: 107).

The task was designed to be two-fold. First, to act as an 'early warning' through monitoring developments concerning national minorities and selecting specific situations for preventative diplomacy and, to facilitate, as appropriate, 'early action' by the OSCE. This mandate required a new and qualitatively different level of intrusiveness into the affairs of the states of East Europe. The HCNM, as a third party, can become involved in a state's affairs at his own discretion without acquiring that state's consent or that of other participating states (Zaagman 1994a: 114–15). For the theorists of international relations the 1992 Helsinki Declaration stands as one of the clearest statements to challenge the post-Second World War conception of state sovereignty (Held 1995: 104–5).

The OSCE's reluctance to develop further commitments in relation to national minorities and the dominance of security concerns at Helsinki and afterwards has provoked criticism from many commentators who feel that human rights issues and national minorities protection in particular have become marginalised (Buchsbaum 1994: 356–7). Many feel that the reason for sidelining the Human Dimension is that western OSCE states have little to gain from it today as added commitments in the Human Dimension can only bring to the fore intra-west divergences rather than putting pressure on the 'new democracies' (Heraclides 1994: 292).

The OSCE has been accused of treating minorities unequally, especially in the case of the HCNM who can only pay attention to the violation of minority rights if they have the potential to develop into violent conflict. It is clear that manifest violations of rights may not involve 'tensions' and therefore fall outside the HCNM's remit no matter how flexibly interpreted (Bloed 1993a: 68). Some commentators clearly approve of the OSCE approach which considers minority rights as 'not exclusively or even primarily a human rights problem, but as a security issue' (Mullerson 1997: 53). Others see this as promoting a negative image of national minorities which are focused on as a source of conflict (Buchsbaum 1994: 339).

An assessment of OSCE policy developments in the 1990s

Bearing in mind the considerations and aims of OSCE policy development in relation to national minority rights, its achievements can be gauged in three areas: the capacity to improve the situation of national minorities; the capacity to manage potential conflict over minority issues in the east; and the creation of a framework for a more unified Europe.

With regard to the situation of national minorities, the OSCE has been highly successful in developing policy on minority rights and pushing this further than any other institution in the early 1990s. However, there have been questions raised over the impact this has actually had on the life-chances of national minorities. It is unlikely that merely introducing normative standards of tolerance towards minorities will resolve tensions generated by social collapse and the struggle for resources in the region (Burgess 1996: 34). Economic and social policy development remains the most important element in conflict resolution at the level of both domestic and international actors.

Another set of questions have been aired over the promotion of 'separate but equal' development for national minorities to foster a separate culture and tradition. For example, at the OSCE Human Dimension Seminar On National Minorities, held in Warsaw in 1993, one of the most controversial areas of discussion was that of constitutional and political arrangements to foster separate minority representation in the legislature. Participants raised two crucial points. First, that special provision for such minorities could be divisive and might foster 'ethnic' parties focused solely on ethnic interests while failing to give minorities a sufficient voice in decision making. To this end, some speakers argued that under a system of equal treatment national minority members would be more inclined to consider issues in a wider context, and second, that collective representation risked permanently marginalising national minorities. The danger of 'separate but equal' policies breeding inequality and inter-ethnic conflict was stressed as well as 'the common risk that only learning the language of the minority could put the members of that minority at a disadvantage for participating in all institutions and structures' of the country and becoming second-class citizens (ODIHR 1993).

In the Balkans, where most attention has been directed to national minority questions, these points would seem to be valid. The focus on Albanians in Serbia and Macedonia being educated in their own language, while making a political point, does little to end the marginalisation and isolation of the Albanian community. In Bosnia and Herzegovina the decentralisation of political institutions and collective representation systems, whereby Serbs, Muslims and Croats must vote for candidates on an 'ethnic key', seems set to increase division as seen by the dissolution of Serbo-Croat and the creation of three 'official' languages in the new state.

Second, in relation to conflict management in the east, of potential concern is the impact that OSCE regulation can have on the relationship between governments and national minorities. As Thomas Buergenthal notes:

> [N]o domestic institution or norm is beyond the jurisdictional reach of the CSCE. Here the traditional domestic jurisdiction doctrine...has for all practical purposes lost its meaning. And this notwithstanding the fact that non-intervention in the domestic affairs of a state is a basic CSCE principle. Once human rights, the rule of law, and democratic pluralism are made the subjects of international commitments, there is little left in terms of governmental institutions that is domestic.
>
> (Buergenthal 1993: 9)

This subordinate relationship to the OSCE and other international institutions can weaken the ability of the state to stand above sectional conflicts because the legitimacy of central institutions can be brought into question in relation to claims based on minority rights. This can create situations where minority/majority conflicts can become more destabilising rather than less so.

In Bosnia and Herzegovina, writers, such as Julie Mertus, argue that there are marked similarities to the destabilising Minority Treaties after the First World War (Mertus forthcoming). The Dayton structures, within which the OSCE plays a crucial role, have both legitimised nationalist differences and at the same time weakened the legitimacy of the Bosnian state through regulation by external international institutions (Chandler 1997: 221–9).

Encouraging minorities to appeal to the OSCE can work counter to more flexible solutions to problems worked out by those on the ground. This also puts governments in a weak position as minorities can go 'forum shopping' and use different institutions to put pressure on the elected representatives. More than one OSCE state believes that special minority rights and the promotion of distinct identities do not resolve problems but instead lead to ethnic strife and disintegration (Heraclides 1994: 186). As we have seen, the danger of exacerbating and internationalising potential problems in cases where minorities may seek to escalate conflict to involve outside parties was a central concern raised in order to restrict the mandate of the HCNM.

Third, there seems little doubt that the OSCE focus on national minorities as an issue of international security does little to overcome a differential treatment of the east. To start with, the assumption that ethnic difference is a cause of conflict 'paints all sides as less rational and less modern (more tribal, more ethnic) than "we" are' and downplays any broader international, social or economic understanding of potential or actual conflict in the east (Bowen 1996: 13). The focus on the security concerns of national minorities rather than minority rights as a broader trans-European or international question bears many similarities to the inter-war period where states in Eastern Europe were treated formally, and in practice, as inferior to the 'developed democracies' of the west.

After the First World War states such as Yugoslavia, Romania and Poland put up a stubborn fight against the Minorities Treaties, claiming that international guarantees of minority rights were an attack upon their sovereignty and an indication of a lack of confidence in their good faith as well as a source of potential danger because minorities would feel that their status rested upon the support of foreign powers. These states demanded to know why similar provisions were not put on Germany, Italy and France (Robinson *et al.* 1943: 154–5).

Occasionally there are similar responses today. These tend to come from leading states which resent being treated differentially, for example, the Czech President Vaclav Havel's response at the European Union-sponsored Conference on Stability in Europe in 1994, that maybe a roundtable should be organised to discuss the Basque and Irish problems under the benevolent eye of the (East European) Visegrad countries. The other group of disgruntled East European states are those that look like being sidelined through the focus on national minorities, such as Croatia and Slovakia. The Slovak Prime Minister, Vladimir Meciar, after being lectured by the HCNM, Max van der Stoel, in 1996, noted that he would like to receive a report on the situation of minorities in EU countries, adding that 'if the results show that there is a higher level of minority rights in other countries we will be glad to adapt' (OMRI 1996).

The major difference today seems to be not so much the divisive character of national minority regulation but that resistance to the regulating role of international institutions such as the OSCE, the United Nations and the Council of Europe is much more muted. The main reason for the lack of negative response has been the desire of East European states to enter European and international institutions and gain the diplomatic and economic assistance that are dependent on international acceptance (Zaagman 1994a: 167). This means that concerns expressed by leading commentators that OSCE mechanisms may become discredited, if seen in Eastern Europe in the same light as the inter-war experiment in minority rights protection, are unlikely to be realised (Bloed 1993a: 87–8; Heraclides 1994: 302–3).

Conclusion

The OSCE-led international consensus on national minority rights protection would appear to be much weaker than the conference agreements and public declarations from leading statesmen indicate. The consensus achieved in the early 1990s on the internationalisation of national minority rights rested on two key elements: the selective interpretation of what constituted a national minority question by western states and the pragmatic acceptance of this framework by Eastern states.

To conclude, it would seem that making and restating commitments in the field of national minority rights costs little in terms of resources and enables states and political leaders on both sides of the old Cold War divide to achieve a higher international standing. However, underneath the veneer of commitment, there is little political will to act when this means upsetting the delicate political status quo in the east or questioning the sovereignty of states in the west.

References

Barcz, J. (1992) 'European Standards for the Protection of National Minorities with Special Regard to the CSCE – Present State and Conditions of Development', in A. Bloed and A. De Jonge (eds) *Legal Aspects of a New European Infrastructure*, Utrecht: Europa Instituut and Netherlands Helsinki Committee.

Bloed, A. (1993a) 'Monitoring the CSCE Human Dimension: In Search of Its Effectiveness', in A. Bloed, A. L. Leicht, M. Nowak, and A. Rosas (eds) *Monitoring Human Rights in Europe*, London: Martinus Nijhoff Publishers.

—— (1993b) 'The CSCE and the Protection of Minorities', CSCE ODIHR Bulletin 1 (3): 4–8.

Bowen, J. (1996) 'The Myth of Global Conflict', *Journal of Democracy* 7 (4): 3–14.

Brett, R. (1993) 'The Human Dimension of the CSCE and the CSCE Response to Minorities', in M.R. Lucas (ed.) *The CSCE in the 1990s: Constructing European Security and Cooperation*, Baden-Baden: Nomos Verlagsgesellschaft.

Buchsbaum, T. (1994) 'The Human Dimension after Helsinki-II', in A. Bloed (ed.) *The Challenges of Change: the Helsinki Summit of the OSCE and its Aftermath*, London: Martinus Nijhoff.

Buergenthal, T. (1993) 'The CSCE Rights System', CSCE ODIHR Bulletin 1 (3): 9–11.

Burgess, A. (1996) 'National Minority Rights and the "Civilizing" of Eastern Europe', *Contention* 5 (2): 17–36.

Chandler, D. (1996) 'The Internationalisation of Minority Rights Protection in Eastern Europe', in I. Hampsher-Monk and J. Stanyer (eds) *Contemporary Political Studies* 1: 103–11, Belfast: The Political Studies Association of the United Kingdom.

—— (1997) 'A New Look at the Democratisation Process: the Case Study of Bosnia-Herzegovina Post-Dayton', in J. Sevic and G. Wright (eds) *Transition in Central and Eastern Europe*, vol. 2: 217–41, Belgrade: Yugoslav Association of Sasakawa Fellows.

Guerra, S. (1996) 'The Multi-Faceted Role of the ODIHR', OSCE ODIHR Bulletin 4 (2): 11–12.

Held, D. (1995) *Democracy and the Global Order*, Cambridge: Polity Press.

Heraclides, A. (1992) 'The CSCE and Minorities: the Negotiations behind the Commitments, 1972–1992', *Helsinki Monitor* 3 (3): 5–18.

—— (1993) *Helsinki-II and its Aftermath: the Making of the CSCE into an International Organization*, London: Pinter.

—— (1994) 'The Human Dimension's Swansong in Helsinki-II: the Normative Aspect with Emphasis on National Minorities', in A. Bloed (ed.) *The Challenges of Change: The Helsinki Summit of the OSCE and its Aftermath*, London: Martinus Nijhoff.

Mastny, V. (1992) *The Helsinki Process and the Reintegration of Europe, 1986–1991: Analysis and Documentation*, New York: New York University Press.

Mertus, J. (forthcoming) 'Prospects for National Minorities under the Dayton Accords – Lessons from History: the Inter-War Minorities Schemes and the "Yugoslav Nations"', in S. Wheatley (ed.) *Minority Rights in Europe?*, Kluwer Press.

Mullerson, R. (1997) *Human Rights Diplomacy*, London/New York: Routledge.

ODIHR (1993) 'CSCE Human Dimension Seminar on Case Studies on National Minorities Issues: Positive Results – Consolidated Summary', Warsaw: Office for Democratic Institutions and Human Rights.

OMRI (1996) 'Slovak Prime Minister meets with OSCE Official', *OMRI Daily Digest* 8, part 2.

OSCE (1995) 'CSCE/OSCE Provisions Concerning Persons Belonging to National Minorities', Warsaw: Office for Democratic Institutions and Human Rights.

Robinson, J. *et al.* (1943) *Were the Minorities Treaties a Failure?*, New York: Institute of Jewish Affairs of the American Jewish Congress and the World Jewish Congress.

Zaagman, R. (1994a) 'The CSCE High Commissioner on National Minorities: An Analysis of the Mandate and the Institutional Context', in A. Bloed (ed.) *The Challenges of Change: the Helsinki Summit of the CSCE and its Aftermath*, London: Martinus Nijhoff.

—— (1994b) 'Institutional Aspects of the CSCE Human Dimension after Helsinki-II', in A. Bloed (ed.) *The Challenges of Change: the Helsinki Summit of the CSCE and its Aftermath*, London: Martinus Nijhoff.

Zaagman, R. and Zaal, H. (1994) 'The CSCE High Commissioner on National Minorities: Prehistory and Negotiations', in A. Bloed (ed.) *The Challenges of Change: the Helsinki Summit of the CSCE and its Aftermath*, London: Martinus Nijhoff.

Part II

Contemporary case studies

7 Catalan nationalism and the democratisation process in Spain[1]

Montserrat Guibernau

Introduction

The aim of this chapter is to offer an account of the re-emergence of Catalan nationalism during the Francoist regime, and to study the process which led to the democratisation of Spain after Franco's death in 1975. The key theme underlying this analysis concerns the distinction between two different meanings ascribed to nationalism, on the one side by Franco and his supporters who almost immediately after their insurrection against the legitimate government of the Second Spanish Republic called themselves 'nationals'; and on the other, by Catalans, Basques and other national minorities included within the Spanish state's territory. I do not want to suggest that all state nationalisms lead to totalitarian, anti-democratic regimes, as was the case with Francoism. Instead, I focus on two recurrent features of these nationalisms: the defence of homogeneity against diversity and pluralism, implying very little if any acknowledgement of national minorities, and the differing access to power and resources of state nationalisms compared with nationalisms of nations without a state.

The chapter begins by analysing the main features of Franco's dictatorship. It then investigates the consequences of the Francoist victory in Catalonia and concludes by studying the processes by means of which Catalan identity was sustained throughout the Francoist regime, offering a detailed typology of the strategies employed to resist the dictatorship.

Francoism: the portrait of a dictatorship

Francoism was the result of a violent confrontation initiated on 18 July 1936 when some sectors of the army revolted against the legitimate government of the Spanish Republic. It was an uprising against democracy, the party system, church–state separation, the autonomy of Catalonia and the freedom and civil rights of the inhabitants of the peninsula. The main objective of the revolutionaries, who almost immediately called themselves 'nationals', was to restore 'order' and erase all trace of the communism and anarchism of what they called *La España roja* (Red Spain). In such a context the end of the Republic was presented as a necessity. As early as September 1936, Pla y Deniel, bishop of

Salamanca, referred to the Civil War as a *Cruzada* (Crusade). This not only implied the distinction between 'good' and 'evil' in the confrontation, but more importantly, it supplied the emerging regime with an ideological legitimisation that it immediately assumed. The 'nationals', with the blessing of God, were fighting the 'reds', the 'infidels' and 'evil'. The 'nationals' proclaimed themselves to be engaged in a war of 'liberation', in a 'crusade', and this became a core element in the building up of the Francoist regime. The exaltation of the victory and the legitimisation of the situation created by it were regularly actualised from the beginning of the war (1936) up to the death of the dictator (1975).

After the Spanish Civil War (1936–9), Franco pursued a strong policy of 'nationalisation' using all resources available to him – physical as well as psychological repression, control of the media and control over elites and bureaucracy – to create what could be termed a 'surveillance state'. Francoism represented the belated emergence of a powerful modern state based upon the repression of internal ethnic diversity. Catalans and Basques were to be assimilated in a Spain based upon Castilian culture, Catholicism and Conservatism. However, Franco's dream of an homogeneous Spain never became a reality. I argue that the tough and highly repressive policy implemented by him could only exacerbate the nationalist feelings of national minorities. The particularly harsh treatment of Basques and Catalans contributed to the creation of a firm sense of community in each case. Thus, the dichotomy between 'us' and 'them' increased dramatically and the measures imposed by the regime, instead of homogenising the population, widened the chasm between an official public sphere and a proscribed private one.[2] In Catalonia and the Basque Country the state's repressive measures often led to internal cohesion and mobilisation, bringing together classes and interest groups which otherwise had little in common with each other.

The supporters of the Franco regime

The Falange

The vital allies of Franco were the Falange party, the army and the Catholic Church. Significant sections of the bourgeoisie also played a fundamental role in backing the new regime. The founder and first leader of the Falange was José Antonio Primo de Rivera, executed by the Republicans in November 1936 and elevated to a quasi-sanctified status in post-war Spain. In its origins, the Falange was a youth movement which advocated a mixture of traditional patriotism and modern authoritarianism. Its aim was to create a national socialist state free from class-struggle. The Falange looked to Italian fascism as its primary source of inspiration and defended the ideal of a greater Spain forged by territorial expansion in North Africa and, above all, the recovery of Gibraltar. They respected the Catholic Church and fiercely denounced Marxism and capitalism, pressing for agrarian reforms and the nationalisation of banks and railways. Franco extracted some of his ideas from the Falange, but mainly used it as a powerful weapon to keep monarchists under control, whilst at the same time appealing to monarchists in order to counterbalance the Falange influence.

The army

The military rising of 18 July 1936 split the army into supporters of the legitimate government of the Republic and those who joined the 'nationals'. The army remained to the end the ultimate guarantor of the Francoist dictatorship. To mention monarchy as one of Spain's traits reflects a tension encountered by the new regime from its very beginnings. Yet, a significant part of the army was monarchist and saw Franco as a transitional figure who would restore the Spanish monarchy; a feature that was only accomplished when in 1969 Franco, who lacked male descendants, decreed that after his death, Prince Juan Carlos de Borbón should take over and become king of Spain.

The bourgeoisie

The new regime gained the support of the industrial bourgeoisie who after a period of turmoil could resume its economic activities. Social order was re-established and all revolutionary or reformist movements eradicated. Large sectors of the bourgeoisie, including those in the Republican area, supported Franco and the conservative policies he represented. The Catalan and Basque bourgeoisie, with very few exceptions, aligned itself with the new regime. Their class interests proved to be above all other factors, national identity included.

The Catholic Church

The definition of the Civil War as a 'Crusade' indicates the immediate position adopted by the Spanish Catholic Church, except in the Basque Country and small sectors in Catalonia, in supporting the military uprising of 1936. Catholicism gave the 'nationals' the most powerful legitimisation for their regime since neither the Falange nor traditionalism alone could have sustained their claim of legitimacy. The bulk of Spanish society was traditional and Catholic. Franco demonstrated outstanding skills in presenting his regime as a stronghold against communism and increasing his contacts with the United States. The Vatican did not discourage Spanish prelates and Catholics in general from reaffirming their support for Franco during the crucial period of ostracism. In 1945, the Allies condemned the Francoist regime in the Potsdam conference and Spain was denied entry to the United Nations. This situation changed progressively with the Cold War around 1948 and the western anti-communist obsession.

Support by the Catholic Church for Franco was challenged by some sectors of the clergy in the Basque Country and in Catalonia. In both places there existed a tradition which linked peripheral nationalism with certain segments of the Church. In the Basque Country, the support of the Catholic Basque people for the Republican cause and the Catholic character of the Basque Autonomous government favoured respect towards the clergy and their institutions during the Civil War, while in other parts of Spain they were severely repressed (Gurruchaga 1985: 154). Catalan nationalism would re-emerge under the protection of certain progressive sectors of the Catholic Church that opposed Francoist National Catholicism.

National Catholicism as a form of ideology

The Catholic faith and Spanish nationalism were inseparable. Nation and culture became identified with Catholicism and tradition; nothing else fitted into the restricted body of Francoism. Spain was considered as a single homogeneous nation, thus ignoring the different cultures, languages and separate historical backgrounds of its constituent parts. The Catholic nationalisation of culture implied the rejection of all kinds of European cultural, political and social move-ments which were considered as anti-Spanish together with a return to the values of the sixteenth and seventeenth centuries.

Franco embodied an organicist conception of the nation as constituting an integral whole. Castile was fully identified with Spain: Spanish history was reduced to the events in which Castile was leader. All languages spoken in the peninsula except Castilian, and all cultures of national minorities, were banned from the public sphere. The Spanish prototype was the traditional Catholic Castilian peasant.

In the National Catholic discourse, the concept of *patria* acquires a tradition-alist meaning since it stresses the connection with the past. Franco incessantly used the term to refer to the Spanish *patria* as a single entity that was ignorant of national minorities and separatist movements. The *patria* became an element of supreme political value. The term *madre patria* (mother *patria*) is charged with an emotional content; it tries to reproduce the mother–child relation and re-direct this intimate relationship into the political arena. As 'good' children who would never jeopardise the legitimacy of their mother and would never dare to insult her, Spaniards should be united in their loyalty to their *patria*. In such a context, Catalan, Basque and Galician minorities seeking independence or autonomy formed the paramount example of the most execrable sin, a separatism that implied the denial of the (imposed) *patria*.

Closely linked with the idea of *patria* is the recurrent appeal to the unity of Spain. The two most feared demons of Francoism and the Spanish right were class struggle and peripheral nationalism. The unity advocated by Franco was meant to apply to all spheres: 'Unity; national unity, religious unity, social unity and political unity, as essential foundation to prevent others from snatching away the benefits of our continuity'.

The idea of empire adopted by Francoism had its origin in the ideals of *grandeur* and supremacy of one's country above others which was also implicit in the Italian and especially in the German fascist doctrine. At the same time, fascism was strongly involved with nationalism as a means of binding together otherwise diverse populations. The reference to imperial claims disappeared from Franco's speeches after the defeat of Germany and Italy in the Second World War. However, the so-called *mito de la Hispanidad* (Hispanic myth), an idea put forward by some intellectuals of *Acción Española* such as Emilio Vizcarra, Ramiro de Maeztu or Isidro Gomá, attempted to recover some sort of Spanish cultural empire based upon the Spanish-speaking Latin American countries, an empire whose foundation was Catholicism. The regime established the *Día de la Raza* (Day of the Race), later called *Día de la Hispanidad* (Hispanic World Day), on 12 October, the date on which Columbus first walked on American soil (still a bank holiday in present day Spain): a date for the remembrance and celebration of the Spanish link with Latin America.

The blessing of the Church compensated for the hostility of the intellectuals, most of whom went into exile. Francoism lacked a common cultural ideological base, and became progressively more concerned with the control of possible alternative cultures than with the creation of an original culture of its own (Carr and Fusi 1981: 105–7).

Chaos and defeat

Three different periods can be distinguished between the end of the Civil War in 1939 and 1950. The first came between 1939 and 1944 and encompassed a period during which Francoism was in the process of consolidation. The new regime was regarded by many as provisional, its fate being closely linked to the outcome of the Second World War. The Spanish army did not enter the confrontation. Franco resisted Hitler's pressure and argued that Spain had just come out of a war and could not engage in another. Misery and destruction were too intense and widespread in the Iberian peninsula. However, Franco supported the fascists up to the point when their defeat could be predicted, then he changed his position to one of neutrality and approached the Allies.

In 1939 the leaders of the Catalan parties defending the Republic went into exile in France. A sharp debate emerged between those who supported the restoration of the Republic and the 1932 Catalan Statute of Autonomy, and those who adopted a radical nationalism defending the independence of Catalonia. The former defended some kind of autonomy for Catalonia and imagined the Catalan community to be included within the Spanish state. The latter displayed a strong anti-Spanish attitude. According to them, 'nothing good could be expected neither from Spain, nor from the Spanish, since all possible alternatives had been exhausted; the only viable political option for Catalonia was the struggle for independence' (Díaz-Esculíes 1983: 30).

The 1932 Statute of Autonomy had contemplated the restoration of the Catalan parliament and government (*Generalitat*) which had been automatically banned by the Francoist regime. Once in exile, the *Generalitat* had its last meeting in Paris in February 1939.[3] Shortly afterwards, its president, Lluís Companys, created the National Council of Catalonia (18 April 1940). However, the Nazi occupation of France forced Catalan exiles to seek protection mainly in the United Kingdom and in some Latin American countries. Catalan resistance in exile was dismantled. The Gestapo arrested Companys and delivered him to the Spanish who tortured and shot him (15 October 1940). Carles Pi i Sunyer, a member of the Catalan Republican Left (*Esquerra Republicana de Catalunya*), the ruling party in Catalonia in 1939, formed a new National Council of Catalonia in London (29 July 1940). The Council received the support of Catalan Communities in Latin America and defended the continuity of Republican legality. The Council advocated self-determination for Catalonia within a federal Spain and, as a compromise accepted to end its existence as soon as the Catalan government could continue its activities. Pi i Sunyer had to dissolve the Council in 1945 when the president of the Catalan Republican Left, Josep Tarradellas, succeeded in creating Catalan Solidarity (*Solidaritat Catalana*), a group including representatives from diverse political factions who agreed to fight to overthrow the Francoist regime and re-establish the Republican legality. They stressed that the national aspirations of Catalonia were not satisfied by the 1931 Republican Constitution and the 1932 Statute of Autonomy (Díaz-Esculíes 1991: 114).

While all political parties were disintegrating as a result of the constant repression exerted by the Francoists, the contact between the interior and those in exile was difficult and led to a breakdown in communication. The National Front of Catalonia (*Front Nacional de Catalunya*) was created in Paris (winter 1939–40) as a resistance movement without a clear-cut ideology. They advocated independence for Catalonia and supported the policy of the National Council of Pi i Sunyer. The most remarkable feature of the National Front is that it managed to organise a link between the resistance within Catalonia and that in exile; it became active and relatively efficient. After the dissolution of the London National Council, the Front was politically isolated and joined the National Council of the Catalan Democracy (*Consell Nacional de la Democràcia Catalana*) (Díaz-Esculíes 1991: 120).

During the period 1945–7, the victory of the Allies opened a period of hope among the Francoist opposition which expected a prompt Allied intervention to overthrow Franco. This hope encouraged the re-organisation of the governments of the Republic and the *Generalitat* in exile. All political parties increased their activity (Molinero and Ysás 1981: 161ff.).

In September 1945, the president of the *Generalitat*, Josep Irla, formed a new government in exile ready to take over after the Francoists had been defeated. However, there was no reaction from the Allies, except for two United Nations (UN) resolutions. The first (12 December 1946) advised the withdrawal of ambassadors from Spain. The second (17 November 1947) denounced the Francoist regime. To the dismay of the opposition, no further action was taken (Díaz-Esculíes 1991: 129–35). The disenchantment of the resistance emphasised important discrepancies between those who strongly supported the re-establishment of the Republic – the Republican Left of Catalonia (ERC) and the Unified Socialist Party of Catalonia (PSUC) – and those endorsing a provisional period in which to discuss the future organisation of the state and the status of Catalonia (de Riquer and Culla 1989: 153).

In turn, the years 1948–50 opened the period of consolidation of the

Francoist regime. The threat of foreign intervention to re-establish democracy in Spain seemed to be over and soon Franco would receive some economic support from the United States (1951) and sign the 1953 Concordat with the Vatican. The Cold War prompted a tolerant attitude towards a dictatorship that presented itself as a guard against the expansion of communism. On 4 November 1950 the United Nations abrogated the 1946 resolution and allowed Spain to enter all international institutions sponsored by the UN. These events created a profound internal crisis among Franco's opponents and forced them to look for new strategies.

The *Generalitat*'s cabinet was dissolved on 24 January 1948. Josep Irla held office as president of the *Generalitat* until 1954 when Josep Tarradellas, after a highly controversial election process, took over the presidency.[4] Tarradellas' first cabinet was to be formed more than twenty years later in the context of a new democratic Spain.

The Francoist opposition directly defeated in the Civil War failed in its attempt to overthrow the new regime. Among the reasons for this were the pervasive and brutal repression exerted by the fascists, the passive tolerance of western countries and the weakness and political mistakes made by the resistance (Vilar 1989: 153). Among the latter I shall distinguish four main issues. First, the Francoist opponents had been unable to offer a united alternative to the new regime. The constant personal and party rivalries springing from their different attitudes and actions, together with the contradictions between exile and interior, contributed to subjective and emotional attitudes that prevented further military action. Second, the opposition took for granted an immediate Allied intervention after the Second World War and based its strategy upon a supposition that never materialised. Third, the defenders of the Republic manifested a considerable lack of sensitivity to the moral and material situation of the working class and the Catalan peasantry. Most of the clandestine press showed optimism about the approaching end of the regime and undermined social support of Francoism. Finally, the opposition equated Francoism with conventional fascism, neglecting a deeper analysis that would have allowed them to plan a more efficient policy.

Breaking the silence

A progressive estrangement from the state permeated Catalonia except among those members of the Catalan high bourgeoisie who renounced their national identity in order to protect their status by defending their class interests. The homogenising policy imposed by the Francoist regime encountered diverse types of reactions aimed at preserving Catalan distinctiveness. As a national minority under threat, the Catalans developed various sorts of counter-strategies to reject the forced uniformity dictated by the state; armed struggle and cultural resistance should be mentioned as major counter-strategies against enforced homogeneity.

Armed struggle did not take shape among the Catalan opposition with the exception of some guerrilla groups, the *Maquis*, comprised of 12,000 armed men operating primarily in the area around the Pyrenees. Their actions were disorganised due to the lack of previous agreement between the mainly communist and anarchist political tendencies they represented. The *Maquis* were particularly active between 1944 and 1950. After that, only isolated groups and sometimes even single *guerrilleros* performed scattered actions around Catalonia.

Cultural resistance, that is the use of all sorts of symbols of Catalan identity in the public as well as in the private sphere, progressed considerably from isolated and risky actions to activities enlisting massive support. The hanging of a Catalan flag, or graffiti written in Catalan, represented a challenge to the Francoist regime and as such a threat. Such actions symbolically broke the control of 'the others' and made clear that the image put forward by the Francoists was not unanimously accepted. In the private domain, resistance was primarily carried out within the family. The Catalan language and culture were taught at home and could only be practised within restricted groups determined by family or friendship ties. However, in spite of the extreme repression exerted by the regime there were still some groups ready to take the risk of speaking out in a different language (Fabré *et al.* 1978).

Four major forms of opposition existed within the public domain: 'symbolic actions', 'interference actions', 'elite actions' and 'solidarity actions'. By 'symbolic action' I mean a single and usually isolated action carried out by a small group or even a single individual whose main objective is to break the control of the public space in the hands of the oppressive regime. In this category I include graffiti, flag displaying and floral offerings suddenly appearing where monuments to Catalan heroes once stood before being removed by the Francoists. Symbolic actions were usually performed in the street and addressed to all occasional witnesses.

By 'interference actions' I refer to single actions executed by small groups during the course of public events. The task of such actions was to challenge the regime at its core by disrupting rituals and ceremonies whose aim was precisely to prove that homogeneity and control had been achieved. 'Interference actions' implied a high degree of risk, since security measures designed to prevent any sort of disturbance were strictly implemented on such occasions. 'Interference actions' envisaged a double reception: on the one hand, they were addressed to those attending the public event, but on the other, they sought the attention of 'alien' observers, such as the international press or foreign representatives, partially or completely unaware of the Catalan situation. There are many examples of 'interference actions' during the long path to democracy which was achieved in 1978. In 1960 during Franco's visit to Barcelona, a concert to commemorate the centenary of the Catalan poet Joan Maragall was organised in the *Palau de la Música Catalana* (Catalan Music Palace). Franco did not attend the concert himself, but four members of his cabinet did. Included in the programme was *El cant de la senyera* (Song of the Catalan Flag), a masterpiece of Maragall with nationalist overtones, that was cancelled at the last minute.

Around two hundred Catalan nationalists, mainly members of the Catalan Language Academy (*Academia de la Llengua Catalana*), demanded the performance of *El cant* and finally began to sing it themselves.[5]

By 'elite actions' I refer to actions and activities carried out by a small but devoted intelligentsia. Their objective was the maintenance and, when at all possible, the development of the Catalan high culture. 'Elite actions' were primarily concerned with the protection of the Catalan language. The Institute for Catalan Studies (Institut d'Estudis Catalans), dismantled in 1939, was reorganised in 1942 by Puig i Cadafalch and Ramon Aramon. Their clandestine activities involved the publication of books and articles on medicine, science and other subjects in Catalan. *Omnium Cultural*, a semi-clandestine institution from 1964, was legally recognised in 1967 and then saw a dramatic increase in membership (from 639 in 1968 to 11,000 in 1971). Among the activities of *Omnium Cultural* were the teaching of Catalan and the sponsoring of the Prize of Honour of the Catalan Letters (*Premi d'honor de les lletres catalanes*).[6]

In the late 1960s and early 1970s the influence of the 1968 student uprisings in France and the 'Prague Spring' favoured the proliferation of radical organisations within the university, and nationalist claims were perceived as bourgeois. Nationalist groups disappeared from the university arena to return only after Franco's death.

The Francoist regime went through different stages, and whilst it is true that it never changed its character as a dictatorship and its conservative ideology, it did certainly modify some of its practices in order to appear more acceptable to the western democracies. The opposition movement took advantage of all possible breaches to actively advance its resistance. The later stages of the regime saw an increase in the number of 'solidarity actions'. The objective of a 'solidarity action' is to show the strength of the opposition by focusing upon a particular demand and presenting it as something that cannot be denied due to the massive support it receives. A fundamental change concerning the context in which actions are performed distinguishes 'solidarity actions' from both 'symbolic' and 'interference actions'. The latter attempt to break the control of the public sphere in the context of a highly repressive discipline surrounding all public activities. The former can only take place when a relative attenuation of the oppressive nature of the regime allows some breaches to take place and the population then dare to gather together challenging the power of the state.

In the context of an eroded dictatorship that strives to present itself as democratic, the use of force has to be carefully calculated. The causes of a demonstration cannot be dealt with by shooting people. 'Solidarity actions' are addressed to the regime officials who are forced to acknowledge the power of the 'different', but at the same time to appeal to the media and to foreign observers who will be attracted by the magnitude of such actions. An example of a 'solidarity action' is the one-million-strong mass demonstration in Barcelona on 11 September 1977 in an attempt to vindicate a statute of autonomy for Catalonia. Franco was already dead and the political reform presented by the prime minister Adolfo Suárez had been ratified by an overwhelming majority.

However, the status that Catalonia might achieve within the new democratic Spanish state was not yet clear. The massive demonstration of 1977 reinforced the Catalan rejection of a simple administrative decentralisation of the state, compelling the government to consider the promulgation of a new Statute of Autonomy for Catalonia.

Cultural resistance within the private domain was, in some cases, particularly among the middle classes and some sectors of the bourgeoisie, a fully conscious activity, a response to the political repression exerted by the regime. I suggest that among the working class and the peasantry the maintenance of the Catalan language and culture was not so much perceived as a specifically resistance activity encouraged by the clandestine circulation of Catalan literature, literary prizes and clandestine Catalan lessons to which these people had no access, but as something much more elemental and less conscious. The working classes and peasants continued to speak Catalan because it was the language they had learned from their parents, the language they used in day-to-day life to express emotions and to describe and talk about their most intimate feelings. They had to learn to use Castilian at work, at school, when shopping or going to court, but once at home they would describe their experiences using their mother tongue. When repeating the 'other's' words they would always use Castilian, the language of the 'alien', the language of power.

The great conspiracy[7]

Nationalism as a form of ideology does not determine which political doctrine its adherents should support. Thus, nationalist parties can have diverse orientations: Marxist, conservative, social-democrat, etc. Where national minorities are faced with a strong homogenising policy that threatens their existence as a distinctive community it is not uncommon to find a certain degree of co-operation and solidarity between nationalist parties which minimise their ideological differences in an attempt to form a solid opposition movement. The capacity of nationalism to overcome internal ideological and political divisions was exemplified by the Assembly of Catalonia (*Assemblea de Catalunya*) formed in 1971.[8]

The Assembly of Catalonia was a clandestine unitary group which brought together three hundred people from diverse social backgrounds and political allegiances. It was the most important unitary movement in Catalonia since the Civil War and had no equivalent in any other part of Spain (Balcells 1991: 180). The Assembly was inspired by Catalan socialists and communists but it also received some financial support from Jordi Pujol's group which later joined it (Balcells 1991: 180). The Socialist Movement of Catalonia (*Moviment Socialista de Catalunya* or MSC) and the Unified Socialist Party of Catalonia (PSUC) played a crucial role in winning over both substantial working-class support and the integration of significant numbers of immigrants from diverse areas of Spain. The message was that democracy, left-wing policies and autonomy for Catalonia had to be part and parcel of the same claim.

The Assembly proposed a common platform with four demands: first, a general amnesty for political prisoners and exiles; second, the upholding of rights and freedoms of speech, the press, of assembly, of association and the right to strike, thus guaranteeing the effective access of the people to economic and political power; third, the provisional re-establishment of the institutions and principles set up in the 1932 Catalan Statute of Autonomy as a concrete expression of the right to self-determination; and fourth, the co-ordination of all peninsular peoples in the fight for democracy (Batista and Playà Maset 1991). The Assembly obtained widespread popular support and the number of institutions and individuals backing it dramatically increased. The Assembly continued its unitary mobilising activity until the first democratic elections to the Spanish parliament on 15 June 1977.

Conclusion: clashing images

Opposing conceptions of the nation and the state were at stake in the Spanish Civil War. The Francoists propounded a highly centralised and uniform image of Spain which condemned any acknowledgement of the existence of national minorities such as the Catalans and Basques. The immediate effects of the Francoist victory over Catalonia entailed not only the suppression of all Catalan political institutions and laws, but also the prohibition of the Catalan language and all sorts of symbolic elements (flags, anthems) of the Catalan identity.

The Francoists, 'nationals', fought to impose a closed 'image' of Spain, an image that emphasised unity and condemned all forms of diversity. Their nationalism emerged as a reaction against modern ideologies such as socialism and anarchism which were threatening the traditional socio-political structure of Spain. During the Second Spanish Republic some progressive policies were implemented leading to the construction of a state within which national minorities were taken into account and conferred a substantial degree of cultural and political autonomy. Francoism halted this process and used a particular form of nationalism to stop the Spanish path towards modernisation while sustaining the traditional structures defended by large conservative Catholic sectors. National Catholicism used tradition to enhance the power of a right-wing political regime.

National minorities such as the Catalans filled the word nationalism with a radically different content. For them, to be nationalists signified the desire to be recognised as different and have the right to express this difference in political as well as in cultural terms. A fundamental distinction between the nationalism instilled by the state and the nationalism of nations without states springs from their different access to power. The state imposes the rules of the game and defines the rights and duties of its members. Furthermore, when it comes to national minorities, the state has the power to acknowledge their existence, allowing them to develop their own specific culture and providing them with sufficient economic and political resources to realise the achievement of various degrees of autonomy. But the state also has the power to decide on the eradication of difference.

The reaction of the Catalans faced with a repression that penetrated all their day-to-day activities turned into passive resistance. They had been defeated. Their country was destroyed and they were living in precarious conditions. They had to confront the presence of a Spanish army and an imported Castilian-speaking bureaucracy. The official public sphere was occupied by the new regime. The same intense force exerted by the 'nationals' to erase difference contributed to the construction of a clear-cut distinction between 'us', the Catalans, and 'them', the Francoists (identified with the Castilians). The subjection the Catalans had to endure in the public sphere increased a 'non-spoken agreement' between them and encouraged a particular sense of solidarity; a feeling that only arises in situations of high risk and shared danger. The Francoist regime and its officials were perceived as a common enemy for all Catalan people, disregarding their social class, since to be 'a Catalan' was enough to arouse the suspicion of the regime. Only some sectors of the upper Catalan bourgeoisie viewed the Francoist victory with relief and supported the new Fascist ideology which would protect their interests.

In the case of Spain, authoritarian rule condemned both democracy and national diversity. As a result, those opposing Francoism in Catalonia, from communists to social-democrats, stood together for the restoration of a democratic regime and the right to cultivate a specific national identity. The dictatorship attempted forced homogenisation and seriously threatened the continuity of the rich Catalan and Basque cultural tradition. The repressive conservative and Castilian character of the regime intensified inter-ethnic tensions between the proscribed national minorities and an arrogant Castilian elite. There were very few exceptions.

The Spanish transition to democracy was initiated after the death of Francisco Franco in 1975. The makers of the new constitution (1978) opted for a model based upon symmetry, what has been called 'coffee for everyone' (*café para todos*), and instead of directly responding to the nationalist claims of Catalonia and the Basque Country as nations, they decided to implement a system which would allow for the creation of seventeen autonomous communities, some historically and culturally distinct – Catalonia, the Basque Country and Galicia – others artificially created where no sense of a separate identity had ever existed – La Rioja and Madrid among many others. Yet, while Catalonia, the Basque Country and Galicia could immediately initiate the process towards full autonomy, other regions had to fulfil a five-year 'restricted autonomy' period before initiating it. Once full autonomy is achieved, however, the Constitution makes no distinction between the communities. This involved assuming the indissoluble unity of Spain while recognising and guaranteeing the right to autonomy of its nationalities and regions.

In many ways, the Autonomous Governments act as states, for example each Community has a regional legislative assembly consisting of a single chamber. Deputies are elected on the basis of proportional representation and usually the leader of the majority party or coalition assumes the presidency of the

Community. The President heads a regional executive of ministers in charge of departments which mostly, but not always, follow the Spanish state's pattern.

After almost twenty years of autonomy, the system deserves a positive evaluation. Even artificially created communities are now enthusiastic about the idea of running their own affairs. Most of them are in the process of searching for symbols and myths which could generate a certain sense of identity among their members. They are busy constructing invented ethnicities. Thus the post-Franco era has not only witnessed a renaissance of Basque and Catalan identities, but has also seen the growth of Andalusian, Canarian and especially Galician consciousness. Although Catalans and Basques are not fully satisfied, because they want to stress their specificity and be recognised as nations within Spain, those groups demanding outright independence find themselves somewhat at the margins, especially in Catalonia. However, the demand for special treatment still exists, and there is increasing reluctance to a blind acceptance of the 'coffee for everyone' option.

At the domestic level the democratisation process has involved the urgent need to re-think Spanish identity which has to be defined in relation to its constituent nations, while these nations are at the same time struggling to recover and develop the key elements of their specific identity suppressed under Franco. At the international level, the Spanish example illustrates how the politics of ethnic accommodation can diffuse potentially volatile situations and contribute to the growth of civil society. As such it provides an example which other countries in Europe might do well to emulate.

Returning to Spain itself, our study shows that it is a country which has re-defined itself in recent years. However, this process of re-definition is not at an end. By defining itself as a nation, Catalonia alters the homogeneous image of Spain defended not only by Francoism but also by those conservative sectors which continue to complain about the substantial autonomy acquired by Catalonia and the Basque Country.

Notes

1 All translations from Spanish and Catalan in this piece are the responsibility of the author.
2 For a detailed analysis of this phenomenon in the Basque Country, see Gurruchaga, A. (1985) *El código nacionalista vasco durante el franquismo*, Barcelona: Anthropos.
3 For a detailed account of the activities of the *Generalitat* in exile illustrated with key documents of the period, see Ferré, M. (1977) *La Generalitat de Catalunya a l'exili*, Barcelona: Ayma.
4 For a detailed account, see Díaz-Esculíes, *El Catalanisme politic a l'exili 1939–1959*, Barcelona: La Magrana.
5 For a detailed account, see Crexell, J. (1982) *Els fets del Palau i el consell de guerra de Jordi Pujol*, Barcelona: La Magrana; see also Muñoz, X. (1990) *De dreta é esquerra: Memòries polítiques*, Barcelona: Edicions 62, 135–44.
6 Vilar, *Història*, 358.

7 This section takes the name of the most recent and accurate account of the activities of the Assembly of Catalonia: Batista, A. and Playà Maset, J. (1991) *La Gran Conspiració: Crónica de l'Assemblea de Catalunya*, Barcelona: Empúries.

8 For a detailed account, see: Batista, A. and Playà Maset, J. (1991) *La Gran Conspiració*; and also Colomer, J.M. (1976) *Assemblea de Catalunya*, Barcelona: L'Avenç. For an evaluation of the Assembly of Catalonia in the twentieth anniversary of its creation see *Debat Nacionalista* 16–17, December 1991–February 1992, Barcelona.

References

Balcells, A. (1991) *El nacionalismo catalán, Historia* 16, Madrid.

Batista, A. and Playà Maset, J. (1991) *La Gran Conspiració: Crónica de l'Assemblea de Catalunya*, Barcelona: Empúries.

Carr, R. and Fusi, J.P. (1981) *Spain: Dictatorship to Democracy*, London: Unwin Hyman.

Colomer, J.M. (1976) *Assemblea de Catalunya*, Barcelona: L'Avenç.

Crexell, J. (1982) *Els fets del Palau i el consell de guerra de Jordi Pujol*, Barcelona: La Magrana.

Debat Nacionalista 16–17, December 1991–February 1992, Barcelona.

Díaz-Esculíes, D. (1983) *El Catalanisme polític a l'exili 1939–1959*, Barcelona: La Magrana.

Fabré, J., Huertas, J.M. and Ribas, A. (1978) *Vint anys de resistència catalana 1939–1950*, Barcelona: La Magrana.

Ferré, M. (1977) *La Generalitat de Catalunya a l'exili*, Barcelona: Ayma.

González Portilla, M. and Garmendía, J.M. (1988) *La postguerra en al País Vasco: política, acumulacíon, miseria*, San Sebastián: Kriselu.

Gurruchaga, A. (1985) *El código nacionalista vasco durante el franquismo*, Barcelona: Anthropos.

Lorenzo, J.M. (1989) *Dictadura y dividendo: el discreto negocio de la burgesía vasca 1937–1950*, Bilbao: U Duesto.

Molinero, C. and Ysás, P. (1981) *L'oposició antifeixsta a Catalunya 1939–1950*, Barcelona: La Magrana.

—— (1991) *Els industrials catalans durant el franquisme*, Vic: Eumo.

Muñoz, X. (1990) *De dreta e esquerra: Memòries polítiques*, Barcelona: Edicions 62.

Riquer, B. de and Culla, J. (1989), in P. Vilar (ed.) *Història de Catalunya*, vol. 2, Barcelona: Edicions 62.

8 Immigration policy and new ethnic minorities in contemporary Germany

Sandra Schmidt

This chapter examines the background to different policies towards various immigrant groups in Germany. Through immigration and nationality laws, different immigrant groups have been ranked into categories in which some groups are regarded as more likely to fit into a society than others. An ethnic hierarchy of migrants has emerged with regard to origin, reflected in legal status, access to the labour market and welfare system. To illustrate the relevance of the idea of the German nation for the formulation of immigration policy, an outline of the specific characteristics of the German nation-state tradition and its implications for the concept of citizenship is presented. Next, the consequences of the concepts of nation and citizenship for policies on immigration are discussed.

The perceived challenge that immigration brings to a political, social and cultural order is highlighted by the persistent denial by German politicians that Germany is a country of immigration. By 1994, almost seven million foreigners were resident in Germany. Today they constitute 8.6 per cent of the total population. Immigrants of Turkish origin constitute 28.1 per cent of this group, followed by immigrants from former Yugoslavia (18.6 per cent). European Union (EU) citizens constitute about 25 per cent of the foreign population. In conurbations, immigrants constitute on average about 15 per cent of the population, reaching over 20 per cent of the population in large cities (Beauftragte 1995: 15–17). In some inner-city areas they form up to 60 per cent of the residents. The increased visibility of immigrants, largely because of the arrival of their families and their concentration in certain regions of the country and in inner-city areas, has led towards segregation. Immigrants are portrayed by politicians and in the media as the cause of domestic social and economic problems. They are accused of taking away work from Germans by undercutting wages and accepting intolerable working conditions. An extreme reaction to the perceived threat of immigration to social order and to the nation's identity has been the rise of extreme-right political groups and the proliferation of racially motivated attacks on foreigners in Germany.

Inter-ethnic relations are a political issue and a source of social conflict all over the world. From an international perspective, the characteristic European nation-state is of great importance. This framework condition is given neither in the classical immigration countries of North America and Australia nor in the multi-ethnic states of Asia and Africa. The question arises of how the nation-state as an organising principle, and in particular the German interpretation of this principle, affects inter-ethnic relations. The formulation of immigration policies is rooted in different traditions of national identity and citizenship. These traditions, or rather the norms inherent in the different concepts, are reflected in a society's attitude towards the admission of aliens. The idea of community usually involves ideas of common descent and language, common history and collective memories, and thus entails that specific legal definitions are embedded in such subjective beliefs.

Membership of a state is legally defined in citizenship laws, yet it is also an expression of the national identity which results from the history of origin of the nation-state. Hence, rights to citizenship are central to the question of who should be included in a national society as a member with full civil rights and who should be excluded and treated as an outsider with lesser rights. Consequently, notions about the concept of national identity and the norms which govern access to citizenship are reflected in immigration policy and attitudes towards ethnic minority groups. In other words, immigration policy is an expression of a state's official attitude on who should be allowed to become its member and under what conditions. In turn, traditions of nationhood, a nation-state's identity, legitimise immigration policy.

Ethnicity and the German nation

When compared with France or Great Britain, the German nation-state developed relatively late towards the end of the nineteenth century. From the middle of the thirteenth century, 'Germany' was a territory loosely united under the name of the Holy Roman Empire, and later, after the Council of Constance in 1417, the Holy Roman Empire of the German Nation. The individual states with a German-speaking majority did not represent the German nation, as either a political or an ethnographic construct.

German nationalism and the idea of an organic nation arose in the context of the Napoleonic wars after the disintegration of the Empire in 1806. The war of liberation against French occupation was perceived as a shared experience by a people. Thus, intimations of a German people preceded the establishment of a German nation-state by half a century. After the restoration of the European order by the Congress of Vienna in 1815, the *Deutscher Bund* (German Confederation) was established, a loose association of thirty-five independent German states and four free imperial cities. There was general agreement on the need for reform of the Confederation among the rulers of the various German states but where the frontiers of the new German state should be was a hotly debated question. In 1871 Bismarck succeeded in unifying German-speaking territories under Prussian leadership, with the so-called *kleindeutsche Lösung* ('little' German solution). He rejected the greater German option that would have included Austria, and thus secured Prussian dominance. Even if it did not include all German-speaking territories, the German *Reich* of 1871 was considered to be the first German nation-state. Yet Bismarck also included Polish territory taken by Prussia which had never been part of the Holy Roman Empire (Mann 1968).

It has been argued that German unification under Bismarck was motivated by military strategic concerns rather than by nationalism. It largely succeeded in fusing the traditions of Prussian statism and German nationalism. Two movements forged German nationalism – the Prussian reform movement and the romantic movement. The Prussian reformers wanted to duplicate the success of France's post-revolutionary military. They sought to mobilise the people around a *Staatsvolk*. This was a rational effort of state building by administrators to create a powerful state along legal-rational lines. For German romanticism, nations are unique, historical narratives of a particular spirit, a *Volksgeist*, that is expressed in its culture, customs, law and the state. Characteristic of the German concept of the nation is the explicit *völkisch*, ethnic understanding of the German nation. German nationhood is thus rooted in the concept of the *Volk* (people) as an organic cultural and racial entity marked by a common language.

Ethnic nationalism developed as an intellectual movement in Germany in the eighteenth century, and became a political ideology and social movement in the nineteenth century. In the nineteenth and twentieth centuries this organic concept of the nation became prevailingly ethnocentric, and led to the identification of the *Volk* with race and the assumption that one's own values and traditions are superior to those of outsiders. As a political ideology, ethnic nationalism strives for congruence between ethnic and political boundaries, a culturally homogenous nation-state. The basic principle of the ethnically legitimised nation-state is the unity of people and state. Multi-ethnic states, any political units that do not correspond to one people, are in this tradition not nations.

The demands of ethnic nationalism often refer to groups of people which represent historically and fictive cultural units. Unity and solidarity are maintained and created in historical projections. The state is conceptualised as a hereditary group of people, related to one another through 'ties of blood'. The unity of the state is based on a sense of kinship, on loyalty to people of a common kind. In connection with a 'self-upgrading', this form of nationalism can produce a strong pressure towards assimilation and open hostility towards the cultural 'other' or even forcible expulsion.

The ethnic nation-state is not only a pattern of legitimation of state organisation but a principle that determines policies towards ethnic minorities. This affects policies on admission and integration, citizenship and naturalisation, as well as the question of political participation. Since the nation is understood as an *Abstammungsgemeinschaft* (community of common origin) with a common culture and history, membership of the nation, nationality and citizenship are tightly bound together. German law uses the term *Staatsangehörigkeit* (belonging to the state). The foundations of this concept are to be found in the concept of *Volk*, and, therefore, the concepts of nationality and citizenship cannot be disentangled. Since an understanding of the state as a distinct ethnocultural unit implies that it cannot admit outsiders indiscriminately, it thus raises the question whom to admit and whom to exclude. In the ethnic view of the state membership is restricted to those connected to it by ties of kinship (common ancestors). This means that if immigrants are admitted they cannot become full members. Even if they obtain citizenship, they remain marginal to the nation and its collective life. On the other hand, all people who are related to the state by ties of kinship but live outside the state's boundaries belong to it in principle. Ethnic nationalism accentuates cultural diversity as undesirable difference and non-adjustment. In this context, ethnicity acquires a central importance as the principle of political and social organisation.

The desire to establish a culturally homogenous nation-state transforms the heterogeneous groups, as defined by the national culture, which live in or migrate to the state territory into ethnic minorities. Since the ethnic ideology assumes that each people owns a specific cultural tradition (*Volkszugehörigkeit*), the immigration of alien people may be perceived as a fundamental threat to the national culture. Admission into such a nation is difficult and has to be understood as an exception. There remains no space for multi-ethnicity or multiculturalism if it is believed that the foundation of the state is the national homogeneity of its citizens. One can only be a German citizen if one shares the common cultural heritage.

This exclusive understanding of German nationhood developed during the twentieth century. German nationalism, having preceded the political organisation of the nation-state, was initially not identified with the state or with the idea of citizenship. As national identity was based on common language and culture, anyone of German descent was after 1871 eligible to be a German citizen whether they had ever lived on German territory or not. Although ethnic ideology dominated the Empire and the Weimar Republic, these were both multi-ethnic states. Minorities of non-German origin had German citizenship as well as special minority rights. The constitution of the Weimar Republic guaranteed the non-German-speaking groups of the population the right to develop their own culture (Hoffmann 1992: 71). In fact, until 1935 citizenship of the states which made up the Empire had priority over the Empire's citizenship. The National Socialist regime institutionalised full citizenship (*Reichsbürgerschaft*), and distinguished it from state membership (*Staatsangehörigkeit*). Full citizenship was restricted to those of German descent, who alone possessed political rights, and explicitly excluded Jews. Yet, in order to explain today's restrictive attitude towards the admission of immigrants in Germany it is important to differentiate between the ethnocultural citizenship law of 1913 and the racial laws of the National Socialist regime (Brubaker 1992: 165–7).

The main elements of today's citizenship law can be traced back to the nineteenth-century notion of an identity of state and nation. The law on attribution of citizenship, the *Reichs- und Staatsbürgerschaftsgesetz*, enacted in 1913, stipulates that nationality is decided according to the principle of *jus sanguinis* which interprets citizenship as being a right transmitted by blood. German descent alone defines the right to citizenship and this right was reconfirmed in the Constitution, the Basic Law (*Grundgesetz*), of the Federal Republic of Germany in 1949. The citizenship law of 1913 was with few modifications retained in 1949. These ties of blood descent are broader than mere parentage for they suggest community with a larger people to whom one belongs in a kind of fictive relationship. Where such notions of consanguinity dominate citizenship law as in Germany, the political system is capable of distinguishing between an acceptable and unacceptable influx of immigrants, without regard either to the numbers or the economic situation in which the immigrants arrive.

The founders of the Federal Republic of Germany emphasised its provisional character in the Constitution. Prior to 1990 the preamble included a commitment to the unity of the German people as well as to the reunification of the two German states. Oberndörfer (1993) argues that through allegiance to the reunification of the Germans in the preamble of the Basic Law, the Federal Republic of Germany renewed allegiance to the notion of a community based on ethnic descent. This is reflected in German citizenship law in two ways. The first consequence, the commitment to German unity, has been the inclusion of all *Volksdeutsche* (members of the German people) or so-called ethnic Germans who live outside the boundaries of the Federal Republic. Article 116 of the Basic Law conferred automatic rights of German citizenship to those who were citizens of Germany within the boundaries of 1937, including their spouses and descendants, and who had not been able to exercise either their right to self-determination or cultural identity as Germans. In other words Article 116 referred to both citizens of the German Democratic Republic (GDR), and to those *Volksdeutsche* in other communist-ruled countries in Europe. Furthermore, Article 116 makes specific reference to ethnic Germans who had long been or recently become citizens of other Eastern European countries. Second, there is only one German citizenship. As the government of the Federal Republic understood itself as the legal successor to the Weimar Republic, citizenship of the former GDR was never recognised in the Federal Republic.

Two elements characterise German citizenship. First, its attribution is still exclusively based on descent (*jus sanguinis*). There is no automatic acquisition of citizenship for children of immigrant origin born in Germany. German citizenship law does not recognise birth on German soil (*jus soli*) as a basis for citizenship. Second, the naturalisation of people of non-German origin, despite some changes in the law, is still rather the exception than the rule. There is no right to naturalisation and citizenship is granted on a discretionary basis. Immigrants have the choice either to assimilate or to remain with a second-class status and be expected to return to their country of origin (Hoffmann 1992: 38–40). This form of ethnically justified discrimination is partly laid down in the German Constitution. The Basic Law contains contradictory universal human rights and particular rights for German citizens only. Article 1 lays down the inviolability and protection of dignity of man as the norm. From this follows the entitlement of all people to the basic rights of liberty, equality, and religious freedom. Article 3 of the Basic Law provides furthermore that 'nobody shall be discriminated or favoured because of gender, descent, race, language, homeland and origin, creed, religious or political beliefs'. However, subsequent articles on freedom of assembly, association and profession as well as on freedom of movement and prohibition of extradition are reserved exclusively for German citizens. This restriction of fundamental rights for German citizens only is incompatible with Articles 2 and 3 of the Basic Law. In this respect, Germany continues to define itself as an ethnic as opposed to civic nation.

Post-war labour migration

Since the end of the Second World War, the Federal Republic of Germany has admitted by far the largest numbers of migrants in Europe with a net intake of more than twenty million people between 1945 and 1992 (Fassmann and Münz 1992: 473). During this period, Germany experienced the immigration by four distinct groups. First, the immigration of approximately twelve million 'ethnic German' *Vertriebene* and *Flüchtlinge* until the early 1960s. Second, the active recruitment of contract workers during the 1950s and 1960s. Third, the immigration of 'ethnic German' *Aussiedler* and *Übersiedler*, and finally the continuing influx of asylum seekers.

After the Second World War, Germany successfully integrated over nine million expelled Germans from former German territory. Additionally, over three million East Germans fled to West Germany for political and/or economic reasons. By 1950, these two groups constituted 14.6 per cent of the population (Benz in Bade 1993: 382). A key strategy of the Allies was the quick integration of the expellees and refugees, an objective which was specified in the refugees law of 1946. The integration of millions of refugees and expellees was certainly helped by favourable economic conditions. Still, it is important to stress that it was achieved not only through the economic miracle but also due to active state intervention. Measures with regard to housing, education and work were implemented which often favoured refugees over the local population. The official attempt to portray a positive image of the refugees and expellees helped to counterbalance social tensions and resentments against this group stemming from poor economic conditions. In 1949, after the establishment of the Federal Republic, the *Bundesvertriebenenministerium* (Ministry for Expellees) was founded to co-ordinate social and economic measures concerning refugees and expellees from former German territory.

The integration of the refugees was seen to be completed by the late 1960s, and the Ministry for Expellees was abolished in 1969 (Benz 1993: 374–86). The establishment of the ministry is characteristic of the way this group of immigrants has been regarded. The expellees and refugees played an important part in the reconstruction of West Germany but officially they were never regarded as immigrants. As *Volksdeutsche* (people of German origin) they belong by definition to the German *Volksgemeinschaft*, and were seen as simply repatriating to their homeland. The immigration of *Aussiedler* continued after the end of the expulsion measures. In 1953, a law was passed that expanded the definition of ethnic

Germans to include those persons who left Eastern Europe or the former Soviet Union 'after the end of the general expulsion measures' (Winkler 1993: 117). A transitional legal provision that granted millions of German refugees admission to Germany after the Second World War became a constitutional right to return for ethnic German immigrants from Eastern Europe. The immigration of almost 1.6 million *Aussiedler* to Germany between 1951 and 1988 was largely unquestioned and integration into German society took place quietly (Bade 1994: 43). The costs of the integration of *Aussiedler*, their different customs and often lack of the German language did not become an issue of public debate until the late 1980s.

The Cold War severely limited the possibility of labour recruitment from Eastern Europe, a development reinforced by the building of the Berlin Wall in 1961 and the closure of the inter-German border. German government officials and employers started to recruit workers from Southern Europe where unemployment was high. Between 1955 and 1968 recruitment agreements were concluded with Italy, Spain, Greece, Turkey, Portugal, and Yugoslavia. Technically, it was official policy to restrict foreign labour to Europeans but other countries such as Morocco and Tunisia also entered into labour agreements, although the numbers involved were small. The recruitment agreements were not the result of long-term planning. Rather, they represented a purely functional response to the short-term requirements of the German labour market. This attitude was best expressed in the term guest worker – by definition guests do not stay. It was generally expected that the migrant workers would return to their countries of origin once they were no longer needed. The recruitment programmes were under government control and work permits were tied to a specific employer. Germany's guest-worker policy did not envisage their permanent integration into German society. The migrant workers lived in special workers' hostels, they had no right to settle or to bring their families nor were they offered services such as language classes and training schemes. The rationality behind the rotation system, which implied that 'guest workers' had to return after two or three years, was to avoid the integration of the foreign workers.

The year 1973 was a turning point in Germany's recruitment policy. Oil crisis and economic recession led the German government, among others in Western Europe, to impose a ban on the recruitment of foreign labour. At that time it had become clear that the policy of rotation had failed. The halt on recruitment, however, did not affect citizens of the member states of the European Community (EC). In 1973, the year of the EC's first enlargement, freedom of movement for workers was already established between the member states. Thus, due to the European integration process, the situation for EC migrant workers and their families improved considerably. Their status is secured by a range of policies. For example, it is not allowed to discriminate against EC citizens in employment, and they have a right to be joined by their families. In turn, however, this process reinforced the inferior position and exclusion of non-EC citizens.

The paradox of the ban on recruitment is that far from inducing migrant workers to leave Germany, it confronted migrants from non-EC countries with a choice they had until now not been required to make. They could either return to their country of origin and thereby forfeit the opportunity to return to Germany or they could stay in Germany on a more permanent basis. Confronted with this choice, most migrants chose to stay in Germany and were joined by their families. By the early 1990s the number of foreign residents had increased by almost 50 per cent compared to 1973, whereas the foreign working population remained stagnant. However, the fact that the former guest workers and their families have settled in Germany has so far not been translated into the German social, political and legal framework. In contrast to the experience of the first post-war German immigrants for whom substantial financial support, housing and education were immediately provided, the German state still treats the migrants as a supplementary workforce to fill gaps in the labour market. This approach is reflected in restrictions on family reunification and access to legal employment for family members of non-EU citizens resident in Germany. Aid for return programmes, though of limited success, has been offered against the background of increasing unemployment during the 1980s and 1990s. Yet the demand for foreign labour did not end with the recruitment ban. Exceptions were made for jobs in certain sectors such as mining and food if no local labour was available. Temporary admission of migrant workers continued during the 1970s and 1980s and has been the compromise between the official policy of the recruitment ban and the demand for migrant labour.

Unification and the new immigrants

The opening of the borders between Eastern and Western Europe following the events of 1989 led to increased immigration to Western Europe. The main recipient has been Germany with almost 1.5 million people from Eastern Europe alone in 1989/1990. This is almost twice the number of immigrants from Eastern Europe than the period 1980 to 1988. By the end of the 1980s, two issues dominated the debate on immigration in Germany.

First, from the 1980s onwards, the constitutionally guaranteed right to asylum has increasingly become a bone of contention in political debate. Against the background of the experiences during the National Socialist regime, the right to asylum was specified in the German Basic Law. Article 16 (2) constituted until its amendment in 1993 the most liberal asylum right in Europe and guaranteed asylum for all those experiencing political persecution. From 1973, non-EU citizens needed a visa to enter Germany, with the exception of *Aussiedler* and citizens of European Economic Area states or states with which Germany has special agreements (Australia, New Zealand, Israel, Japan, Canada and the USA). Consequently, the only way to enter Germany legally apart from with a tourist visa has been to apply for political asylum. Until the 1970s, the number of asylum seekers was small and almost all came from Eastern European countries. During the 1980s, the number of asylum seekers increased significantly and a shift in the countries of origin occurred, with less than one-third of all applications from Eastern Europe and the majority from the developing world (BMI 1993: 49). Many have been employed during the asylum procedure or as *de facto* refugees. Large numbers of migrant workers arrived as tourists when the visa obligations for citizens of Poland, Hungary and former Czechoslovakia were abolished in 1991.

Second, the collapse of communist regimes in Eastern Europe and the abolition of most obstacles on migration led to large numbers of *Aussiedler* arriving in Germany. The number of *Aussiedler* emigrating to Germany increased rapidly in 1987. In 1988, over 200,000 *Aussiedler* came to Germany, and in 1989 the number reached 377,055. The high number of 'ethnic Germans' emigrating to Germany from Eastern Europe and the former Soviet Union, combined with the economic recession, contributed to a shift in attitudes towards this immigrant group. *Aussiedler* have increasingly been seen as taking advantage of the economic opportunities and the welfare benefits afforded in Germany and not as people escaping tyranny. Their lack of ability in the German language and their different customs have led to criticisms about their 'Germanness' and their right to enter Germany as Germans. Concerned about the strong hostility towards *Aussiedler*, the government carried out an information campaign in 1989 to win support for the immigration of *Aussiedler*. They have been presented as a cultural, economic and social benefit to the country in contrast to the image of non-German immigrants who are seen as a threat to the social order and economic well-being. *Aussiedler* have been proclaimed to be the solution to Germany's demographic problem and vital to the future of the pension scheme. The second development was a massive increase in the immigration of *Übersiedler* from the GDR which contributed to the fall of the Berlin Wall. In 1989, 343,854 *Übersiedler* registered, and in the first half of 1990 a further 238,384. Including the *Übersiedler*, in 1989 alone Germany admitted almost three-quarters of a million new German citizens or immigrants of German origin (Bade 1993: 403–5). Since 1987, almost 50 per cent of migrants have been either *Aussiedler* from Eastern Europe or *Übersiedler* from the former GDR.

Against the background of economic recession, high structural unemployment, racist attacks on foreigners, and the electoral success of extreme-right parties, the German government asserted its position to limit the admission of non-EU immigrants with the reform of the foreigners' law in 1990. The legal status of immigrants and migrant workers had been specified in a special *Ausländergesetz* (foreigners' law) in 1965 which regulates the granting of work and residence permits, naturalisation criteria, and expulsion. This law is also a means of controlling the influx of new immigrants, both by defining visa policies and regulations concerning family reunification and by specifying exceptions to the general ban on recruitment of migrant workers. The revision of the foreigners' law in 1990 was officially presented as a codification of the ban on recruitment and Germany's restrictive immigration policy. The German government argued that immigration of people from alien cultures is not in the national interest as social and political stability are tied to the national homogeneity of the state

(Hoffmann 1992: 71). Yet at the same time the rules on employment of foreign labour were amended allowing for a range of exceptions to that ban. The relevant decree, the *Anwerbestoppausnahme-Verordnung*, can be read as a catalogue of all the new forms of temporary employment of foreign labour used during the 1980s. In particular, agreements on seasonal work have been concluded with several Eastern European countries. Foreign workers are entitled to similar working conditions as German workers. Another form of flexible labour is cross-border work. Czechs, Slovaks (since September 1990) and Poles (since January 1991) have the possibility to work in Germany within the border zone up to fifty kilometres from the frontier provided they return home every evening (Groenendijk and Hampsink 1994: 30–40).

In 1993, official anti-immigration rhetoric culminated in the abolition of the constitutionally guaranteed right of asylum. The government claimed that only a change in the Constitution could lead to a reduction in the number of asylum seekers. The conservative–liberal coalition government and the main opposition party, the Social Democrats (SPD), agreed on the so-called asylum compromise. In the end, the 'asylum compromise' went further and became a 'migration compromise' which illustrates the blurring of asylum and immigration issues in political debate. Apart from the abolition of the constitutionally guaranteed right of asylum, it also included significant agreements on naturalisation and the immigration of *Aussiedler*. Changes in pattern of immigration of ethnic Germans stopped short of an abolition of the constitutional right to return home, as demanded by the SPD. The introduction of an annual quota for the immigration of *Aussiedler* and indirect administrative steering possibilities led to the admission of no more than around 210,000 ethnic German immigrants per year. Potential *Aussiedler* now have to apply from their country of residence to ensure that only 'Germans' are arriving. Additionally, the services offered to *Aussiedler*, first restricted in 1991, when the changing political climate made this decision possible for the government, were further limited (Bade 1994).

A further measure was the consolidation of changes in the naturalisation regulations of 1990. Immigrants living more than fifteen years in Germany and children of immigrants between the age of sixteen and twenty-three can become naturalised if they fulfil certain conditions and give up their former citizenship. Neither knowledge of the German language nor identification with German culture are any longer prerequisites for becoming naturalised. Commentators have interpreted this as a positive step towards liberalisation of the *jus sanguinis* principle. However, the rejection of dual nationality and the introduction of residence permits in January 1997 for children of immigrant origin born in Germany, mainly affecting Turkish citizens, sends the wrong signal to immigrant communities.

A fourth development, almost unnoticed by the public, was the extension of the temporary employment system for migrant workers. The German government responded for foreign policy reasons to the migration pressure from neighbouring East European states with the introduction of quotas for migrant workers. From 1989 on, Germany concluded bilateral agreements with several

East European countries which offer the possibility of employment for up to three years. The agreements provide for an annual quota of workers for each country. German employers sub-contract to employers in Eastern Europe for a defined, temporary project in Germany. The foreign companies employ their own staff. Again, as with the recruitment programme in the 1950s and 1960s, a characteristic feature of these agreements is the principle of contract work, i.e. migrant workers have to sign a contract with a specific company and their residence permits depend on this employment contract. Furthermore, these foreign workers are excluded from German social security provisions, and often receive lower wages than workers employed by a German company. Former contract workers have to spend at least two years abroad before they can again take up employment in Germany.

These agreements should not be simply regarded as a means of satisfying labour demand. The formal aim of the system, including seasonal and cross-border work, is to improve relations between Germany and the neighbouring countries but should also be interpreted in the context of the new German *Ostpolitik*. In the changed geopolitical situation after the fall of the Iron Curtain, Germany is trying to co-opt its poorer Eastern European neighbours by bilateral agreements designed to control migration movements and to reduce illegal immigration and employment by providing the temporary labour needed after unification in Germany. Given that Germany acts as unofficial ambassador to the EU for many of these countries, such co-option has proven to be fairly successful.

Further reasons brought forward were that providing the workers with hard currency and improving professional qualifications would assist the economic development and the democratic reform process in the sending countries. Similar aims were formulated to legitimise the recruitment of temporary migrant workers from Southern Europe three decades earlier. In order to protect the domestic labour force, the quota was reduced when the unemployment rate in Germany increased. After a decline in the employment of foreign contract workers in the 1980s, there was a rapid increase as from 1989. In 1993, as part of the asylum compromise, the annual quota for contract workers was limited at an average of 100,000. Several measures were introduced to make the system less attractive following the rapid rise in unemployment during 1993. These new groups of migrants are also confronted with the guest-worker ideology. Yet again, significant numbers will turn an initial temporary position into permanent status. However, concern over the import of cheap labour has also been voiced by trade unions with regard to workers from EU member states with lower wages and less social protection who benefit from the freedom of movement within the EU (Groenendijk and Hampsink 1994).

The creation of a migrant hierarchy

There is a clear division of policies directed towards ethnic Germans on the one hand and non-German immigrants on the other. Whereas the German government maintains that the 'boat is full' in justifying the closure of its borders against the influx of non-German/non-EU migrants, its policy regarding the immigration of ethnic Germans contradicts this stance. The fundamental principle guiding government policies on immigration is the differentiation between those who are 'ethnic Germans' and those who are not. This doctrine has been maintained by all main political parties. Ethnic Germans or *Volksdeutsche* (people of German origin) are officially not perceived as immigrants. This view is best expressed by Alfred Dregger of the Christian Democratic Union, when he stated that Germany is the '*Heimat* [homeland] of all persecuted and oppressed Germans' (Tichy 1993: 34). This doctrine is constitutionally institutionalised in Article 116 Basic Law. The provision is unique within the field of EU immigration law. The central distinction in the treatment of these two immigrant groups has been the application by the German state of the principle of ethnicity (or *Volk*) to the question of citizenship. This concept deprives the government of a policy framework to deal with the dilemma of settled guest workers. The policy implication of the right to return home for ethnic Germans is the provision of state support programmes to guarantee a smooth and quick integration. In addition to support schemes and financial contributions, this means above all the automatic acquisition of German citizenship.

The situation is fundamentally different for immigrants lacking German roots. Policies relating to them are essentially exclusionary, either internally in the form of their legal status and the absence of integrative measures, or externally, by implementing measures to stop further immigration of these groups. Whereas immigrants from Italy, Greece, Portugal or Spain are accepted today, and their legal status has improved due to their status as citizens of an EU member state, immigrants from Turkey are perceived as problematic. The debate on the reform of the citizenship law focuses on this part of the immigrant population. The thrust of the debate is of a cultural nature. The main factor appears to be that the majority of these immigrants are Muslims and that their lifestyle and many of their values are incompatible with a secular, modern, industrial society.

Restrictive measures are necessary, so runs the official argument, in order to guarantee public order. This is conveyed through a language and imagery of threat: the lack of space and resources to accommodate more foreigners, the jeopardising of social peace through *Überfremdung* (foreign domination), and the inability or unwillingness to integrate. The exclusion of the non-German minority and the striving for ethnic homogeneity, particularly reflected in the *Aussiedler* policy, shows a way of thinking that continues in the tradition of the ethnic nation-state. Historically, nation-building and identity formation in Germany have resulted from a process of exclusion. Today, the motor of this process is a feeling of threat (unemployment, lack of housing, 'foreigners' crime'). In particular the perception of material threat plays a large role in the hostility against minorities. In times of empty public purses, narrowing economic possibilities and cuts in welfare provisions, the living conditions of the national majority are noticeably affected and tolerance towards ethnic minorities is declining.

The transformation of migrant workers from a temporary workforce to a settled immigrant population is still not accepted. The presumption that categories of migrants, such as contract workers and asylum seekers, would only stay temporarily has been a way to bridge the gap between policy statement and reality. The refusal to accept ethnic diversity has its roots in the prevailing image of the German nation which has been challenged by the settlement of large immigrant groups. Yet, as has been shown, labour market policy and foreign policy considerations play a significant role in determining admission policies. However, the German understanding of ethnicity and what it signifies to them as Germans affects strongly the formulation of integration policies and naturalisation regulations. A report by the Interior Ministry defines integration as 'incorporation into German conditions', and identifies as the essential preconditions adaptation to the social values and norms, knowledge of the German language and 'renunciation of exaggerated national-religious behaviour' (BMI 1993: 13). These demands are equivalent to assimilation. The giving up of one's original citizenship as requirement for naturalisation underlines this.

According to this rationale, naturalisation is seen as the end of an integration process and not as a means of integration. This is expressed in the fact that there is no automatic right to citizenship in Germany, and for many non-EU immigrants naturalisation remains a discretionary act by the German authorities. The government argues that dual nationality could lead to loyalty conflicts in times of crisis between Germany and the country of origin as well as to practical problems such as military service. This is well illustrated by the one *de facto* exception made to the dual citizenship rule. Due to the fact that nearly all ethnic Germans remaining in Poland after the Second World War were deprived of their German citizenship in 1945, and re-classified as ethnic Poles, today both governments have decided to let sleeping dogs lie, and ignore an anomaly which contradicts the legal code of both countries. This system works well, and has helped to staunch the flow of migration from Poland to Germany, but it has created a situation in which a small number of ethnic Germans resident in Poland have demanded the right to complete their national service in the armed services of their choice.

European perspectives

The establishment of an EU citizenship in the Maastricht Treaty has created new boundaries and contributed to the relative decline in the status of resident third country nationals. The treaty prohibits any discrimination on grounds of nationality between nationals of member states. EU citizens resident in Germany have the same economic, social and cultural rights as German citizens. They have the right to vote and stand in local and European Parliament elections, whereas in 1989, the right of resident third country nationals to vote in local elections was ruled unconstitutional by the German Constitutional Court. In contrast to EU immigrants, non-EU citizens have no right to move and reside freely within the EU, and family reunification has become more difficult.

European citizenship has no significance for third country nationals living in Germany. Member states continue to determine national regulations of immigration and citizenship rules, and as such determine who can and who cannot become a citizen of the EU. Access to political participation on the national as well as on the European level remains linked to citizenship law.

The continuing legal insecurity and disadvantage for migrant workers who originate from outside Europe or from Central and Eastern Europe is in stark contrast with the experiences of migrants who are citizens of EU states. Yet, third country nationals are again divided into those who enjoy more favourable provisions under bi- or multilateral agreements between their country and Germany or the European Union. EU Association Agreements (e.g. with Turkey, the Maghreb countries), agreements with the Central and Eastern European countries and bilateral co-operation agreements between Eastern European countries and Germany have conferred certain rights to citizens of these states employed legally in Germany. However, the diversity of these agreements and the rights they confer to individuals means that they cannot be seen as a model for the future. It is arguable that their patchwork approach is insufficient in achieving equality between non-EU migrant workers and EU citizens. Those agreements that give limited free movement rights for some non-EU immigrants such as Turkish workers have led to the creation of a higher 'intermediate' status for this group. Now, with the new forms of temporary employment prevailing since the 1980s, many migrant workers are excluded from social rights such as the eligibility for welfare state programmes or family reunification. This process will lead to further social stratification unless it is clearly seen to be part of a process towards full integration of all non-EU immigrants and their families. Well-meaning declarations by politicians to counter racism are flawed if non-German immigrants are officially marginalised. Short of citizenship entitlements, integration requires the granting of rights comparable with those held by EU citizens working and living in Germany.

The discrimination against non-EU immigrants is inherent in the temporary migration policy. This is particularly evident in the employment restrictions imposed on migrants in terms of geographic and professional mobility. Language difficulties and lack of education further contribute to the inferior status of these migrants in the receiving society. Given the lack of freedom of movement and choice, these migrant workers cannot take advantage of the same opportunities that the labour market offers German and EU citizens. Thus, immigration regulations have not only economic consequences but also a direct effect on the migrants' integration into German society.

Constraints on other rights in the economic, social and political spheres further marginalise migrant workers and their families. Poverty, poor housing and inadequate education are some of the more profound consequences. General discrimination in the workplace, in the allocation of housing, and other aspects of their daily lives, is also experienced by long-term resident immigrants. Principles of equality and claims to human rights challenge the tendency of the ethnic nation-state tradition to exclude a part of the people – in the sense of population – from political participation.

In essence if Germany is to effect a change in its attitude towards nationality and citizenship, it will have to adopt a model of civic nationhood which it rejected in the nineteenth century. The character of the German nation itself would inevitably change. Yet, as long as citizenship rights are granted on the basis of ethnicity, the social and political tensions resulting from such mechanisms of inclusion and exclusion will continue. As immigration into Germany will continue despite restrictive immigration policies, the question of how to deal with demands by resident immigrants for equal rights, a process that has been facilitated by the European integration process, will be high on the agenda.

References

Bade, K. (1993) *Deutsche im Ausland, Fremde in Deutschland. Migration in Geschichte und Gegenwart*, Munich: C.H. Beck.

—— (1994) *Ausländer, Aussiedler, Asyl in der Bundesrepublik Deutschland*, Berlin: Landeszentrale für politische Bildungsarbeit.

Beauftragte der Bundesregierung für die Belange der Ausländer (ed.) (1995) *Bericht über die Lage der Ausländer in der Bundesrepublik Deutschland*, Bonn.

Brubaker, R. (1992) *Citizenship and Nationhood in France and Germany*, Cambridge, MA: Harvard University Press.

Bundesministerium des Innern (BMI) (1993) *Aufzeichnung zur Ausländerpolitik und zum Ausländerrecht in der Bundesrepublik Deutschland*, Bonn.

Fassmann, H. and Münz, R. (1992) 'Patterns and Trends of International Migration in Western Europe', *Population and Development Review* 18 (3): 457–80.

Gellner, E. (1982) *Nations and Nationalism*, Oxford: Blackwell.

Groenendijk, K. and Hampsink, R. (1994) *Temporary Employment of Migrants in Europe*, Nijmwegen: Katholieke Universiteit.

Hoffmann, L. (1992) *Die unvollendete Republik: Zwischen Einwanderungsland und deutschem Nationalstaat*, 2nd revised edn, Köln: Pappy Rossa.

Mann, G. (1968) *The History of Germany since 1789*, London: Penguin Books.

Miles, R. (1982) *Racism and Migrant Labour*, London: Routledge & Kegan Paul.

Oberndärfer, D. (1993) *Der Wahn des Nationalen. Die Alternative der offenen Republik*, Freiburg: Herder.

Smith, A. (1991) *National Identity*, London: Penguin Books.

Tichy, R. (1993) *Ausländer rein! Deutsche und Ausländer – verschiedene Herkunft, gemeinsame Zukunft*, Munich: Beck.

Ulrich, H. (1986) *Geschichte der Ausländerbeschäftigung in Deutschland 1880 bis 1980: Saisonarbeiter, Zwangsarbeiter, Gastarbeiter*, Berlin: Dietz.

Winkler, B. (1993) *Zukunftsangst Einwanderung*, 3rd revised edn, Munich: Beck.

9 Parties, elections and the Slovene minority in Austria

Boris Jesih

Introduction

The Slovene minority of Austria constitutes one of Europe's lesser-known ethnic minorities. Although small in number, as we shall see, the land on which they reside has often provided an arena for mutually exclusive Austrian and Yugoslav claims. That their presence no longer excites the passions it once did is the consequence of diligent policy-making and the careful if sometimes not completely painless implementation of minority rights policies. For reasons of space, this chapter focuses on one element of the relationship between ethnic Slovenes and the host Austrian society. That element is the participation of the minority in the electoral and party political processes of Austrian politics. As we shall see, such participation may have broader implications for other such minorities in Europe.

The legacy of history

The Slovene minority in Austria is to found in the federal *Länder* of Carinthia and Styria. The exact number of ethnic Slovenes in either *Land* is a matter of dispute, with estimates varying in 'several tens of thousands' in Carinthia to 'a few thousand' in Styria.[1] This text deals mainly with the status of Slovenes in Carinthia, although reference to the Slovenes of Styria will be made as and where appropriate.

After unsuccessful attempts at annexation on the part of Yugoslavia, after both World Wars, the areas of Austria in which the Slovene minority resides are nowadays recognised as an integral part of Austria with adequate international legal protection for the minority being provided within the terms of the Austrian State Treaty of 1955. This chapter provides a detailed analysis of the post-1945 period, with emphasis being placed upon the dilemmas which faced and continue to face the minority. In order to provide a clear focus, the later analysis deals almost exclusively with issues concerning the political organisation of the Slovene minority, their modes of electoral participation, the relationship between Slovene political organisations and the national party system, and the interaction between the minority and Yugoslavia/Slovenia.

After the dissolution of the Austro-Hungarian monarchy in 1919, the Slovene nation was divided between four states: Italy, Austria, Hungary and the Kingdom of Serbs, Croats and Slovenes, later the Kingdom of Yugoslavia. In Austria, Slovenes remained settled in the southern parts of Carinthia and Styria. In Carinthia there was a plebiscite on 10 October 1920, the result of which was, according to some sources, that due to the falsification of a few thousands of votes, the southern part of Carinthia remained within Austria.[2] The implications of the plebiscite were both ethnic and political, since inhabitants were also deciding upon the form of the state they wished to live in. Allegations of falsification to one side, contrary to the expectations of the adherents to primordial nationalism, the newly emerged Austrian republic was undoubtedly more attractive than the conservative, dynastic and non-developed Yugoslavia.

The status of all minorities in Austria was thereafter regulated with the provisions contained in Articles 62–9 of the Treaty of Saint-Germain. The plebiscite result and the annexation of Carinthia to Austria gave rise to the expansion of German nationalist organisations in the *Land*, including the Kärntner Heimatdienst (KHD) (The Patriotic League of Carinthia) which is active to this day.[3] Despite such unfavourable circumstances, Carinthian Slovenes established their own political organisation: The Catholic Political and Economic Association of Slovenes in Carinthia, later renamed the Political and Economic Association of Carinthian Slovenes. Initially the Slovenes had two deputies in the Carinthian *Landtag*. Contacts were also maintained with the Austrian political parties, especially the social democrats and the communists. Between 1925 and 1930 there were negotiations aimed at securing cultural autonomy for Carinthian Slovenes, which ultimately proved to be unsuccessful.

After the *Anschluss* of 1934 and the subsequent invasion of Yugoslavia in 1941, Carinthian Slovenes were exposed to Nazi terror, their organisations were banned, and a programme of mass deportations of Carinthian Slovenes ensued. By 1942 armed partisan resistance on the part of Carinthian Slovenes had begun in tandem with Tito's Partisan movement.

For the Carinthian Slovenes, the end of the Second World War was marked by the expectation of unification with Yugoslavia. In a 1947 Memorandum on the Carinthian question, Yugoslavia demanded 2,470 square kilometres of Carinthia, an area which contained some 18,000 inhabitants, together with 130 square kilometres of Styria with a population of around 10,000. Despite diplomatic endeavours it soon became obvious that these demands would not be granted. The most significant result of the subsequent negotiations was Article 7 of the Austrian State Treaty,[4] which remains to this very day the basis for the rights of the Slovene minority in Carinthia and Austrian Styria (Stourzh 1980).

The signing of the Austrian State Treaty on 15 May 1955 guaranteed the Slovene minority equality before the law, the right to elementary and secondary schooling in their mother tongue, the equality of Slovenian with German as an official language in areas of minority residence, the right of minority participation in cultural, administrative and legal institutions, and the prohibition of anti-Slovene organisations. However, inevitably the implementation of these principles has not proven to be so easy, and even today there are areas in which Slovene activists claim that discrimination exists.

In post-war Austria, Carinthian Slovenes developed two main political organisations: the National Council of Carinthian Slovenes (NCCS) and the Union of the Slovene Organisations in Carinthia (USOC), two main cultural and educational organisations, and a range of ancillary organisations. At the local level the Uniform List of Carinthia (ULC), together with independents, began to contest elections. In addition three publishing houses and two bookshops were established. There is also a Slovene language press, and most importantly, a research institute, The Slovene Scientific Research Institute.

With regard to the treatment of the minority since 1945, we can note the following turning points: the abolition of compulsory bilingual education in 1949, the establishing of the Federal Secondary School for Slovenes in 1957, the passing of the Law on Bilingual Topographic Signs in 1972[5] and, in reaction to the activities of Austrian right-wing extremists, the special population census in 1976, the Three-Party Agreement in 1976, various legislation in July 1976/7, and finally, the reform of bilingual schooling with the segregational school law in 1988.

However, from the Slovene perspective, Austria has yet fully to implement the necessary legislation through which these objectives can be realised. As a result it is claimed that the minority is in effect faced with unwelcome assimilatory pressures. It is further argued by minority activists that this implementation gap has arisen because of nationalist pressure upon the national political parties.

Slovenes in Austrian Styria

Slovenes of Austrian Styria are to be found in the southern parts of the Austrian *Land* which, in 1919 when the new Austro-Yugoslav border was drawn, remained within the Austrian state under the terms of the Treaty of Saint-Germain. In Slovenian the territory is known as the *Radgona kot* (Radgona Corner) or *Trikotnik* (Triangle), and in German as the *Radkesburger Winkel*, and is comprised of some villages around Radgona (Radkesburg) as well as the town itself. Most Slovenes in Styria in fact speak only a regional dialect of their mother tongue the exception being younger intellectuals who have learned literary Slovene at their own initiative.[6]

Although the Treaty of Saint-Germain guaranteed minorities in Austria a certain level of minority rights, Austria refused to grant such rights to the Slovenes of Styria, unlike in Carinthia where they were at least partly granted. The sole permitted minority organisation was the Slovene Educational Association, which in fact had been founded in 1910. Indeed, the Association was quickly abolished in 1919 upon the assassination of its president. The result was that the Slovenes of Styria were unable to maintain their cultural uniqueness, and found it difficult to maintain contact with their fellow Slovenes in Carinthia and Yugoslavia. During the Second World War the Slovene population of Styria was also subjected to Nazi violence, and wherever possible lent its support to the Partisans. In 1945 there were a few attempts to organise the population in favour of Yugoslavia. However, as with Carinthia these endeavours were to prove futile.

Despite Article 7 of the Austrian State Treaty, the position of the minority did not in any way improve. The sheer numeric weakness of the Styrian community, combined with assimilatory pressures, seemed to signal that it had no long-term future. It was due to a group of younger activists who, at the end of the 1970s, founded their own minority organisation, that the minority survives at all. The group submitted a framework programme of the project of Slovene revitalisation in Styria to the political authorities of the then Yugoslav republic of Slovenia. The Slovenian leadership showed no interest in the group's ideas, which served to re-enforce the suspicion that the Yugoslav government had no interest in the Styrian Slovenes and the unfavourable attitude of the parent nation-state towards the Styrian as opposed to the Carinthian Slovenes.

Nevertheless, in 1988 the Article Seven Association of Styrian Slovenes was established. Faced with serious difficulties, it survived to become an important organisation of the Styrian Slovenes. A turning point came with the conference 'Slovenes in the Austrian Federal *Land* Styria', held in the Slovenian city of Maribor in 1993 as a joint event of the Institute for Ethnic Studies, University of Maribor, and the Austrian Institute for Eastern and South Eastern Europe. The significance of this conference was in the fact that, for the first time, academics from both Yugoslavia and Austria addressed the issue of the Styrian Slovenes. In turn, the conference was followed by a series of cultural and other events in Austria (Jesih 1994a).

Although there is a degree of hostility towards the minority on the part of the majority Austrian population in Styria, it may nevertheless be said that Austria has officially acknowledged the legitimacy of the Article Seven Association, and thus also the existence of the Slovene minority in Austrian Styria. In 1994 two minority representatives were co-opted onto the Advisory Committee for Carinthian Slovenes with the Austrian Federal Chancellor. The Association has had an office in Graz since 1993, and in 1995 the Association bought a house which in 1997, with the help of Slovenia, became a cultural centre. Finally, we should note that the issue of the Slovene minority in Styria is also tied to Austrian demands that Slovenia change its policy towards its German-speaking citizens, who are a remnant of the wider German community of pre-1945 Yugoslavia (Stenner 1997).

Minorities and their political participation

Turning to our main theme, we can begin by stating that the issue of minority political participation is one of the basic issues of democracy. The main problem that poses itself is whether a minority should, because of its characteristics, enjoy a specific status in the political life of a country, and to what extent should they participate in the decision-making of a state. For example, should any special status refer only to matters concerning the realisation of specific minority rights, or also to issues concerning their wider social environment, since all issues concerning such an environment also concern the minority settled there? Within this context, guarantees enabling minority participation, and the specific status minorities might occupy in the bodies of representative and executive authority, are of crucial importance. With regard to the Slovene community of Austria, various methods have been tried. We shall now examine each of these in turn.

The first is to take part in elections via a Slovene political party. A typical example of such a party is the German minority party in South Tyrol – *Südtiroler Volkspartei*. Such parties have their disadvantages, mainly due to the parochial range of their activities. It may also be the case that the minority is split over whether or not 'their' party actually embodies the interests of the community as a whole. Two competing parties both of which claim to represent the interests of the minority may arise, thus causing cohesion to be weakened. There is also the question of which elections such a party should contest. Such parties can expect to be most successful at local or regional elections. However, it is a matter of debate as to whether a minority party can actually claim to be the authentic voice of the community, particularly if the minority is socio-economically differentiated. Moreover, if a minority choose to tread this path, it becomes difficult to expect other political parties to be involved with the solving of minority problems. In other words the national arena and the diverse interests of voters must always be taken into account.

The second way of co-operation is by minority activists working together with an established national party, whilst maintaining organisational independence. Usually this co-operation takes place with minor political parties which, apart from having a degree of sympathy with a given minority, need to maximise their potential electorate. Such votes are ensured by the minority party. A good example of this kind of participation is found in Denmark where in 1974 the German *Schleswigsche Partei* established electoral co-operation with the Danish Centre Democrats, thereby facilitating the election of an ethnic German to the Danish parliament.

The third way of asserting minority demands is for the minority to lend its support towards all parties which claim to be in sympathy with it. Minority members nearly always give their votes to more than one political party, precisely because as with the titular ethnic group their members are socially stratified and differentiated. Of course the criteria of decision-making employed by members of minorities when making such decisions will not necessarily be the same as those employed by members of the host community. The political status of a party is very important as well, whether it be at local, regional or national level, as a ruling party has an automatically privileged status.

However, the formal equality of a minority in election processes, and how it chooses to participate in elections, is but one part of the democratic process. In order for a minority successfully to participate in the political life of a country, there must exist freedom of political assembly, the right to free speech, non-discrimination and the like. Group Rights' activists argue that special conditions must be created which make it possible for minority communities and their members to participate as equals in the political process. Thus they advocate special clauses which facilitate the representation of ethnic minorities in the various tiers of government that a state might possess. They also argue that there should be no laws, such as that passed in Carinthia in 1979, which altered constituency boundaries in such a way that it made it difficult for the UCL to participate as an equal in elections for the Carinthian *Landtag* (Jesih 1992).

Finally, within this context we should mention the interesting, and in a way unique, method of minority political participation in Slovenia, which guarantees mandates for a member of both the Italian and Hungarian minorities in the Slovene parliament, along with the right of veto over matters which could alter the rights of those minorities (Jesih 1994a: 22–4). The Slovenian alternative enables the minorities to enjoy direct parliamentary representation, but at the same time does not forestall the possibility of ethnic Hungarians or Italians from voting for other parties. As such the Slovene model provides a convenient answer to many of the above-stated dilemmas, but it would be difficult to offer it as a solution to other states, since it was created in conditions specific to Slovenia which are unlikely to repeat themselves elsewhere.

Carinthian Slovenes, political parties and participation at elections

As was mentioned earlier, the Slovene minority in Carinthia is divided into two central political organisations, the left-of-centre-oriented USOC, and the right-of-centre NCCS. Until the 1960s, the NCCS sought political support from the Austrian People's Party (ÖVP). Nowadays, it maintains a stance of equidistance from all the mainstream parties,[7] although some Slovene voters still give their votes to the ÖVP. In addition, the ULC has often stood at elections in coalition with mainstream parties. In 1986 it stood alongside the Green Alternative List (GAL) and succeeded in its objective of securing the election of an ethnic Slovene to parliament.

In 1995 it formed a coalition with the Liberal Forum (LiF), but on this occasion the success of 1986 was not repeated. In both cases, these coalitions were rather unnatural, given that the GAL is decidedly left of centre, that the LiF is anti-clerical, and that the Slovene minority is religious as well as conservative. Within this context we should note that at the local level, the ULC enjoys the largest share of the Slovene vote.

For its part, the USOC, despite an early flirtation with the communists, has traditionally been closer to the Socialist Party of Austria (SPÖ), although in recent years it has made overtures to the GAL. Indeed, for some years there has been a special Slovene section within the SPÖ. The SPÖ and GAL as a result became involved in a political struggle for the votes of the Slovenes which has played a negative role in the development of Austrian–Slovene inter-state relations. Since 1988, USOC has been in favour of an integrationist, inter-cultural model of co-operation whilst deliberately avoiding a formal alliance with either party.

On the other hand, the NCCS advocates that the Slovene community seeks to obtain independent representation in national politics. Within this context we should note two basic differences between the NCCS and the USOC. First, as just mentioned, the NCCS favours independent Slovene representation in parliament. Whereas the USOC continues to favour the representation of Slovene interests through the mainstream political parties. The NCCS also favours the establishment of a quota system for appointees to public bodies. Whereas USOC is not opposed to this idea in principle, it sees no scope for it within the current legal framework.

There is of course also the question of power and political influence, ascension to which is the means to securing funds from both the Austrian and Slovenian governments. At present the NCCS enjoys more support in Slovenia, and all parties in Slovenia are keen to parade their patriotic credentials and interest in the fate of Slovenes abroad. In fact, it could be argued that domestic parties have a vested interest in ensuring that the NCCS and USOC continue to be unable to find common cause (Jesih 1995).

Returning to the theme of electoral participation in Austria, we have already noted the activities of the ULC in 1986 and 1995. With regard to the Carinthian *Landtag*, in 1949 and 1953 two Slovene lists stood, and in 1959 and 1965 only one. The ULC first contested this level of election in 1975, but narrowly failed to gain election. In 1979, despite boundary changes which placed the Slovenes in several different constituencies, the ULC stood again, although once more without success. The same has been true of all subsequent *Land* elections. Slovene activists have argued that the constituency boundaries were changed for the 1979 elections in order to forestall the possibility of the ULC gaining a mandate. It should also be stressed that the ULC did not have the support of the entire community. USOC was increasingly inclined towards co-operation with mainstream Austrian political parties and the NCCS was divided on how best to proceed.

Inevitably, Carinthian Slovene candidates do best at local elections. In 1973 Slovene lists stood for election in nineteen communes and gained a total of forty mandates. In 1979 they increased their representation to forty-four mandates in twenty-three communes. Following the 1985 elections, the number of mandates remained unchanged, and actually increased in the elections of 1991 and 1996. Besides paying attention to issues of specific concern to the minority, Slovene candidates addressed themselves to issues that were of concern to all the inhabitants of Carinthia. A considerable number of Slovenes stood for election as candidates of the mainstream parties, demonstrating the diversity of attitudes which exists within Slovene society in Carinthia (Jesih 1992).

At the local level, the extent to which the politics of ethnicity dominates is dependent above all on the national political mood. The campaigns of 1973 and 1975 were marked by misuse of the minority issue by mainstream parties who had an eye open to a wider national constituency. The reasons for the politics of ethnicity playing such a major role during these years were a growth in nationalism among a section of Austrian society, and a similar phenomenon being evident among part of Carinthian Slovene youth. The situation was aggravated by an acrimonious debate over the adoption and alleged non-implementation of the 1972 Law on Bilingual Topographic Inscriptions. Attempts to implement this law triggered attacks by the *Heimatdienst* on the few bilingual signs erected by the authorities. The ugliness of the situation was evidenced by a fall in support for the Carinthian SPÖ which condemned the attacks unreservedly, and the resignation of Hans Simat, the SPÖ's president in Carinthia.

In the wake of these events, common sense began to prevail as was evidenced in 1976, when Carinthian Slovene organisations and Austrian political parties signed what was known as the Three-Party Agreement. However, the rise of Jörg Haider and the Freedom Party of Austria (FPÖ) has inevitably meant that the politics of ethnicity has once again come to the fore, as Haider seeks to manipulate pan-German nationalist sentiment.

Unlike the other main parties, the FPÖ is not interested in votes from ethnic Slovenes. Although some sections of the ÖVP have sought to emulate Haider's rhetoric in order to minimise the seepage of votes to the FPÖ, so far the major parties as parties have not followed Haider's dangerous precedent in order to head him off. Having said that, contacts between the Slovene community and the ÖVP and SPÖ tend to be minimal outside of campaign times. The one party that does attempt to maintain continuous contact with the Slovene community is the GAL. Up until 1991, the GAL worked particularly closely with supporters of the ULC, and as was previously mentioned, an ethnic Slovene has sat in parliament in Vienna as part of the GAL faction. Unfortunately, since 1991, the two have begun to drift apart.

With regard to voting behaviour, we find that the distribution of votes in Carinthia is somewhat different from the rest of the country. The bilingual areas of the *Land* are of course particularly infertile ground for the FPÖ. Conversely, the SPÖ achieves some of its best results in the said area, as usually does the ÖVP. This indicates that the two major parties still retain a large degree of residual loyalty among Carinthian Slovenes.

Co-operation and conflict

The Three-Party Agreement of July 1976 laid the formal and legal foundations for the future policy of Austria towards its Croat and Slovene minorities. Some Slovene activists claim that the situation of the Slovene community actually deteriorated in the wake of the Agreement. The Agreement supports the use of consociational mechanisms for the resolution of issues of concern to the minority. It also facilitated the holding of a special census in 1976, which was held in an attempt to discover just how many Slovenes there are in Carinthia. The main complaint from Slovenes about the Agreement and its ramifications is that too many decisions about their fate are in fact taken without any reference to the needs of the community itself.

Regardless of the form of co-operation with mainstream Austrian parties, results for the Carinthian Slovenes have been mixed. It may be argued that both the strategy of independent representation within such parties, and the strategy of forming electoral pacts with such parties, have their uses. Indeed for a short while the co-operation between the GAL and ULC brought a large number of benefits to the Slovene community.

The emergence of the green movement introduced essential qualitative changes in Austrian–Slovene relations. However, due to its lack of numbers, and corresponding minimal political weight, the Slovene minority found it had difficulty in articulating its voice within the GAL. Yet it must be acknowledged that the emergence of the Greens did stimulate changes in attitudes on the part of the mainstream parties towards the Slovene minority.

There is no reason to assume that the Slovene community will ever lend its support *en masse* to a single Austrian party. It is too sophisticated and internally differentiated for such crass behaviour. However, neither is there any real possibility of any Slovene organisation gaining a seat in the national parliament. Both the electoral law and numeric weakness of the community see to that. In reality, the Slovene organisations are going to have to content themselves with representation at the local and possibly *Land* levels. Although in the latter case there is the issue of whether constituencies have been gerrymandered to the detriment of the Slovene community. In the short term, then, the local arena will remain the most viable avenue of representation. In order for there to be a single Slovene party there would have to be a degree of group solidarity which at present simply does not exist. Moreover, the greater the sensitivity of the mainstream parties to the Carinthian Slovenes, the smaller the political space for any such hypothetical party. Besides, the situation at local and *Land* level, where Slovene lists oppose parties which themselves field Slovene candidates, is a situation that only a primordial nationalist would find objectionable.

Conclusion

The issue of political participation of the Slovene minority in Austrian politics is of vital importance to all citizens of Austria. For the minority itself it is the most important issue and constitutes a constant source of irritation within both the minority itself, as well as in wider society. The idea of establishing a kind of ethnic assembly, which has been discussed for the past few years, represents a conceptual novelty; whether it also represents something positive is quite another matter.

In any case, Carinthian Slovenes have not yet found the recipe which would solve the problem of their relationship with the mainstream political parties. Not that this is a problem peculiar to this particular case. In the opinion of the author, the least favourable option is for the minority to channel its resources in a single direction. It is essential that such relations be multi-layered, and not tied exclusively to one party, since all previous unidimensional strategies have failed to achieve any tangible benefits. Clearly there is no ideal prescriptive path that may be followed. What is needed is for there to be a series of activities which allows for the articulation of different interests, but does not lead to the neglect of the interests of the community as a whole.

On the other hand, if the minority were to become alienated from the main body politic, any such development would in large part be due to attempts by nationalist forces to abuse the presence of the Slovene community for their own ends. The legacy of previous such attempts has been to make difficult the participation of ethnic Slovenes in wider Austrian politics. This in turn has led them to develop autonomous forms of political activity, which so far have had little success outside of the local level.

Notes

1 In Austrian censuses, population is not classified according to ethnic origin, but according to the language of communication. Some estimates claim that there are several times more Slovenes in Austria than is revealed by the census data. According to the 1991 population census there were 16,000 Slovenians in Carinthia. In other words, 16,000 people gave Slovenian as their mother tongue.

2 The Carinthian plebiscite took place on 10 October 1920. 15,279 (40.96 per cent) voted for Yugoslavia, and 22,025 (59.04 per cent) for Austria.

3 Supporters of the KHD carried out attacks against Carinthian Slovenes during and after the plebiscite. They advocated increased German settlement in Southern Carinthia, and were involved in the falsification of census data regarding the language of communication. Even before the *Anschluss* of 1938, the KHD contained influential Carinthian Nazis and after the annexation the first secretary became a member of the provincial government. He then organised the deportation of about 200 Carinthian Slovene families. The KHD was active until the end of the Second World War. After the war, only the SPÖ was consistent in its demand that it be banned. After the signing of the Austrian State Treaty in 1955, it was re-established despite it being technically illegal. Today it rather fancifully claims a membership of around 100,000 and is linked to other ultra-rightist organisations in Austria.

4 Article 7 of the Austrian State Treaty (1955) defined the rights of the Slovene and Croatian minorities in Austria.

5 In 1972, the socialist government of Bruno Kreisky adopted The Law on Bilingual Topographic Inscriptions. The implementation of this law triggered attacks by the KHD against the few bilingual inscriptions erected by the authorities. In the face of public hostility the SPÖ then backed down from its previous support for bilingualism in southern Carinthia

6 According to the 1910 census in the autochthonous Slovene region of Austrian Styria there were 2,644 persons who used Slovenian as their language of communication among a total of 5,146 Slovenian speakers in the entire province. The number has drastically decreased in the intervening years until, according to the 1991 census, there were only 246 Slovenian speakers left. According to the estimates of the Slovene Article Seven Association, there are today in Austrian Styria anything from 3,000 to 5,000 bilingual inhabitants.

7 At the *Land* elections of 1965, the NCCS stood as the Carinthian Electoral Community. This decision marked the parting of the ways for the NCCS and the ÖVP. By the elections of 1986, the NCCS had switched its support to the left-oriented GAL.

References

Austrian State Treaty of 1955.

Barker, T.M. (1984) *The Slovene Minority of Carinthia*, New York: Columbia University Press.

—— (1990) *Social Revolutionaries and Secret Agents: the Carinthian Slovene Partisans and Britain's Operations Executive*, New York: Columbia University Press.

Brezigar, B. (forthcoming 1999) *Between Alps and Adriatic. The Slovenes in the European Union*, Brussels: European Bureau for Lesser Used Languages.

Devetak, S.M. and Jesih, B. (eds) (1988) *Minority Education in Carinthia: Co-existence or Fragmentation?* (selected Documents), Ljubljana: Institute for Ethnic Studies.

Fischer, G. (1980) *Das slowenische in Kärnten*, Klagenfurt: Slowenisches informations Zentrum.

Fritzl, M. (1990) *Der Kärntner Heimatdienst: Ideologie, Ziele und Strategien einer nationalistischen Organisation*, Klagenfurt: Drava.

Gombocz, W. (1990) 'Der Artikel-VII-Kulturverein Steiermark', *Europa Ethnica* 2: 94–8.

—— (1992) 'Outlawed: The Republic of Austria's Permanent Violations of Human Rights in Styria', in *Razprave in gradivo: revija za narodnostna vpraanja* 26–7: 200–38.

Jesih, B. (1992) *The Political Parties in Austria and the Minority Question*, unpublished M.Sc. thesis, University of Ljubljana.

——(1994a) 'Political Participation', in V. Klocic and J. Stergar (eds) *Ethnic Minorities in Slovenia*, Ljubljana: Institute for Ethnic Studies.

—— (ed.) (1994b) *Slovenci v avstrijski zvezni dezeli Stajerski*, Ljubljana: Slovenska akademija znanosti in umetnosti.

—— (ed.) (1995) *Manjsina kot subjekt*, Ljubljana: Institute for Ethnic Studies

Necak, D. (1978) 'Die Wahlen in Kärnten nach dem zweiten Weltkrieg', in *Jahrbuch für Zeitgeschichte*, Vienna: Löcker Verlag.

Pernthaler, P. (1985) 'Ein Modell fur eine selbststandige politische Vertretung der Karnter Slowenen zum Landtag', *Europa Ethnica* 4.

—— (1992) 'A Model for an Autonomous Representational Body Based on Public Law for the Slovene Ethnic Group in Carinthia', in P. Apovnik (ed.) *Eine autonome Vertrettung für die Kärntner Slowenen*, Klagenfurt: Verlag Land Kärnten.

Reiterer, A.F. (1996) *Karntner Slowenen: Minderheit oder Elite? Neuere Tendenzen der ethnischen Arbeitsteilung*, Klagenfurt: Drava.

Stenner, C. (ed.) (1997), *Slowenische Steiermark. Verdrangte Minderheit in Österreichs Südosten*, Vienna: Bählau Verlag.

Stourzh, G. (1980) *Geschichte des Staatsvertrages 1945–1955*, Cologne: Styria Verlag.

Wakounig, M. and Larcher, D. (eds) (1989) *Lage und Perspektiven der Volksgruppen in Österreich. Bericht der Arbeitsgruppe*, Vienna: Österreichische Rektorenkonferenz.

10 Democratisation and ethnopolitical conflict: the Yugoslav case

Agneza Bozic

Ethnopolitical conflict

The bloodiest war in post-Second World War Europe broke out in the Balkans following the dissolution of multinational Yugoslavia in 1991. Most analysts describe this conflict as being driven by incompatible ethnic demands. The term 'ethnic' has become the popular descriptive term for conflicts among ethnic groups who reside in multiethnic states. In the most general sense, the common assessment of the conflict in Yugoslavia – that it erupted because of deeply ingrained differences in religion, culture and state traditions which fed into 'age-old ethnic hatreds' – is misleading. While the role of historical factors is dealt with elsewhere, the contention of this analysis is to demonstrate that ethnic differences are normal features of different ethnic groups rather than being inherent sources of conflict. The concern of this chapter is to see how ethnic differences can be and are being utilised as a tool by political elites and opportunist leaders to achieve political ends and, consequently, why ethnicity has become so salient in the process of the decline of communist power, and in its immediate aftermath, in the former Yugoslavia.

The political utilisation of ethnicity, like conflict itself, may be both positive and negative. Positive uses of ethnicity in the political arena include the assertion of ethnicity to effect a more equal distribution of resources or for improving the positions of disadvantaged groups through cultural and political autonomy. Negative uses of ethnicity emphasise intolerance and exclusion and result in destructive politics. Such negative utilisation of ethnicity is evident in mass violence aimed at the members of other ethnic groups, the forced expulsion of innocent people, and the destruction of other groups' cultural and religious sources of identity. Our concern is with the destructive side of ethnic politicisation.

This analysis argues that referring to contemporary inter-ethnic conflict as 'ethnic' distorts the conflict into a phenomenon that is not conducive to effective conflict management. Current attempts towards conflict resolution have not been fruitful because both the ethnic and political dimensions of the conflict are not fully understood. Because of that, existing analyses provide little basis for prevention of ethnopolitical conflict. Consequently, it is necessary to demythologise the burdened concept of ethnicity and to distinguish between the ethnic and the political aspects of inter-ethnic conflict. Such separation allows for the determination of when and how ethnic identity becomes politicised.

Furthermore, simply to use the term 'ethnic' for a phenomenon that is deeply political is an inadequate description for the true nature of conflict which is set in action by what Rothschild (1981) would term the 'politicisation of ethnicity'. The term 'ethnopolitical' is a more appropriate description of this conflict since it is the result of politics that deliberately use ethnicity in the struggle for power and control over the territory and resources of a Yugoslav state. According to Rothschild (1981: 2), politicisation of ethnicity involves the political transmutation of ethnicity from 'a psychological or cultural or social datum into political leverage for the purpose of altering or reinforcing such systems of structured inequality between and among ethnic categories'. The fundamental issue of politics – 'who controls the resources of the state' – is most often at the core of the processes that bring about conflict among ethnic groups. Thus, while the issues often are identified with the ethnic groups, and are referred to as being concerned with ethnic attributes, the roots of the conflict are found in politics.

This indiscriminate use of the concept of ethnicity reveals that the concept itself frequently acquires a pejorative meaning. Moving beyond borders of the former Yugoslavia to the former Soviet Union, Rwanda, Bangladesh, India, Sri Lanka and Northern Ireland, to name just a few contemporary examples of such conflicts, one is easily led to believe that in all these 'ethnic' conflicts, ethnicity is the cause of war and unimaginable atrocities. Ethnicity is promoted as the main culprit: the source of irrationality and deep divisions that lead to horrible bloodshed, genocide, forcible transfers of people, and in general to chronic instability within multi-ethnic societies. This view is narrowly uni-dimensional and neglects not only the positive aspects of ethnicity, but also the inherent latency of its political nature. Only when we 'demythologise' the concept of ethnicity, determining in which circumstances and by which mechanisms ethnicity is manipulated or transformed into political force, will we be able to deal effectively with the phenomenon so inadequately termed 'ethnic conflict'.

The nature of ethnic identity in the context of ideological and power vacuums provides fertile ground for radicalisation, but it is only through the mechanisms of ethnic politicisation that these identities become radicalised and confrontational. Paradoxically, the politicisation of ethnicity in the former Yugoslavia occurred during the time of nascent democratisation and emerging civil society in some parts of the country. In part these changes were stimulated by internal factors such as the need to provide answers to Yugoslavia's pressing economic problems. They were also stimulated by the Gorbachev reform process which called into doubt the future of communist political systems regardless of form.

Since the reform of the federal system of the late 1960s, the party's control of the state was diminishing at the same time that the power of society, measured by the autonomous activity of its members, was increasing (Irvine 1997). Thus, in the late 1980s and early 1990s the assertiveness of nationalist leaders was unhampered by communist control. Throughout its rule, the Yugoslav League of Communists (YCL) initiated processes of liberalisation, but these processes were introduced in order to keep the power of the various nationalists at bay and to insure the monopoly of the party. As Klein and Klein (1981) point out, swings towards centralism were associated historically with Serbian politics, while liberalism was generally associated with Croatian and Slovenian demands.

The analysis in the following sections will focus on the essence of ethnicity and ethnic identity and those elements of politicisation which utilise the most vulnerable aspects of ethnicity in pursuit of radicalism and open conflict with the members of other ethnic groups. The elements that are seen as central to the politicisation of ethnicity in the context of emerging democratisation are the mass media, political rhetoric, and political entrepreneurs. Analysis of the emergence of ethnopolitical conflict in the former Yugoslavia will be based on the historical and analytical assessment of the relationship between and relative influence of these three variables in the violent break-up of the country.

What is ethnicity?

'Ethnicity', in the sense used in modern social science, is a term which surfaced in the 1950s. The modern meaning of ethnicity centres on the idea of 'familiar groups of people sharing a culture, an origin, or a language' (Chapman 1993: 15). Ever since earliest civilisations the meaning of *ethnos* implied a lack of individuation, the lack of internal differentiation within a group that develops in response to the perception of 'other'. This meaning and function of ethnicity as a tool for the classification of people into 'us' and 'them' remains. Ethnicity is seen as an entity whose major function is to stress and reproduce basic social similarities and differences among groups of people (Eriksen 1991; Hobsbawm 1992; Chapman 1993).

Equally powerful, and perhaps a part of 'differentiation', is ethnicity's unique function as a provider of self-identity and a sense of belonging. In this sense some describe ethnicity as primordial or primitive. While there is a debate as to the meaning of primordialism, this chapter subscribes to Rothschild's (1981) treatment of primordial feelings as those that denote identification with cultural symbols (e.g. religion, language), with symbolically significant physical attributes (e.g. pigmentation) and with communal or tribal membership. These are identities or self-perceptions people obtain before they acquire explicit political and economic identities and loyalties (1981: 25–7). Hobsbawm describes ethnicity as a form of social organisation whose crucial base is cultural (1992: 63–5). In his words it is 'something' that binds together, that provides bonds and a sense of collective belonging to people who may or may not live in the same territories and who lack a common polity.

Smith (1988) offers the most systematic definition of ethnicity: while placing a similar emphasis on ethnicity as the communal identity of people who share common history, social customs and physical attributes, he also advances a set of fundamental criteria of ethnicity: a name, a myth of common ancestry, shared memories, a common culture and economy, a link with a historic territory and a measure of internal solidarity. Some of these criteria are very helpful in understanding how ethnicity becomes politicised, and thereby used by political actors in order to produce a political agenda structured around ethnicity.

By taking into account such considerations, it is easier to understand the importance of cultural/ethnic identity and why it is such an important part of contemporary reality. The appeal of ethnic identity is 'rooted in the conditions of modern life' (Gellner 1994). It is a response to the immense changes occurring in the world, an attempt to maintain emotional gratification and support from membership in a special community of shared values and customs in an age of mass society, industrial universalism, transient relationships and alienation. As it becomes increasingly difficult for individuals to find 'satisfactory selfhood' in large entities, they become alienated from the larger whole and begin to search for identity in smaller units (Glynn 1993). It is important to note that ethnicity is only one source of identity. As Hobsbawm (1992: 123) argues, 'people cannot choose collective identification as they choose shoes, knowing that one could put on [only] one pair at the time'. People have several loyalties, several sources of identity, simultaneously: the family, class, religion, professional and political associations, all related to various aspects and problems of life. Eriksen (1991) refers to these phenomena as 'segmentary identities'. Which one of those loyalties will be most prominent is largely dictated by the social context in which an individual happens to be.

In an attempt to determine what seems to be the mysterious character of ethnicity that produces emotionally grounded and politically significant solidarity, ethnicity as an 'identity provider' appears to be an answer. According to Smith (1988), ethnicity can shape individual identity and self-respect because of the 'myth–symbol' complex which endows ethnicity with special qualities and durability. Equally important is ethnicity's simultaneous existence with other aspects of everyday life and sources of identity. This makes ethnicity particularly vulnerable to mass appeals by those who may decide to present economic, political and social issues as a threat to the ethnic group (Esman 1989; Eriksen 1991; Rothschild 1981).

The politicisation of ethnicity

The preceding descriptions help us understand what ethnicity is. So armed, and in order to complete the task of conceptual clarification, we need to stress that the articulation of an ethnic identity is not necessarily integral to a nationalist project. Such a conflation often appears both in journalistic jargon and in scholarly works dealing with 'ethnic conflict' (e.g. Horowitz 1985, 1993, 1994; Jalali and Lipset 1992). These authors operate within a conceptual predicament which endows ethnicity with a political power and destructiveness that ethnicity alone simply does not have.

Ethnicity, however, is neither impotent nor passive. On the contrary, the psycho-cultural appeal with which ethnicity often successfully competes for loyalty among other sources of identity testifies to its potential power. Yet, the power of ethnicity is latent and not inherently destructive. Through politicisation this power can become a source of hatred, of stereotyping and ultimately be mobilised into confrontational nationalism. The following is an attempt to describe how nationalism exploits ethnicity and transforms its power into a destructive force.

Nationalism

Over the last few decades, we have heard about ethnicity most frequently in the context of ethnopolitical conflict, in the relation to the state or the part(s) of it which certain ethnic groups claim to be rightfully entitled to control. In light of the fact that the modern bureaucratic state represents the most powerful actor in the domestic and international arena, this is not surprising (Motyl 1992). The modern state is seen as an entity which controls the resources and values for which members of society compete. The resources that a state controls and distributes, such as participation in politics and access to the offices, and its role as the ultimate guarantor of cultural status and economic opportunity, make it understandable why any group would want to have the resources of the state at its own disposal (Skocpol 1985). Preoccupation with the state, however, does not bear a natural and immediate connection with ethnicity.

Ethnicity, as described above, has no particular historical relationship to the formation of a nation-state. Until recently, very few modern national movements were actually based on strong ethnic consciousness (Hobsbawm 1992: 64–5). Most of the states created after the First World War, supposedly through application of Woodrow Wilson's criteria of national self-determination, were not the product of the primordial aspirations of people who had been under foreign rule, but were usually the constructs of intellectuals who often studied abroad (Hobsbawm 1992; Gellner 1983). Indeed, 'nation-states' are often in fact not nation-states, that is, the geographic boundaries of the ethnic group that supposedly created the state *Staatvolk*, and the territorial borders of the state, rarely coincide. The state is usually either larger or much smaller than the area inhabited by its *Staatvolk*, or its corresponding nation. This simply means that the modern world is dominated by the multi-ethnic states (Hobsbawm 1992; Ra'anan 1989).

Hobsbawm (1992) argues that the imprecise use of the word 'nation' has made the task of finding a consistent definition of nation a difficult, almost impossible, task. For the sake of some conceptual clarity, this chapter will use a political definition of nation as suggested by Gellner (1983), Anderson (1991) and Hobsbawm (1992). These authors define the nation as a recent invention, an artefact or 'imagined community'. In this view, the nation is a recent historical phenomenon fostered by the technological and economic developments of modernisation such as printing, mass literacy and education. The nation is a product of nationalism. 'It is a social entity only insofar as it relates to a certain kind of modern territorial state, the nation-state' (Hobsbawm 1992: 9–10).

In essence the modern ideology of nationalism can be described as a fusion of the ideas of popular sovereignty and ethnic solidarity. This set of beliefs, rooted in the Enlightenment principle of popular sovereignty, extended the democratic right of self-determination to a national grouping created to justify the right to a state. Yet nationalism does not necessarily seek to express this principle through democratic means. In order to achieve the proclaimed goals of a nation, some nationalist leaders do not hesitate to use violence even when the majority of citizens opposes them. As to the source of the rights of a nation, the argument of nationalists is tautological. The rights of an entity, that is, a nation, do not stem from the collective will of its adherents, but from its very existence as a nation; they are presented as inherent (Ben-Israel 1992: 372–4).

Ben-Israel (1992) claims that there is a striking correlation between the extent to which ethnicity is stressed and the propensity for making war because of the unifying force of ethnicity. This particular type of nationalism, by treating the nation as the supreme object of devotion, justifies the most serious crimes and atrocities in the eyes of nationalists as long as they serve national ends (Braunthal 1946; Hobsbawm 1992). When this type of nationalism exerts resource claims on another group, it becomes confrontational and provokes ethno-political conflict. The use of nationalism in former Yugoslavia is such an example. However, this kind of nationalism is not a permanent feature of the nation.

It is necessary to point out that while nationalism may be competitive by nature, it does not always involve reliance on violence and negative use of ethnicity. Some nationalist movements do not even claim the right to independent statehood. While there are very few modern cases of nationalism which do not politicise ethnicity towards destructive or exclusionary ends, it is necessary to recognise their existence. For the sake of clarity, we will refer to the type of nationalism that does not exert resource claims on another group as benevolent or benign. Historically, this was the case with national movements of Slovenia and Croatia when they joined the Kingdom of Serbia, Croatia and Slovenia in 1918 (Banac 1984).

Many scholars emphasise the dual nature of nationalism. Geopolitically, nationalism is an ambiguous ideology. It can be aggressive and expansionist both within and outside state boundaries. At the same time it can serve as a peacekeeping and culturally integrating force in a nation-state or a region. This latter universalist nationalism, in line with the principles of the Enlightenment, emphasises equality and individual human rights. Particularist nationalism, on the other hand, denies non-citizens or culturally different citizens full human rights and, in extreme cases, denies them membership in the community of people.

This suggests two important points regarding the relationship between ethnicity and nationalism. First, the ideology of nationalism is different from that of ethnicity, which is more precisely described as a subjective feeling of belonging. The second point responds to the argument advanced by Eriksen (1991), who claims that the difference between nationalism and ethnicity is only one of degree. His justification of the difference – that many political movements are both ethnic and nationalist in character – does not recognise the fact that ethnicity is often used as a criterion for nationalist aspirations: establishing the state *based* on a specific culture.

As the example of Yugoslavia demonstrates, ethnicity provides both nationalist and non-nationalist elites, as well as their individual leaders, with an instrument that can be utilised and manipulated for any number of ends. The goals and mechanisms for the achievement of these ends may range from peaceful coexistence and tolerance within one territorial unit (of which Yugoslavia was an example until 1987), to radicalism, exclusion, and violence (when Milosevic's rhetoric initiated a struggle for the resources of the Yugoslav state). The following section will focus on those mechanisms of politicisation, mass media and political rhetoric, by which political entrepreneurs utilised the most vulnerable aspects of ethnicity in pursuit of radicalism and which led to ethnopolitical conflict in the former Yugoslavia.

Elements of politicisation

Based on the case of Yugoslavia, the elements that appear to be particularly salient to the analysis of ethnopolitical conflict are mass media, political office-holders, and the political rhetoric of demagogic and charismatic leadership. These three elements capitalised on the difficult socio-political environment following the demise of communism, the rapidly deteriorating economic situation and the collective and individual disorientation which this deterioration accentuated, and on the vulnerabilities of ethnic identity. They are important factors whose visibility allows for early diagnosis and advanced prevention of ethnopolitical conflict.

An understanding of inter-ethnic conflict within multi-ethnic states and, in the case of the former Yugoslavia, in the context of the ultimate demise of multi-ethnic communist states, is incomplete without consideration of the character of ethnic or national identities. The notion of ethnic identity as elaborated in the earlier sections incorporates culture, religion, any state traditions and various historical events that are reflected in popular values and political myths and symbols, often embodied in national heroes or represented in epic events and/or literature. They shape the character and aspirations of the ethnic group and inevitably influence how these may be politicised. No less important is the fact that they also shape and colour the perceptions of neighbouring groups which may be seen as either contenders for power or as legitimate sharers of that power.

The psychological nature of ethnic identity of some groups, its emotionally grounded solidarity, and its capacity to arouse and engage the most intense and private emotional sentiments, may lend itself to politicisation or radicalisation. In the case of radical nationalism, politicisation directs an ethnic group to build boundaries between itself and other groups (Esman 1989; Rothschild 1981: 13). In those instances, the differentiating role of ethnicity is imbued with intolerance and exclusionary relations to other groups. Those are the cases when segmentary identities, people's loyalty to several communities simultaneously, which in normal times facilitate peaceful coexistence of different groups within polity, turn into binary identities with clear boundaries between 'us' and 'them' and may ultimately come into conflict with one another (Eriksen 1991). Whether the ethnic groups will resort to conflict depends largely on the historical and political environment, the role of mass media, the nature of the present leadership of the state and the opportunity for the emergence of charismatic or dogmatic leaders. Thus, ethnic identity with its primordial characteristics and potential for differentiation between 'us' and 'them' is a necessary but insufficient cause for the mobilisation of ethnic groups into militant political actors.

Political context and officeholders

The political and economic context is important to the extent that it describes the characteristics of the regime within which ethnic groups reside. If demands articulated through conventional channels of communication lead to responses that the discontented find inadequate, they are increasingly likely to use demonstrative, sometimes violent, actions. Applying this theory to Yugoslavia, it is interesting to see to what extent the leaderships of Serbs, Croats and Slovenes responded differently to the regime's perceived inability to meet their demands. Croats and Slovenes were dissatisfied with the deteriorating political and economic life of the country, but their requests for improvement centred on reform of both economic and political systems (Ribicic and Tomac 1989). On the other hand, the centralist forces who rose to power in Serbia did not hesitate to call 'solidarity meetings' (*mitinzi solidarnosti*), massive demonstrations of Serbs and Montenegrins. These meetings were used as political means to justify the removal of the governments in the provinces of Kosovo and Vojvodina, and the Republic of Montenegro, in order to achieve the ideologically monolithic structure of Serbian government and impose their vision of Yugoslavia on other parts of the country (Andrejevich 1989). These meetings were also used in order to 'rejuvenate' the Serbian nation in order that it could fulfil its 'historic mission' of creating a Greater Serbia.

The leadership of the state has a powerful role in organising its economy. In multi-ethnic states the underlying dynamics of inter-ethnic relations is a constant competition over resources. Whether the resource competition will result in pluralism, co-operation, or conflict is largely determined by the political influence of leaders. Frequently, various ethnic boundaries are associated with 'economic production niches' (Nagel 1984: 422). In some cases, leaders deliberately exploit economic differences as delineated by ethnic boundaries in order to perpetuate the sense of exploitation and exclusion held by subordinate ethnic groups. The economic dimensions of inter-ethnic relations provide leaders with a mechanism to distribute resources either on the basis of ethnic segregation or on a more just basis. In cases of the former, the power of resource allocation endows the leadership of the state to perpetuate inter-ethnic hostility. Ethnic groups who suffer discrimination can use their position to strengthen their solidarity and eventually rise in violent opposition against the status quo. Although as Kosovo shows, whether such groups can actually achieve their individual and collective goals is another matter.

In Yugoslavia the huge disparities in regional development between 'north' and 'south' persisted despite communist rhetoric of equal development and prosperity. It is important to note that the first signs of inter-republic conflict, and conflict within party leadership, rose in the 1960s over the issue of federal control of the economy (Bilandzic 1985). Increasingly, economic complaints were presented in national/republican terms, and consequently, social differentiation became interpreted in terms of national inequality. The frustration of the more developed republics, Croatia and Slovenia, over the payments they were forced to make to the federation, which in their view did not always use them productively, would become a permanent feature of the Yugoslav federation (Magas 1993). Another grave concern of these republics was that decisions concerning the allocation of investment funds were handled through subjective criteria from Belgrade, both the federal capital of Yugoslavia and of the republic Serbia. This led other federal units to believe that the Serbian nation was favoured and that little had changed compared with the pre-1941 state (Bilandzic 1985). Yugoslavia represented a good case of Eriksen's (1991) 'segmentary loyalties' until 1987. But when Milosevic initiated the phase of nationalism in Serbia, and especially after December 1990, when the Milosevic government illegally took $1.8 billion from the federal bank to finance the Serbian economy, other republican leaders felt threatened and began to convey binary, us/them identities.

Mass media

The power of the mass media lies in their role as mass communicators of news and ideas, and in their ability to penetrate large numbers of people and influence their belief systems. Modern societies have created and used mass media for rapid dissemination of political information to large numbers of people. Many governments either own or control the mass media because they firmly believe that their ability to govern authoritatively is closely related to the nature, quality and quantity of information disseminated to the public (Graber 1992). Hobsbawm (1992) argues that the use of the mass media is one of the most significant aspects of modern nationalism. The mass media became the means by which popular ideologies were not only standardised and easily transmitted but also exploited for the purposes of deliberate political propaganda. Moreover, the mass media have become an instrument which transmits national symbols as part of the everyday life of individuals and thus reinforces ethnic identification. In contemporary multi-ethnic societies media can serve as an instrument in reinforcing stereotypes, 'hostile attitudes and over sensitivity to differences [which] lead to distorted views that may intensify and perpetuate conflict' (Deutsch 1991: 43).

A good example of propaganda – deliberate use of the mass media to create malevolent impressions of 'others' – is the Serbian media coverage of the Kosovo crisis at the end of the 1980s. Deliberate lies created rising animosities between the Serbian and Albanian populations and led to the open discrimination against Albanians by Serbs. This development led the Slovenian – and later Croatian – alternative media to react. Slovene and Croatian journalists and intellectuals claimed that Serbian media coverage was distorted and in clear violation of human rights of the Albanian population. This 'war of words' lasted for several years between Serbia and two northern republics (Bozic 1990). In many ways, this media conflict was the prelude to open war in Slovenia, and then in Croatia. As soon as Franjo Tudjman assumed power in Croatia after the spring 1990 Croatian elections, he took control of the media and used them to promote his appeals to Croatian national pride at the expense of Croatia's Serbian minority. The power of the media was crucial in the spreading of the war to Bosnia. Participants in the conference 'Making War and Peace in the Balkans: The Role of the Media', held at the University of Michigan in October 1995, contend that the multi-ethnic Bosnian society was deliberately destroyed by a war inflamed and fuelled by the sophisticated use of radio and television. Tom Gjelten, National Public Radio correspondent in Bosnia during the recent war, claims that capture of a Bosnian television tower in 1991 was crucial to Serbian nationalists' strategy in Bosnia. Control of Bosnian television allowed the Serbs to invoke a version of history and folk myths concerning Turkish/Islamic occupation of Serbia. The aim was to instil fear and suspicion of (Bosnian) Muslims in order to convince as many Serbs as possible that the Muslims were conspiring to create an Islamic state.

Political rhetoric

Throughout history political rhetoric has been associated with an effort to persuade and induce some sort of political control and deliberate outcome (Nimmo and Swanson 1990). In order to achieve political goals, political orators engage interests, values, emotions and aspirations. Messages designed for political persuasion use arguments that are linked to values, facts that are linked to interests and descriptions that evoke emotions (Graber 1981). The potential for conflict between ethnic groups gives rise to leaders who recognise the circumstances in which the potential psychological intensity of ethnic identities, anxieties and aspirations can be made pertinent.

The relevant subject for the purpose of this study is a leader whose political rhetoric thrives on emotional appeals to the group. Graber (1981) refers to this type of rhetoric as charismatic. The timing of the oratory is carefully selected and it occurs in the context where the audience – potential future supporters – is already emotionally charged. In the midst of lost hope and feelings of neglect by the state, the orator offers solutions to the problems. Indeed, in his visit to Kosovo in the spring of 1987, Slobodan Milosevic deliberately utilised charismatic rhetoric as a means of mobilising the wider Serb population behind him as the embodiment of the Serb nation and its destiny.

Charismatic leadership can turn into a demagogic one (Graber 1981). Demagogues use available social problems to advance their personal position and power. A most important characteristic of such leaders is their use of propaganda – 'intentional use of suggestion, irrelevant emotional appeals, and pseudo-proof to circumvent human rational decision-making processes' (Johannesen 1989: 37). This type of rhetoric appeals to emotions on a baser level, like prejudice, hatred and bigotry, and due to opportunistic goals, the appeals have little to do with truth and fairness (Graber 1981).

In times of a perceived threat to the ethnic group, the power of rhetoric based on ethnic appeal is immense. Not only do such leaders manage to persuade their ethnic kinsmen to perceive their destiny in ethnic rather than in individual or class terms but their power of mobilisation is particularly important (Rothschild 1981). It is at such moments that people's identity may shift from a 'segmentary' status (multiple sources of identity) into a 'binary' status (ethnicity as the predominant source of identity) (Eriksen 1991). This power of a demagogue stems from his knowledge of what his followers perceive as the most serious threat to their security, self-esteem and physical well-being (Deutsch 1991). Demagogues with rhetorical skills can persuade people to organise themselves into communities with a strong sense of solidarity, perceived as the only way to preserve their values, customs, uniqueness and survival in the midst of real or imagined dangers coming from other ethnic group(s). In this case, the rhetoric of Milosevic was designed to create a sense of Serbian solidarity from which all outsiders were excluded. As the case of Serbia shows, the wider promise to address the injustices incites the people to follow their leader unconditionally, even to the point of desecrating graves and raping women. Graber (1981) expresses the fear of dogmatic leadership by saying that political messages may be especially dangerous when they turn into action itself.

The political rhetoric of Slobodan Milosevic appeared to have such a strength – to turn the promises given to his kinsmen into actions that ultimately caused one of the bloodiest wars in post-Second World War Europe. While his ascendancy to the role of a populist leader was somewhat accidental, the opportunist in Milosevic quickly grabbed the opportunity given to him in 1987, when the Serbs of Kosovo Polje demanded to be heard by Serbian leaders. Milosevic's speech delivered at Kosovo Polje in April of 1987 'transform[ed] his image from a faceless bureaucrat to charismatic Serb leader' (Engelberg 1991: 32). His speech, which would later be characterised as legendary, used emotionally charged statements that were aimed at assuring people that he understood the seriousness of the problems affecting Serbs in Kosovo. Milosevic shaped his rhetoric to transform powerful myths and symbols into the sorts of experience that can be utilised for political purposes. Reference to historical events, especially the defeat of the medieval Serbian Kingdom by the Ottoman Empire at Kosovo Polje in 1398, promoted the view that the solution to the Serbs' 'problem' could be achieved only by force. Statements such as '[Albanian separatists] should know, there will be no tyranny on this soil anymore' and 'Yugoslavia and Serbia will not give Kosovo away' (Milosevic 1989) reflected the sense of abandonment among the Serbs of Kosovo and touched on Serbian national pride. In the midst of a crisis which was deliberately inflamed in order to meet a personal political agenda, Serbs were encouraged to shed themselves of all loyalties except to those of their fellow Serbs and Orthodox co-religionists.

Milosevic openly endorsed the mass 'meetings of solidarity'. In his speech to the seventeenth Session of the Central Committee of the Serbian League of Communists in 1988, it became obvious that as a communist he was promoting radicalism and Serbian nationalism. At these mass meetings and in response to other Milosevic speeches, the audiences shouted slogans such as 'All Serbs must live in one state', 'It is Serbian land wherever there are Serbian graves', 'Muslims are Serbs'. Milosevic used the grievances of the Serbs and their sense of oppression and mistreatment in Yugoslavia to promote the Serbs' insistence on greater jurisdiction over Kosovo and Vojvodina, but he refused to call this a plea for centralism or unitarism. In December 1989, having been re-elected Serbia's State President, Milosevic reiterated his promise to establish a state where all Serbs would live together. In the steadfast quest for Greater Serbia he followed a single strategy. Each step began with rhetoric stressing injustices committed against Serbs, and by portraying Serbs as victims (Engelberg 1991). As a key component of his campaign to unite all Serbs in one country and create one Serbian state, he proclaimed himself the saviour of Yugoslavia, which to almost everybody else in Yugoslavia but Serbs meant a Greater Serbia and Serbian hegemony. Yet the 'Western powers' stood silent as the plan unfolded. Their reasons for so doing are moot. However, it is not beyond the realms of possibility that above all they feared that self-determination in Yugoslavia would lead to wider destabilisation throughout the continent. If that is the case, then so far they have been proven wrong. Indeed, it is not unreasonable to argue that if Nato had called Milosevic's bluff in 1991 or 1992, they would have discovered that he held a very weak hand.

Conclusion

Based on the study of the former Yugoslavia, this chapter offers a case study of a country where democratisation, economic crisis and the decline of communist power brought about ethnopolitical conflict and the subsequent violent dissolution of the country. Current attempts and strategies towards the resolution of ethnopolitical conflict have not been fruitful because both ethnic and political dimensions of conflict are not fully understood. Labelling conflict as 'ethnic' adds to the misperception of mythical insolubility of the phenomenon.

An analytical clarification of the factors that lead to the politicisation of ethnicity, and the singling out of mechanisms by which it occurs, can, if dealt with, assist in advanced conflict resolution. By clarifying the meaning of the burdened concept of ethnicity and distinguishing between the ethnic and political aspects of 'ethnic' conflict, advanced prevention of conflict becomes more feasible. Through an analysis of ethnic identity and certain potentials of it, it is possible to determine when and how ethnic identity becomes politicised. Some ethnic identities lend themselves to radicalism. This chapter argues that necessary to recognise the importance of the mechanisms, such as mass m and political rhetoric, by which leadership can manipulate and politi ethnicity. The recognition of these mechanisms and their early detection could assist in prevention of violent ethnopolitical conflict. This analysis is not intended to be the final word on the causes of the conflict, but is offered in the hope that the variables explored provide a means by which attempts towards conflict management and prevention might stand a chance of success.

References

Anderson, B. (1991) *Imagined Communities: Reflections on the Origin and Spread of Nationalism*, revised edn, New York: Verso.

Andrejevich, M. (27 June 1989) 'Slovenia Offers Reconciliation', *Radio Free Europe, Situation Report, Yugoslavia*.

Banac, I. (1984) *The National Question in Yugoslavia*, London: Cornell University Press.

Ben-Israel, H. (1992) 'Nationalism in Historical Perspective', *Journal of International Affairs* 45 (2): 365–97.

Bilandzic, D. (1985) *Historija SFRJ* (History of Yugoslavia), Zagreb: Skolska knjiga.

Bozic, A. (1990) 'Kosovo kao problem komunikacije' (How the Kosovo Problem Can be Interpreted as a Problem of Communication), unpublished Diploma paper, Croatia: University of Zagreb.

—— (1992) 'The Rhetoric of Slobodan Milosevic and War on the Territory of Yugoslavia', unpublished Master's thesis, Kalamazoo, MI: Western Michigan University.

Braunthal, J. (1946) *The Paradox of Nationalism: an Epilogue to the Nuremberg Trials*, London: St Botolph.

Chapman, M. (ed.) (1993) *Social and Biological Aspects of Ethnicity*, New York: Oxford University Press.

Davies, J. (1969) 'The J-Curve of Rising and Declining Satisfactions as a Cause of Some Great Revolutions and a Contained Rebellion', in H.D. Graham and T.R. Gurr (eds) *Violence in America: Historical and Comparative Perspectives*, New York: Praeger.

Deutsch, M. (1991) 'Subjective Features of Conflict Resolution: Psychological, Social and Cultural Influences', in R. Vayrynen (ed.) *New Directions in Conflict Theory*, London: Sage.

Engelberg, S. (1 September 1991) 'Greater Serbia', *The New York Times Magazine*.

Eriksen, T.H. (1991) 'Ethnicity Versus Nationalism', *Journal of Peace Research* 28 (3): 263–78.

Esman, M.J. (1989) 'Political and Psychological Factors in Ethnic Conflict', in J.V. Montville (ed.) *Conflict and Peacemaking in Multiethnic Societies*, New York: Lexington Books.

Gellner, E. (1983) *Nations and Nationalism*, Oxford: Oxford University Press.

—— (1994) *Encounters with Nationalism*, Oxford: Blackwell.

Glynn, P. (1993) 'The Age of Balkanization', *Commentary*, July.

Graber, D. (1981) 'Political Language', in D.D. Nimmo and K.R. Sanders (eds) *Handbook of Political Communication*, Beverly Hills: Sage Publications.

—— (April 1992) 'News and Democracy: Are Their Paths Diverging?', Roy W. Howard Public Lecture in Journalism and Mass Communication Research, Indiana University.

Gurr, T.R. (1970) *Why Men Rebel*, Princeton, NJ: Princeton University Press.

Hobsbawm, E.J. (1992) *Nations and Nationalism Since 1780*, Cambridge: Cambridge University Press.

Horowitz, D.L. (1985) *Ethnic Groups in Conflict*, Berkeley, CA: University of California Press.

—— (1993) 'Democracy in Divided Societies', *Journal of Democracy*, 4 (4): 18–38.

—— (1994) 'Ethnic and Nationalist Conflict', in Klare, J. and Thomas, M. (eds) *World Security*, 2nd edn, New York: St Martin's Press.

Irvine, J.A. (1997) 'State–Society Relations in Yugoslavia, 1945–1992', in M.K. Bokovoy, J.A. Irvine and C.S. Lilly (eds) *State–Society Relations in Yugoslavia, 1945–1992*, New York: St Martin's Press.

Jalali, R. and Lipset, S.M. (1992) 'Racial and Ethnic Conflicts: a Global Perspective', *Political Science Quarterly* 107 (4): 585–606.

Johannesen, R.L. (1989) 'Perspectives of Ethics in Persuasion', in C.U. Larson (ed.) *Persuasion: Reception and Responsibility*, Belmont: Wordsworth.

Klein, G. and Klein, P. (1981) 'Nationalism Versus Ideology', in G. Klein and M. Reban (eds) *The Politics of Ethnicity in Eastern Europe*, Boulder, CO: East European Monographs.

Magas, B. (1993) *The Destruction of Yugoslavia*, London: Verso.

'Making War and Peace in the Balkans: the Role of the Media' (1995) International conference organised by the University of Michigan Working Group on War and Peace in Southeastern Europe, Ann Arbor, MI: University of Michigan, 19–20 October.

Milosevic, S. (1989) *Godine raspleta* (The Years of Solution), Belgrade: Beogradski izdavacko graficki zavod.

Montville, J.V. (ed.) (1989) *Conflict and Peacemaking in Multiethnic Societies*, New York: Lexington Books.

Motyl, A.J. (1992) 'The Modernity of Nationalism: Nations, States, and Nation-States in the Contemporary World', *Journal of International Affairs* 45 (2): 307–23.

Nagel, J. (1984) 'The Ethnic Revolution: the Emergence of Ethnic Nationalism in Modern States', *Sociology and Social Research* 64 (4): 417–34.

Nimmo, D.D. and Swanson, D.L. (eds) (1990) *New Directions in Political Communication: a Resource Book*, Newbury Park, CA: Sage Publications.

Ra'anan, U. (1989) 'The Nation-State Fallacy', in J.V. Montville (ed.) *Conflict and Peacemaking in Multiethnic Societies*, New York: Lexington Books.

Ribicic, C. and Tomac, Z. (1989) *Federalizam po mjeri buducnosti* (Federalism to the Measure of the Future), Zagreb: Globus.

Rothschild, J. (1981) *Ethnopolitics: a Conceptual Framework*, New York: Columbia University Press.

Skocpol, T. (1985) 'Bringing the State Back In: Strategies of Analysis in Current Research', in P.B. Evans, D. Rueschemeyer and T. Skocpol (eds) *Bringing the State Back In*, Cambridge: Cambridge University Press.

Smith, A. (1988) *The Ethnic Origins of Nations*, New York: Blackwell.

11 The Albanian communities in the post-communist transition[1]

Hugh Miall

Introduction

Surrounded by more powerful neighbours and riven by divisions among themselves, the Albanian experience to date has been one of failure in state-building, nation-building and democratisation. Among the poorest people in Europe, they are divided between three states: Albania itself with smaller minorities resident in Montenegro and Greece, and a significant diaspora in many others. In the face of an adverse history, and extraordinarily difficult contemporary problems, democratisation has been partial and incomplete. The two million Albanians in Kosovo and the third of a million in Macedonia have experienced ethnic conflict, while the three million in Albania have experienced the collapse of their economy and their state. In spite of these calamities, the Albanian communities have managed to preserve their ethnic affiliation, in a way that represents a distinctive adaptation to the more fluid conditions governing sovereignty, economic organisation and political mobilisation in the new Europe.

Blocked from constructing a conventional nation-state, they have used the opportunities provided by democracy and market structures in the West to find ways to survive and express an Albanian identity. Precisely because of their fusion of pre-modern and post-modern elements, the Albanians have succeeded in constructing a loose affiliation of communities that lacks clear leadership, pays little attention to borders, operates informally, has strong international contacts and depends heavily on its diaspora. This is not a basis for a conventional nation-state, but in a new Europe increasingly distinguished by internal nations and sub-sovereign nationalism, the Albanian accommodation to their circumstances can be seen as distinctive and contemporary. Theirs is a national movement without a coherent national programme, a beneficiary of democratisation lacking in democratic legitimation, a non-state 'nation' that has nevertheless found a niche in the conditions of globalisation, open borders and fragmentation in the 1990s.

The question of ethnicity and democratisation in the Albanian communities is worth examination because it goes to the heart of one of the key regional security issues facing Europe and the international community. The complex of linked problems in Kosovo, Macedonia and Albania clearly has the potential to trigger instability in the Balkans in the way that the Kosovo issue did in the former Yugoslavia. The West has relied primarily on a mixture of diplomatic intervention, containment and preventive deployment to avert an overspill of armed conflict, but in the longer term it strives also for ethnic accommodation and the construction of viable, democratic, pluralistic states in order to prevent a further round of fighting and ethnic cleansing in the Balkans.

Achieving ethnic accommodation and democratisation, however, has not been easy. Indeed, in so far as democratisation has taken place, one of its effects in the Balkans appears to have been to fuel ethnically driven conflict. The shift that has happened since 1989 is better interpreted as a transition from communism to post-communism, a 'transitional' political form that may have a long future. The quasi-democratisation that has taken place has led to new and distinctive forms which are a development from the communist framework and of older forms of political culture (which in the Albanian case include an authoritarian tradition, clans, and a well-established culture of patronage and clients). As in other parts of southern Europe, a veneer of democratic forms masks the reality of more traditional lines of influence and control.

Throughout the Balkans, the adoption of democratic forms of government raised the question of who was to be the *demos*. Where the existing state contained a mixture of peoples, as it did in most countries in the region, efforts to establish western-style nation-states immediately triggered ethnic competition. In both Kosovo and Macedonia, the development of ethnic politics accompanied steps away from communism towards a form of multi-party system. In the absence of notions of class solidarity which transcended ethnicity, and by way of testimony to the failed attempt to create an over-arching sense of Yugoslav identity, political parties formed along ethnic lines. The beginnings of party competition within ethnic groups set the conditions for a potentially protracted ethnic demarcation of the political system. Already Macedonia, for example, has competition between more radical and more moderate parties within the Albanian section of the vote, creating electoral pressure on the moderates not to agree with the (ethnic) Macedonian parties (Horowitz 1985; Mitchell 1995).

At the same time the Balkans saw the resurrection of political programmes. for 'Greater' states, aimed at incorporating all the members of an ethnic group into one state. With the break-up of Yugoslavia leading to a profound sense of insecurity among the Balkan national groups, the political support for demands for 'Greater Croatia', 'Greater Serbia', etc., were understandable, even if these programmes were ultimately destined to lead to violence. They create fear and suspicion among those who are threatened by them. The fear of a 'Greater Albania', even if this seems an unrealistic prospect with little open support at present among the Albanian communities, underlies attitudes by other states towards Albanian ethnic movements.

The western democracies have adopted a 'twin-track' approach to ethnic conflicts in the Balkans, relying on diplomatic intervention and if need be the use of force on the one hand, and on support for development and democratisation in the long term. In the former Yugoslavia, the west chose the path of *realpolitik* by negotiating with the leaders of ethnic parties and accepting their programme for an ethnically based territorial future. In Albania, Macedonia and Serbia, too, short-term diplomatic priorities have tended to overshadow the long-term policy of encouraging democratisation. The west for a long time supported former president Berisha in the interests of regional stability despite his authoritarian and anti-democratic internal policies. Similarly the west's attitude towards Albanian claims in Kosovo was governed by the priority given to Bosnia, the need for Milosevic's co-operation, and the overriding wish to avoid any further change in borders, constrained its support for Albanian claims. The strains between the twin tracks have at times been evident (Carnegie Endowment for International Peace 1996).

Ethnic accommodation and democratisation are essential if the peoples of the southern Balkans are to resolve their conflicts, overcome their past and move towards Western Europe. Yet the Albanian communities lack many of the preconditions of democratisation that Western European societies enjoyed, in terms of social, cultural and economic development; and in the short term, post-communist democratisation has fuelled ethnic mobilisation.

This chapter argues that applying West European models of democratisation and nation-building wholesale to the Albanian circumstances is likely only to foster conflicts with other national projects in the area. However, there are alternative models of national expression and democratic organisation, which may be better fitted to contemporary Albanian and European realities. Considering in turn Kosovo and the Albanian diaspora, Macedonia, and Albania, the chapter explores the difficulties the Albanian communities face in finding a basis for legitimacy, consent and self-government. Yet it may be that the wider European setting offers an opportunity for finding a way towards a transnational and civic democracy.

A pre-modern nation in a postmodern Europe

Before analysing the political construction of ethnicity and democratisation in the Albanian political space, it is worth first reviewing briefly the formation of the Albanian nation, the nature of the states in which Albanians live in the Balkans, and the meaning of democratisation in Balkan circumstances.

Albanian-speaking people have occupied their mountainous domains continuously for over two thousand years (Vickers 1995). They trace their history back to the Illyrians, contemporaries of the ancient Greeks, who shared a similar culture. Scholars are divided over whether this claim is fact or myth, but certainly the Albanians have had a linguistic and cultural identity and have occupied a common territory for centuries. Yet, with the brief exception of the period of rebellion and unification under the national hero, Skanderbeg, they have always lived under foreign rule: under the Byzantine Empire until the fourteenth century, under the medieval Serbian Empire during the fourteenth, under the Ottoman Empire from the fifteenth to the twentieth century, under Italian rule in Albania until the Second World War,

Yugoslav rule in western Macedonia until 1991, and Serb rule in Kosovo until now.

Albanian households were traditionally organised in clans, with the head of the household ruling over an extended family, with groups of clans linked for mutual protection under tribal leaders. The key to their political system was the *Kanun of Lek Dukagjini* (Kanun 1989), a medieval body of customary law, which regulated relations between the households. The central notion in the *Kanun* was that the overriding duty of the Albanian male was to preserve his household's honour ('A man who has been dishonoured is considered dead according to the *Kanun*'). Hospitality was essential. Breaches of hospitality and other rules governing relations between households would have to be repaid through compensation, or failing that, by blood. Real political sovereignty lay not at the state or national level, but at the level of the clan. Disputes between sovereign clan-leaders resulted in bitter and protracted feuds that continued through generations. For many centuries, therefore, including up to the middle part of the twentieth century, Albanians were used to being armed, self-reliant, locally self-governing, unco-operative with their rulers (who were usually foreigners), unruly, and difficult to govern or unite.

This lack of unity made the Albanians easy prey for foreign rulers, but foreign government was rarely effective. However, the Albanians were forced to adapt to their foreign rulers. The population became Catholic in the north where Italian and Vatican influence was strong, Orthodox in the south under Greek influence, and Muslim in the plains of the Albanian coastal strip and Kosovo, where the Ottoman *beys* held the land. These religious divisions, together with educational and economic backwardness, explain why Albania was the last of the European peoples to develop a nationalist movement. When it developed, in the late nineteenth and twentieth centuries, it was based in Pristina in Kosovo rather than the more backward Tirana. But Kosovo fell under Serbian rule as soon as the Ottomans were evicted. The rump of Albania which became independent in 1913 left a third of the Albanian population outside of its borders, and soon plunged into almost continuous warfare and then Italian occupation.

From the time of the First World War, the historical experience of the Albanian communities began to diverge. In Albania, following the collapse of the Italian and German occupation, the partisan take-over led to a communist regime under Enver Hoxha, which remained Stalinist long after post-Stalinist relaxation in the Soviet Union and most other East European states. In Yugoslavia, the Albanians in Kosovo experienced harsh rule by the Yugoslav communists, partly because of their animosity to Serbian rule, and partly because they were considered ideologically unreliable after supporting the fascists during the war in an effort to win independence.

In both Albania and the Albanian-populated areas of Yugoslavia, communism brought a form of modernisation that changed society, but differed radically from modernisation in the west. Industrialisation and urbanisation increased, but although Albania and Kosovo were both industrialised, the effects on a still predominantly rural society were not so profound as they had been in

Western Europe. People came from the surrounding valleys to work in newly built industries, and retained links with their rural backgrounds and their families. A modern, urban form of life developed in the towns, with smaller households, but remained confined to a minority of the population. The Albanian dictator Hoxha deliberately retarded the rural to urban transition, so that as late as 1990 two-thirds of the population lived in the countryside, and traditional forms of village life co-existed with communist rule. There was no middle class, with the exception of the communist urban elite. Even the communist political system, which stamped its authority ruthlessly on Albania, cloaked pre-modern elements. Hoxha's victory was a classic take-over by a dominant clan, bringing to power his southerner associates. The savagery of the repression, including the punishment of whole families for the political offences of the head of the household, can only be interpreted in terms of traditional culture. Hoxha's intense suspicion of Yugoslavia and his isolationist policy meant that the Albanians in Albania and those in former Yugoslavia became totally cut off from one another.

In Yugoslavia, the Albanian-populated areas enjoyed the benefits of a more open and developed society. They could travel abroad relatively unhindered, and a subsidised economy and welfare system, if undeveloped by the standards of Yugoslavia generally, nevertheless provided significant opportunities for Albanians. By 1991, therefore, the Kosovars enjoyed a higher standard of life, and a considerably greater awareness of the modern world than their kinfolk in Albania. They also enjoyed a period of relatively unhindered self-government from 1974 until the mid-1980s, after Tito's 1974 constitution granted the Albanians *de facto* autonomy under an Albanian communist administration. The slow break-up of federal communist rule in Yugoslavia after Tito's death, which was accentuated by the overall collapse of communist regimes in Eastern Europe, together with the rise of Milosevic, put paid to these liberties, and from 1987 Kosovo came under increasing Serb repression.

Milosevic planned to kick-start the Serbian economy by re-colonising Kosovo. Unemployed Serbs from the rest of Yugoslavia were to be encouraged to migrate to Kosovo with guarantees of accommodation and employment. In 1991, about 70 per cent of Albanians in employment were sacked. The result was total and irreconcilable Albanian alienation from Serbia. More than a fifth of Serbia's 1991 budget was absorbed in policing the once autonomous province and subsidising the importation of Serb and Montenegrin workers. Restrictions were placed on land sales to Albanians and the legal code was altered to make some crimes anti-constitutional if perpetrated by Albanians.

Just as a process of liberalisation was being ushered in within the Soviet itself, Hoxha's death in 1985 left Albania an isolated and capital-starved communist system which was on the verge of economic and political collapse. A popular democratic movement, made up of students, disaffected communists, writers, intellectuals and other representatives of the urban elite, forced the communist regime to announce multi-party elections in 1991. In the countryside, the peasants celebrated the end of communism with a spontaneous orgy of destruction, smashing up collective farms, irrigation systems, greenhouses and tractors. The Democratic Party won a sweeping victory in elections in 1992, but it was soon clear that the dominant group were themselves a faction of the former Communist Party. With no previous tradition of political parties, a political class educated in communist methods, and a political culture in which opposition, criticism and political liberties were unknown, the conditions for democratisation were unfavourable.

In retrospect it is clear that western hopes for an immediate and easy adoption of democracy in Eastern Europe were misplaced and ahistorical. Albania slipped into its own distinctive form of post-communism, a compromise between outwardly western political forms, communist-style methods of internal control, and relationships between government and opposition and within the governing group that were more typical of modified clan politics than of parliamentary government. Some of the typical characteristics of the post-communist model of democracy were soon to be seen in Albania, as in Serbia and Macedonia: strong presidents, weak parliaments, intense political polarisation, government control of the media (especially television and radio), and political interference with the judiciary, police and civil service (Schöpflin 1994).

These were among the conditions which have made an appeal to exclusive nationalism attractive and feasible as a means of mobilising political support in the Balkans and Central and Eastern Europe. Nevertheless, the political use made of ethnicity depends on context. In the Albanian circumstances, given Albania's political and military weakness, a challenge to Serbia was impossible. Recognising this, Berisha distinguished himself by his moderation on the issue of Albanian 'minorities' outside Albania. In Macedonia too, moderate Albanian leaders and the Macedonian leadership handled the ethnic conflict between Albanians and Slav Macedonians with caution. In Kosovo, while Albanian political development was forced to take the form of a resistance movement, it has nevertheless been marked with non-violence and restraint until the spring of 1998.

There is no likely prospect in the short term of the unification of the Albanian communities in one state. In the Balkans, where the state is seen as the main agent of decision and organisation, and a hankering after strong states is associated with the quest for stability (Tzenkov and Georgiev 1995), this may seem a constraint on the expression of Albanian national identity. Yet in a Europe which is marked increasingly by the co-existence of a variety of states and nations at different stages of development, failing to meet an imagined West European or East European norm for statehood may not be such a crippling handicap. In the shadow state, and the network of Albanian communities in the Balkans, the United States and Europe, the Albanians appear to be engaged in a new kind of nation-building: one which ignores borders and mobilises the support of both the diaspora and the international community. While West European states are suffering the corrosive erosion of their powers and their borders by the process of globalisation, and internal nationalism and transnational social movements are growing phenomena, the conditions for this new type of nation-building seem favourable (Miall 1994; Foucher 1993). Nationalism remains a potent force in an era of globalisation, but it seems increasingly redundant for it to take a specific territorial form. The aspiration for a particular territory can provide an organising myth for a movement that need no longer be confined to or even draw its strength from a particular territorial area.

The shadow state and the diaspora

It is Kosovo, appropriately, which became the centre of this new form of nation-alist movement. This occurred, because within Serbia the opportunities for political mobilisation remain limited. It was also Kosovo which was the most open and relatively modernised of the Albanian communities, and the one in closest touch with the diaspora. Its shadow government operated partly inside and partly outside Kosovo, with centres in Bonn, London and Washington.

The Kosovar Albanians have not yet experienced democratisation. As part of their policy of boycotting Serbian institutions, the Albanians deliberately abstained from participation in Serbian elections. They were living under martial law and arrests and beatings of Albanians in Kosovo were common. The Serbian authorities abolished Kosovo's autonomy in 1989–90, and closed the schools and universities. With much reduced investment in Kosovo from the rump Yugoslavia, together with the impact of sanctions on Serbia, living standards in Kosovo fell steeply to levels comparable with those of Albania. The threat of conscription of army-age boys into the Yugoslav army also led to an annual exodus of Kosovar Albanian youth, who in any case held few favourable opportunities if they stayed in Kosovo.

In response to the repression, the Kosovar Albanians set up a shadow state, with an underground government (mainly based outside Serbia). The university professors continued to operate classes in private homes, unofficial schools operated, and a limited health service was offered. The Kosovar Albanians claimed they had a democratic basis for their declaration of independence from Serbia, since this was based on the referendum they carried out in 1991. But a shadow democracy cannot easily be exercised under martial law. In Kosovo, though, the struggle for democracy, self-governance and the status of the Albanian ethnic group are all linked. The Democratic League of Kosovo and the smaller militant parties are clearly ethnic parties.

The Kosovar Albanian demand for independence hardened with the continued resistance to what is perceived as a brutal and oppressive colonial regime. Nor, despite hints that Serbian authorities might be prepared to consider some form of autonomy, was there much Serbian willingness to compromise their control of the province. The importance of Kosovo to Serbia as the cradle of the Serb nation remains very high; the Serbian churches and monuments in Serbia are considered as part of Kosovo; there are important mines and mineral resources; and there is a significant (approximately 10 per cent) Serb minority within Kosovo, together with a larger group of Serbs who in recent years have left but retain claims on the area. Given that Milosevic built his political career on support for this group, it would be a remarkable reversal, even by his standards, for him to abandon them.

It might seem that greater democratisation in Serbia and Kosovo could help to resolve this conundrum. In principle there might be scope for a breakthrough, if the Kosovar Albanians exercised their votes in Serbian elections, for combined with the Serbian opposition they might have sufficient strength to bring down Milosevic's Socialist Party. If the Serb opposition could reach an agreement on Kosovo acceptable to the Albanians, they could at once exorcise one of the chief sources of undemocratic rule in Serbia and lay the basis for a democratic Serbia. However, the Serbian opposition, like the government, remains strongly attached to the principle that Kosovo is part of Serbia and appears loth to abandon the province. Negotiations between the Kosovar Albanians and Serb opposition leaders in New York in 1997 broke up in acrimony, amidst rivalry between the Serb leaders who were nervous of doing anything to sacrifice their chances in an eventual presidential contest. As elsewhere, when electoral politics and ethnic politics coincide, concessions were seen to cost votes.

Another possible resolution of the Kosovo issue might come from a sudden reversal of policy by the Serb government. In a re-assessment of the value to Serbia of Kosovo, the Serbian Academy of Sciences suggested that Serbs might be in a minority within Serbia by the early decades of the twenty-first century given the growth rate of the Albanian population. A choice might have to be faced, it suggested, between letting Kosovo go, and reaching a new political structure which could accommodate the Albanians. In the short term, however, the Serbian government has overwhelming military, police and political power in the province and shows no sign of giving it up.

The United States and the European Union (EU) have pressed for a compromise solution of autonomy on both sides, or a new status within a re-balanced rump Yugoslavia. The autonomy idea has divided the Democratic League of Kosovo. The Kosovar leader, Ibrahim Rugova, has struggled to preserve unity between those favouring compromise and the hard-liners favouring independence, but the hard-liners appear to have the upper hand.

While the deadlock in Kosovo persists, support for Rugova's policy of non-violent resistance is increasingly coming under pressure. Popular resentment against the international community for abandoning Kosovo peaked when the Dayton Accords failed to require Serbia to change its policy in Kosovo. Some have urged a Kosovo *intifada*, a policy that would be certain to lead to a violent Serbian response. A small terrorist group has also appeared and carried out a number of assassinations and bomb explosions in 1997, which in turn provided Milosevic with the excuse he needed to launch his crackdown in March 1998. Indeed, given that at the time of writing (June 1998) both the scale of the repression and armed resistance to Serb control, in the shape of the Kosovo Liberation Army (KLA), are increasing, the potential for a peaceful resolution to the conflict is bleak.

The risk that the deadlock and repression in Kosovo could be a *casus belli* for a violent conflict with the potential to spill over into Macedonia, Albania and the wider Balkan region is now higher than ever. However, it is clear that the Albanians themselves would have the most to lose from such an escalation. The quest for an accommodation should involve a willingness on all sides to examine a variety of possibilities, including radical changes, without preconditions. As in other situations involving double minorities, there are legitimate interests on both sides that are closely interdependent. A framework is needed which recognises both the validity of Serb interests in Kosovo and the aspiration of the Albanian community to govern itself and to develop relations with other Albanian communities.

To the extent that an 'Albanian political space' can be developed, based on contacts between the Albanian communities, movement across borders, and co-operation, the pressure for a violent bid for unification may be reduced. The more a triangular transnational relationship evolves and deepens between the communities, and the more the communities can rely on their diaspora and on international support, the more possible it seems that an alternative path of development to violent confrontation can be developed. Of course this depends on a relaxation and eventual removal of the present asymmetrical and violent relationship between the Serbs and the Albanians; and this in turn requires international support and pressure. The project of developing a nation internationally, using both Albanian space and the wider western democratic space, appears to offer the best hope of finding a way towards an accommodation avoiding war.

Here the Albanian diaspora becomes important. It is the size and significance of the diaspora which gives the Albanian national movement its 'post-modern' character. There are a third of a million former Albanians now living in the United States as Albanian-Americans, who provide a significant lobbying effort in Congress for human rights and national independence for Kosovo. In Europe the biggest communities are the 100,000 Kosovar Albanians in Switzerland and the 120,000 in Germany (Vickers and Pettifer 1997: 151–2), with smaller communities in Scandinavia and other parts of Western Europe. They provide a major source of income for Kosovar families, financing the parallel institutions in Kosovo, and also offering the most important opportunities for permanent or temporary employment, capital investment, and political finance. There are more Albanians from Montenegro now living in the Bronx than in Montenegro itself, while Albanians from Albania can be found working in Italy, Greece and other European countries: the numbers in Greece have been put at a third of a million at any time. Of course, the diaspora includes among its numbers some of the most ardent Albanian nationalists. It also creates the possibilities of links between a dispersed Albanian nation and the wider international community. On this diversity of communities and contacts, much of the Albanian potential for wealth and nationhood depends. It also became an opportunity for a darker side as crime, drug smuggling, arms smuggling and trade in illegal immigrants became a growth industry (Milivojevic 1995).

Macedonia's ethnic trials

On the other hand, Macedonia offers a more clear-cut case of a link between democratisation and ethnic conflict. As elsewhere in Eastern Europe, democratisation was towards a post-communist model, at least a multi-party system with free elections has operated. Hitherto Macedonia has avoided the perils of violent ethnic conflict and has managed to sustain a multi-ethnic conflict, though tensions between the ethnic communities have been significant (Mickey and Albion 1993).

As in Kosovo, the 1980s saw a deterioration in relations between the Albanian minority and the Yugoslav government, as the educational rights and political benefits granted in 1974 were withdrawn. When Macedonia became independent in 1991, Albanians perceived a loss of status. The new state was declared to be 'a national state of the Macedonian people', prior to 1989 it had been the 'state of the Macedonian people and the Albanian and Turkish minorities'. The Albanians, who make up about a quarter of the population, felt grievances over their opportunities for education in their own language (especially higher education), employment opportunities, the constitution, and over their claims to local self-government and autonomy. The Macedonians felt threatened by the complaints and threatened autonomy (which was seen as a step towards secession), which they feared would fragment an already small and vulnerable state.

Despite these fears, the majority Albanian party was prepared to work with the Macedonian government, and the Gligorov government sought to make a workable multi-ethnic and pluralistic state. The EU, United Nations (UN) and Organisation for Security and Co-operation in Europe (OSCE) showed their concern for the situation respectively through support for the 1994 census, through the stationing of UN troops on Macedonia's borders, and by the efforts of the High Commissioner on National Minorities and an OSCE Mission to negotiate agreements on education and citizenship.

Nevertheless, inter-ethnic relations are poor, and incidents such as police action against Albanian demonstrators demanding a university and Macedonian counter-demonstrations have maintained tense relations (Pettifer 1992; Vickers and Pettifer 1997: chapter 9). The Macedonians have offered compromises in further education but were unwilling to yield on the more politically sensitive university issue. On both the Albanian and Slav Macedonian sides, political parties compete within their own ethnic groups, tending to result in electoral competition between moderate and hard-line parties and creating an unwillingness to compromise. While Macedonia has avoided a violent ethnic conflict, it remains a vulnerable state, particularly as Kosovo slides into open warfare.

Democratisation certainly did not create the ethnic tensions in Macedonia, since they were well established before 1991. Its effects on ethnicity have been mixed. On the one hand the formation of ethnic parties, and intra-ethnic competition for votes, have encouraged an unwillingness to compromise, and set up the potential for a protracted ethnopolitical conflict. On the other hand, the parliamentary arithmetic which has made the governing coalition dependent on the support of the Albanian parties has been the most powerful factor enforcing a degree of moderation on the government, and a willingness to work with the government on the Albanians. As Western European experience makes clear, majority democracy by itself is no guarantee of accommodation in ethnically divided societies; but it is possible to manage a workable multi-ethnic political system if democratic forms can be supplemented by consociational practices, political incentives for accommodation, and pluralistic institutions that offer a political space for ethnic groups to work out their futures together (McGarry and O'Leary 1993).

Albania: from democratic revolution to rebellion

The Albanian communities in Kosovo and Macedonia had great hopes for the future when the democratic revolution in Albania overthrew the communist regime and broke the isolation into which Hoxha had plunged the country for so long. The west, too, was well disposed to the new regime, and in the first years of the Democratic Party's rule the country enjoyed a honeymoon of international approval, small-scale inward investment, and the highest rate of economic growth in Central and Eastern Europe (albeit from the lowest base). Albania was the only state to recognise the independence of Kosovo, and Berisha maintained close relations with both Rugova's Democratic League of Kosovo and with the Albanian parties in Macedonia. Although he was careful to insist on Albania's acceptance of OSCE principles, including the inviolability of existing borders, Berisha gave strong support to the Albanian communities abroad in his public pronouncements.

Within Albania, however, the democratisation process ran into trouble (Miall 1995). Berisha's Democratic Party had begun as a broad-based coalition, but splinter groups began to break away as some came to resent Berisha's autocratic style. While an intense war of words developed between the two main parties, the Democratic Party and the Socialist Party, critics argued that Berisha's ruling style reflected his own communist past. In classic post-communist fashion, the government removed former communists from the civil service, police and judiciary, appointing Betisha's supporters in their place. As a result state institutions became the province of the governing party, and Berisha appointed northerners from his own region and clan to the main posts. He retained the dreaded secret service, the SHIK, turning it against his political enemies. When local elections produced mixed results for the Democratic Party, he moved to undermine the local governments under Socialist Party control by establishing a new tier of prefects under his personal control. The prefects were also given control over election arrangements, which therefore fell under Democratic Party rather than state control. As elsewhere in the Balkans, the governing party controlled television and radio and used them blatantly for political purposes. They also used the courts against their enemies, imprisoning the leader of the opposition, and entering into a prolonged battle with the Head of the Supreme Court, a former Berisha supporter, over the independence of the judiciary. The judge was eventually forced to flee the country. When public opinion began to move against Berisha, especially after he lost a referendum on a new constitution which would have concentrated new powers in the presidency, he intensified his moves against critics in the press, frequently arresting journalists who wrote critical pieces, and using taxes on newspaper operations and later secret police raids to attack the independent press. These illiberal moves came to a climax in the election of 1996, when Berisha's party manipulated the pre-election rules and election arrangements to such an extent that the OSCE declared that the conduct of the elections had violated OSCE principles and Albanian law. The opposition parties withdrew and Berisha continued to rule with a parliament packed with his own supporters, and power over the media, the judiciary, the police, the secret police, parliament, local and central government now concentrated in his hands.

Although he might have had an incentive and certainly had the opportunity to play a 'Greater Albania' card, Berisha refrained from doing so. Support for a 'Greater Albania' certainly exists at an emotional level in some Albanian political circles, although only the Republican Party and right-wing groups are prepared to express this openly. The original Democratic Party programme supported an eventual union with Kosovo, and Berisha was quoted as supporting it in 1992, but he took a more cautious approach from 1993 on, denying that the idea of Greater Albania was considered seriously. Despite his post-communist leadership style, the context did not favour a bid at ethnic mobilisation.

Within Albania itself a number of non-Albanian ethnic groups formed significant minorities, with a Greek minority of some 60,000, significant numbers of Macedonian Slavs, Vlachs and Roma, and small populations of Serb/ Montenegrins and other peoples. Following the end of communism several of these groups began to seek better treatment, and especially education in their own language. A serious political conflict over the Greek minority appeared to be in prospect in 1993, when the Albanian police arrested a Greek priest and Greece expelled thousands of ethnic Albanians from Greece. The dispute was complicated by residual territorial disputes between Greece and Albania, the developing tensions between Greek Orthodoxy and the Muslim religion in Albania, and the brutal habits of Albanian police at the expense of human rights groups. The two governments at first fanned the dispute, but following interventions by the OSCE High Commissioner on National Minorities, the United States and European governments, the dispute was calmed, and a series of Greek–Albanian commissions dealt with some of the outstanding issues. On the ground, community relations between ethnic Greeks and Albanians remained largely friendly, and in any case many of the Greeks left to take advantage of economic opportunities in Greece. Because most of the minorities were relatively small, and were no worse off and in some cases better off than most Albanians, inter-ethnic relations did not become a source of violent conflict within Albania. As elsewhere in the Balkans, it was the Roma who received the worst treatment, but even they found opportunities in the new conditions of a market economy.

These relatively minor conflicts over ethnicity were overshadowed by the much greater tensions between the polarised political parties. They also seemed less important than the regional differences within Albania, between the Gheg north, from which the Democratic Party drew its main support, and Tosk south, which was the heartland of the Socialist Party. Berisha's position after the elections appeared outwardly strong, but the government had lost its international approval and what remained of its internal legitimacy. When the pyramid savings crisis unexpectedly hit the country, Berisha's own supporters in the police and army, as well as people in the south, turned against the regime. The institutions of the state, which had been so comprehensively taken over by the governing party, were suddenly powerless, and Albania was exposed as a country close to the heart of Europe in 'state failure'. In the Tosk (and Greek minority) area, south of the river Shkumbi, the government lost its authority altogether. In the aftermath of the rebellion, one million guns were in free circulation in a country of only three million. Albania appeared to have reverted to its pre-war form, when every Albanian man had a gun, clans and armed gangs controlled local areas, and central government was difficult or impossible to achieve. Whether the decisive victory of the Socialist Party in the June 1997 general election will have opened the potential for a period of stability remains to be seen, but with politics still deeply polarised, politicians preoccupied with settling past scores, and institutions and civil society only weakly developed, the prospects for 'real democratisation' remained bleak.

The collapse of the one state they had came as an unpleasant shock to the Albanian communities in Kosovo and Albania. Their position appeared to be weaker than ever with police and army authority in Albania crumbling and the population dissolving into armed gangs. The disintegration of Albania seemed to dash dreams of eventual unification. Certainly the deep divisions within Albania, the weakness of the state there and the lack of effective institutions created little basis for building a wider polity.

Conclusion

While the Albanian communities remain weak, divided, insecure and subject to foreign influence or rule, state- and nation-building on traditional West European lines appears to be a remote prospect. The recovery of the state in Albania will be a slow process. Albania badly needs independent institutions to separate the state from political parties, but even organising the basics of a civil society is difficult in the chaotic and mistrustful conditions which prevail. The possibility of achieving some form of accommodation in Kosovo seems more remote than ever, while in Macedonia democratisation has brought a mixed harvest of conflict together with inter-ethnic accommodation. In the case of Kosovo in particular there is a case for establishing some kind of international or inter-state minority regime. However, not only do such plans only exist in the realms of ideas at present, past practice indicates that such regimes are fraught with difficulty.

Although their numbers in the Balkans will put them on an equal footing with other Balkan peoples early in the next century, the Albanians still lack the basis of a modern state and even of a modern nation. Without them, the best conditions for Albanian development are offered by international opportunities for movement between states, transnational organisation, and a cross-border movement of people, capital and political ideas. In default of nation-building options on the ground, this seems to be the direction offering prospects for Albanian nationalism to develop, as well as one which offers hope of a peaceful outcome.

Note

1 I would like to thank the following individuals for their help and insightful comments: Dr James Butterfield, Dr Patricia Klein, Dr Barbara McCrea, Dr William Ritchie and Dr Robert Stauffer.

References

Carnegie Endowment for International Peace (1996) *Unfinished Peace: Report of the International Commission on the Balkans*, Washington DC: Carnegie Institute.

Foucher, M. (1993) *Fragments d'Europe* (Fragments of Europe), Lyon: Fayard.

Horowitz, D. (1985) *Ethnic Groups in Conflict*, Berkeley, CA and London: University of California Press.

Kanun (1989) *Kanuni I Leke Dukagjinit*, New York: GjonLekaj.

McGarry, J. and O'Leary, B. (1993) *The Politics of Ethnic Conflict Regulation*, London: Routledge.

Miall, H. (1994) *Shaping the New Europe*, London: RIIA/Pinter.

—— (1995) *Progress and Constraints in the Transition Process in Albania*, The Hague: Netherlands Development Organization (SNV).

Mickey, R.W. and Albion, A.S. (1993) 'Ethnic Relations in the Republic of Macedonia', in I. Cuthbertson and J. Liebowitz (eds) *Minorities: the New Europe's Old Issue*, Prague: Institute for East–West Studies.

Milivojevic, M. (1995) 'The Balkan Medellin', *Jane's Intelligence Review* 7 (2).

Mitchell, P. (1995) 'Party Competition in an Ethnic Dual Party System', *Ethnic and Racial Studies* 18 (4).

Pettifer, J. (1992) 'The New Macedonian Question', *International Affairs* 68 (3).

Schöpflin, G. (1994) *Politics in Eastern Europe*, London: Blackwell.

Tzenkov, E. and Georgiev, A. (1995) 'The Troubled Balkans', *Redefining Europe*, London: RIIA/Pinter.

Vickers, M. (1995) *The Albanians: a Modern History*, London: I.B.Tauris.

Vickers, M. and Pettifer, J. (1997) *From Anarchy to a Balkan Identity*, London: Hurst & Co.

12 Minority rights and Roma politics in Hungary

Martin Kovats

Minority rights have become an increasingly common feature of international law. If we consider the factors behind this development we can see that the adoption of these rights often reflects more the interests of the authorities rather than those of minority individuals and communities. Such a perspective enables us to understand why Hungary has been so keen to incorporate minority rights into its own domestic legislation. As well as enabling the country to fulfil its international obligations, Hungary's Minorities Law provides a means of controlling minority political activity, in particular that of its Roma population.

The development of minority rights in international law

In international law, minority rights have moved away from the simple prohibition of discrimination on ethnic grounds as represented by the United Nations Charter and the Universal Declaration of Human Rights, towards covering a variety of areas perceived as central to minority existence (Thornberry 1994). These rights, contained in documents such as the Charter of Paris (OSCE 1990) and the Framework Convention for the Protection of National Minorities (Council of Europe 1995) are fundamentally culturally based and promote cultural expression, education, language use, self-organisation and contacts with other communities sharing the same culture. A number of questions are still unresolved, such as a comprehensive definition of 'minority' and whether minority rights should/do apply to groups as well as individuals (Gyurcsík 1993). However, a basic principle has been established, that identity is a matter of choice. As membership of a minority is conceived as an election to associate with certain characteristics, minority rights focus only on those areas of life where minorities 'differ' from the majority.

In part the extension of minority rights is a result of greater awareness of the multiple dimensions of minority existence and the limitations of universal rights and legal protections in accommodating these. For example, the universal right to education does not necessarily lead to educational provision in accordance with the needs and wishes of minorities. It is also a recognition that minorities often experience inequality in exercising universal rights for reasons such as a lack of resources or the cultural 'bias' of mainstream institutions. Minority rights are, therefore, seen as a way of making societies more sensitive to diversity. Such an approach is advanced by Kymlicka, who argues that 'a comprehensive theory of justice in a multicultural state will include both universal rights...and certain group-differentiated rights or "special status" for minority cultures' (Kymlicka 1995).

However, the rapid evolution of minority rights is a product of its age, and is related to tackling ethnicity-based political conflicts which are seen as an increasingly significant area of contemporary politics. Outbreaks of violence in the former Soviet Union and Yugoslavia and lower intensity troubles from Spain to the Baltic are considered serious sources of economic, political and military instability. At its meeting in Roima in 1991, NATO identified 'ethnic tension' as a threat to security. The provision of legally enforceable measures for minority protection is seen as a way of managing such conflicts in a peaceful manner.

Minority rights need also to be seen within the context of wider political change in Europe, which is characterised by the relative decline of states and the growth of supra-national political, economic and juridical institutions. Political boundaries are often not coterminous with 'ethnic' boundaries, and history has left many national groups in states that are not (but usually border) their 'mother country'. It would facilitate the process of European 'integration' if a mechanism could be found for reducing tension between states with regard to 'their' minorities abroad. Furthermore, minority rights provide a means of supporting all European languages and cultures in an anticipated future when the primary mechanism for their preservation and promotion (for the past century or so), the nation-state, is superseded and all the Continent's people become 'minorities' within a single European citizenry. For these reasons, the Council of Europe now requires minority protection as a pre-requisite for the recognition of new states (Christopulos 1994).

The adoption of minority rights in Hungary

The purpose of the discussion so far has been to show that the provenance of minority rights lies fundamentally with governing authorities (supra-national institutions or states) rather than with (minority) citizens. The growth of the issue is related to the European 'project', in particular the negotiation of the relationship between the west and the former socialist states of Eastern Europe. With regard to the construction and application of minority rights, we can adopt Barbalet's assertion (made in respect of civil and political rights) that 'the choice taken can be explained in terms of whether it enhances the state's capacity to rule' (Barbalet 1988). The rest of the chapter uses this approach to examine the adoption of minority rights in Hungary and their effect upon the country's largest minority population, the Roma (Gypsies).

Post-communist Hungary has enthusiastically embraced minority rights. In 1990, the Constitution was amended to acknowledge the minorities as 'constituent elements of the state' and to require government to bring forth legislation on minority rights (Bugajski 1995). This reached the statute book in July 1993 with overwhelming parliamentary approval for Law LXXVII on the Rights of National and Ethnic Minorities (hereafter, Minorities Law). Its sixty-five clauses grant the thirteen recognised minority populations rights covering anti-discrimination, culture, education, language, contacts, media access and political participation. The Law is not only considered a 'model' by the Hungarian government but also by international observers (*Népszabadság* 1995). The most interesting aspect of the Minorities Law, from the perspective of the political scientist, is its recognition that rights, in themselves, are of little value and that a mechanism is needed to transform them from paper into practice. The mechanism created by the Minorities Law is the system of minority self-governments. Self-governments are legally recognised elected institutions. Their two main functions are to realise the cultural 'autonomy' of minorities and to represent the interests of minority individuals and communities. As a result of elections in 1994 and 1995, there are currently 817 local self-governments and eleven national bodies.

Hungary's enthusiasm may seem odd for a country usually considered one of the most ethnically homogenous in Eastern Europe and where the majority's (Magyar) ethnic identity is so central to the identity of the country. However, from the perspective of foreign policy, the position becomes more understandable. Never 'at home' in the Soviet bloc, Hungary has traditionally looked westward for economic, political and cultural ties. Entry into the European Union is the primary foreign policy goal of post-communist governments and the main issue of consensus amongst the mainstream political parties. Hungary's commitment to 'Europe' is signalled in the Preamble to the Minorities Law which anticipates a 'Europe without borders'.

Minority rights is a good issue for Hungarian governments to promote because it helps protect Magyar minorities abroad, demonstrates the country's commitment to 'democracy', shows up its neighbours and provides long-term security for the Magyar language and culture. The Treaty of Trianon in 1920, led Hungary to lose half its population, leaving substantial Magyar minorities in neighbouring states. Since the 'change of system' in the late 1980s, Hungary has shown its commitment to regional stability by concluding treaties with neighbouring states, each of which includes provisions for minority protection (Lábody and Íjgyártó 1996). These provide Hungarian ministers with (moral as well as some real) authority to examine the activities of other, sovereign governments. It does not harm a government's standing at home, or elsewhere in Europe, if they can point out the failings of neighbouring regimes with whom they are in competition for early accession to supra-national institutions. Having accepted that the quality of their nation-state is likely to change (or even ultimately disappear), governments can make provision for preserving the distinctiveness of Magyar culture by helping establish pan-European mechanisms for its protection.

Though foreign policy considerations predominate, it would be a mistake to ignore the domestic political factors behind Hungary's embrace of minority rights. The state has long recognised the existence of certain 'national' groups and during the communist period the German, Romanian, Slovak and southern Slav minorities all had their own cultural associations (Föglein 1996). However, the most politically significant minority today is the Roma, who account for around 5 per cent of the country's population and over 50 per cent of its non-Magyar citizens. The importance of the Roma lies not so much in their numbers, but in the circumstances of the population and the fact that, since the 1980s, they have been engaged in their own political mobilisation. Minority rights provide the state with an opportunity for managing this new participant in the country's political life.

The Roma minority

Over the last decade, Hungary's Roma population has been dramatically affected by economic, political and cultural change. The re-introduction of a 'market' economy has led to the reappearance of mass unemployment and poverty. Only just over 30 per cent of adult Roma men now have a job and the figure is even lower for women (Havas *et al.* 1995). However, the facts behind the statistics paint an even more depressing picture. Roma unemployment is structural in character and unlikely to vanish in the short or even medium term. Roma are heavily over represented amongst unskilled workers, and the greatest contraction in the demand for labour has been in the low-productivity occupations they used to fill. In the poorer northern and eastern counties where most Roma live job opportunities are scarce. This has led the Ministry of Labour to consider a new category in the division of labour: Gypsy (Ágoston 1994). Nevertheless, whilst most Roma have seen their income and opportunities decline, a small section of the population has maintained their position or even accumulated wealth.

Roma have benefited from a number of initiatives aimed at confronting racism such as the 'Act against Hatred' campaign. However, they are also recipients of the negative consequences of a reformation of Magyar identity consequent of the recovery of 'national independence'. Roma are the main victims of a skinhead movement that emerged in the mid-1980s and reached its peak in 1993. There have also been a number of less ideologically motivated attempts to expel Roma from neighbourhoods (Guglielmo and Waters 1996). Impoverishment reinforces main pre-existing stereotypes (such as the Roma being work-shy or prone to criminality) and so further undermines their already low social status. An opinion poll, in 1994, found the Roma to be the least popular 'ethnic' group in the survey with only 18 per cent of Hungarians saying they would be willing to have a Roma as a friend and only 15 per cent as a neighbour (Lendvay and Szabó 1994). The link between poverty and prejudice leads many, including the government, to expect an increase in 'ethnic tension' in the years to come.

Roma politics

Coinciding with a severe deterioration in living standards, Roma have been quick to exploit greater opportunities for self-organisation. Since 1990 over two hundred Roma organisations have been formed, ranging from large, national bodies down to village-level initiatives. Since the passage of the Minorities Law, Roma have formed 477 local minority self-governments (almost 60 per cent of the total number of these institutions) and, in April 1995, elected the first fifty-three-member National Roma Self-Government. There are now over two thousand Roma individuals who derive some or most of their income from their public duties.

Roma politics has its origin in the communist period and the dramatic failure of policy aimed at assimilating the Roma out of existence. Rising incomes, greater access to public services and healthier living conditions enabled the Roma population to rise from a pre-Holocaust total of 100,000 to around half a million. Improved educational opportunities and means of communication saw the emergence, from the 1970s, of a number of Roma writers and other artists who were able to express and promote a positive conception of Roma identity (Lemon 1996). Perhaps just as importantly, communist modernisation led to the destruction (often physically too) of Roma communities and to an historically unprecedented level of dependence of Roma on extra-communal institutions (employers, local government, banks, public utilities etc.) for their means of existence. 'Integration' meant Roma had to negotiate with institutions in order to secure services and resources. It also brought into sharp focus inequalities in distribution and heightened the debilitating effects of anti-Roma prejudice.

Minority rights and the Roma

Roma politics reflects the interests of Roma people, based on their contemporary existence. It seeks to develop and promote a Roma identity, enabling Roma people to define the meaning of their identity and to control its expression. It also seeks for prejudice to be confronted and to overcome the obstacles it places before Roma people in its tangible form of racial discrimination. Roma politics is also about securing, for Roma people, a fairer share of society's resources, which can be conceived of broadly as to include investment, income, services and opportunities.

One of the primary functions of rights is to define the relationship between those who possess them and the state. Therefore, minority rights, in the form of the Minorities Law, have a pivotal role in determining how Roma are able to achieve those changes they wish for themselves as represented, primarily, by Roma politics. Two aspects of this mechanism can be identified. First, minority rights have an important role in constructing the agenda for minority political activity, and more general public claims. Rights usually confer positive entitlements rather than proscribe actions, but what is included and what is left out has important legal and political implications for those who possess and interpret them. Second, the Minorities Law constructs a framework for minority political activity, the competence of which, therefore, affects the lobbying capacity of those who use it.

At the heart of the Minorities Law is the acknowledgement of the equal citizenship and cultural value of Hungary's (recognised) minorities. This is a positive development for the Roma, whose culture and identity have for centuries, been formally condemned as either non-existent or worthless. The Law seeks to establish 'cultural autonomy' for the minorities which, though nowhere defined, can be considered the right to control their own cultural expression and development. For this purpose, the minorities are entitled to establish their own festivals and monuments and to set up institutions such as libraries, museums and publishing houses. They are also allowed to develop their own written and electronic media and have access to public broadcast networks. Emphasis is placed on the development and use of the minority languages, though this is less relevant for most of the Roma population, three-quarters of whom speak only Hungarian. The minorities are also entitled to establish their own educational institutions and parents may elect what kind of education their children receive. The fundamental aim of these rights is to 'halt and even reverse the process of assimilation' and enhance the viability of minority identities (Boda *et al.* 1994).

Flaws in the Minorities Law

Despite the positive approach represented by minority rights, and provision of many important entitlements, there are a number of problems in the agenda set by the Minorities Law, especially from the perspective of the Roma. In part, these stem from the Law's almost total failure to acknowledge the differences in size, circumstances and needs of Hungary's different minority populations, but also because of its limited focus on culture, rather than broader issues which affect minority individuals and communities.

Economic rights

In recent years, most Hungarians have experienced a decline in their standard of living. Many have lost their jobs, and most in employment have seen prices rise faster than their income as well as the withdrawal of benefits and services which were previously free or offered at a subsidised rate (Fóti 1994). Poverty is not minority specific and even the different minority populations experience it to varying degrees. However, in a society in which social relations are increasingly defined by wealth, economic opportunity is fundamental to both individuals and communities. Yet, the Minorities Law contains no right of minorities to a decent standard of living or even one on a par with the rest of society. Not only is there no basis for any legal claim for an improvement in living standards, but the issue is excluded from the agenda set for minority political activity. Economic opportunity is an area where most Roma are severely disadvantaged. Government acknowledges that there are a number of particular factors contributing to

Roma poverty, such as low educational and skill levels, high levels of disability, family structure, settlement pattern and discrimination (Ágoston 1994), yet this is not reflected in the Minorities Law. The omission is not because the Law cannot distinguish between the minorities, as it explicitly recognises the particular problems of the Roma with regard to education (paragraph 45(2)).

It might be argued that rights are not appropriate to resolve economic problems, which must be left to the 'market'. However, this is incompatible with the fact that the Minorities Law does grant some rights with regard to economic interests and activities, most notably the right of minority self-governments to set up their own businesses, the profits of which can be used to support their communities. In reality, government does recognise the particular economic problems of the Roma and has taken steps to address these. In 1995, the Co-ordination Council of Gypsy Affairs was set up to make policy in this (and other areas) more efficient. A number of programmes have been launched to provide Roma with training, employment and agricultural self-sufficiency (*Lungo Drom* 1997). The point is that these measures are disconnected from rights. The reasons behind this are not hard to find. The Hungarian government is under enormous budgetary pressure at a time when Roma needs require substantial investments by the state. The establishment of economic rights, which Roma people could use to make immediate legal claims and as a basis for political action, is incompatible with the government's position that 'it would take the Gypsy community at least two decades to reach the level of [economic] integration which had developed by the late 1980s, and the full-scale integration of the Gypsy community is conceivable only in a historical perspective' (Szilágy and Heizer 1996).

Discrimination

As the main victims of racial discrimination in Hungary, the anti-discrimination provisions of the Minorities Law could be of great use to Roma, not only for increasing economic opportunity, but in many other areas of life too. Paragraph 3(5) prohibits 'all kinds of disadvantageous discrimination' against minorities. This is largely a restatement of the Constitutional guarantee of freedom from discrimination, but it is included as a fundamental tenet of the agenda set by minority rights. Though its inclusiveness is admirable, the opportunity has not been taken to develop the concept. Unlike the UK Race Relations Act, no attempt is made to define what constitutes discrimination. Does the Minorities Law cover only explicit racist statements or actions? Or can it be applied to 'indirect' discrimination, such as when a condition (say, job applicants must have a degree) is unnecessarily applied and which an ethnic group is disproportionately unable to satisfy? Or can these anti-discrimination clauses be invoked to promote a radical change of any system, such as public education, which produces an unequal outcome? If the right not to be discriminated against is to be applied in practice, these issues will have to be resolved and it is a pity that the Minorities Law does not contribute to this difficult task.

Cultural autonomy

One of the most innovative aspects of minority rights for Hungary is the explicit acceptance of the right of the minorities to 'practise and develop their languages and traditions and to protect and promote their...culture' (paragraph 16). As well as asserting the value of the minorities' culture, the Law goes into great detail as to how this 'autonomy' is to be enjoyed, including the establishment of institutions for the purpose. The minority self-government system is conceived of as a means of channelling resources towards cultural projects. The Law also created a source of finance in the Foundation for Minorities, as well as identifying other potential supporters.

Resources are necessary if the minorities are to 'promote' their culture and identity. Yet again, Roma are at a disadvantage (in comparison with other minority populations), due to mass impoverishment and the lack of a 'mother' country (and the poverty of the Roma diaspora). In order to organise events, Roma require the 'approval' of others (in the form of financial or other support) such as the state, local government and private benefactors such as George Soros. This situation clearly limits their 'autonomy'. Nevertheless, minority rights give Roma greater moral and legal authority to attract support for such projects, as well as greater control over the allocation of resources, once they have been made available.

However, the emphasis on cultural 'autonomy' exposes a tension in certain areas, between the respect for 'difference' and the right to be treated equally. Education provides a good example. The Law goes into great detail about how minorities can set up their own education facilities, yet it nowhere establishes the right to (let alone methods for achieving) an equal standard of education with the rest of society. The former (Roma) MP, Aladár Horváth, notes that 'Roma schools are a form of self-segregation, but at least they give Roma parents a choice of where to send their children' (*Guardian* 1996). However, even more important than the existence of a choice is the basis on which the choice is made. Is it right to ask Roma to decide whether to stay within the state education system that usually fails them or, no doubt with the encouragement of some local authorities glad to be rid of responsibility for teaching Roma children, enter an unknown educational environment in which the standards only have to be no lower (paragraph 47) than they were before? Indeed, it is a fundamental weakness of minority rights that, while they 'empower' minorities with regard to certain aspects of their lives, they do not tackle the fundamental inequalities which undermine people's lives.

The minority self-government system

It is not fair to criticise the Minorities Law for not providing detailed answers to complex questions. The method by which minority rights can be applied, in practice, is through a process of negotiation between those who claim them, the minorities and their representatives, and those who arbitrate or guarantee them, national and local government and other institutions. The necessity of a Roma input into decision-making processes was recognised (in institutional form) in 1986 with the creation of Gypsy Councils. Since 1990, Roma have exploited opportunities to organise (including the availability of financial support from the state) and founded a large number of organisations seeking to represent their interests at both the local and national level. This expansion was accompanied by a qualitative development in the creation of a number of 'umbrella' organisations which sought to co-ordinate and improve the lobbying effort. Since the passage of the Minorities Law, self-organisation has been superseded by the minority self-government system, reflected by a decline in the level of attention and the amount of money devoted to self-organised groups (Kovats 1997).

The extent to which the Roma (and the other minorities) are able to utilise their rights, including having their interpretation of them accepted, is largely dependent on the authority of their representatives, primarily self-governments. By providing every minority community with the right to establish its own representative institution, the Minorities Law has brought more Roma into public life. The status of Roma interests is increased as self-governments are legally recognised bodies which are 'legitimated' by public election. Furthermore, self-governments possess rights which self-organised groups do not, including that authorities respond to their representations, and they may also veto certain decisions. The 'official' status of self-governments probably also increases their chances of attracting financial and other support from outside agencies.

The authority of local self-governments

There are two main criticisms of the system. These relate to the position of self-governments within the country's administrative system, and the Law's effect upon the political development of the minorities. The term 'self-government' is somewhat misleading as these bodies cannot pass legislation, raise taxes or take over the statutory responsibilities of other institutions. Their two main functions are to articulate the minority's interests and to establish its cultural 'autonomy'. Noszkai has argued that self-governments have not been 'built into' the system of administration and that there is no explicit juridical mechanism by which they can compel other authorities to acknowledge their 'rights' (Noszkai 1994). Local authorities have an important role in determining the activities of self-governments, such as the attention they give to a minority's representations or to let its representatives participate in the work of the local authority.

A similar structural weakness can be found with regard to the financing of self-governments. Every year the state provides a minimal budget to each self-government, regardless of the size and need of the minority community (in 1995 this amounted to around £1,000). Though a number of potential sources of finance are identified by the Minorities Law, in practice the main one is the corresponding local authority. This state of 'dependency' is deliberately constructed in order to avoid the emergence of parallel institutions and to encourage co-operation between self-governments and local authorities (Boda *et al.* 1994). This situation represents a particular problem for the Roma whose low social status and lack of money means that there may be little desire on the part of a local authority to be constructive. A consequence of the current structure is that the first years of the self-government system have seen a wide variation in practice across the country.

Political development

As well as being a means of increasing mutual understanding, the self-government system also puts issues of disagreement more prominently into the public domain. It is inconceivable that disputes should not arise between self-governments and their local authority. The absence of a clear legal mechanism for resolving these means that they must be sorted out politically. There is a danger that two institutions in dispute may seek to mobilise their supporters and thus increase inter-communal tensions rather than reduce them. However, it is unlikely that a self-government would wish to engage in a protracted legal or political battle with its local authority as this might threaten the future viability of the self-government. A further limitation faced by minority representatives lies in the electoral system. All citizens may vote for a self-government and, in 1994, less than a quarter voting for Roma self-governments were themselves Roma (Boda *et al.* 1994). Representatives must be careful about advocating actions which may be portrayed as 'harmful' to the majority, as this could lead them to lose their posts at election time. In effect, the current state of the Law perpetuates the structural weakness of minorities in the interests of limiting inconvenience to local authorities, and creates an incentive for local politicians to undermine minority political development.

Just as important is the effect of the Minorities Law on the political direction of the minorities in general, and the Roma in particular. The self-government system has essentially replaced self-organisation and minority interest representation has been redefined and limited to 'the practice and tasks laid down in the Minorities Law' (Boda *et al.* 1994: 32). As we have seen, the Minorities Law deals only with certain aspects of Roma needs and excludes any reference to the most pressing problem, a lack of resources. Furthermore, with its emphasis on cultural difference, the Law fails to enforce the equality of the minorities with all other citizens. The effect is to direct Roma politics away from fundamental, and more expensive, issues, towards other important, but cheaper, ones. While this may help the Roma's lobbying capacity through the creation of a more coherent Roma identity on which it may draw, it also erects obstacles to the pursuit of a politics with which the Roma may find allies in the wider society on issues such as fighting poverty and the decline in public services. In effect, minority rights manoeuvre Roma politics into an ethnic ghetto and reduce pressure on the Hungarian government to address social and economic inequalities.

Conclusion

In recent years, minority rights have become a notable feature of international relations and agreements. In part, this is an attempt to adjust legal mechanisms to take account of increasing cultural diversity. However, it also reflects wider political developments, particularly the creation of a 'united' Europe. Minority rights play an important role in the negotiation of the relationship between Western Europe and the former socialist states. An examination of the forces contributing to the development of minority rights leads to the conclusion that they are designed, primarily, to reflect the interests of authorities rather than those of (minority) citizens.

For over a decade Hungary has been extending the number of rights available to its non-Magyar citizens. The high point of this process to date was the passage, in 1993, of the Law on the Rights of National and Ethnic Minorities, which expresses Hungary's unequivocal commitment to the European 'project'. Minority rights also enable Hungary to protect the interests of Magyar citizens in other states, as well as to secure the long-term viability of Magyar language and culture. Whilst Hungary's enthusiasm for minority rights is primarily related to foreign policy considerations, it also has consequences for domestic politics. The Minorities Law enables the state to set the agenda for minority political activity and constructs a framework within which this activity must take place.

Hungary's largest minority population, the Roma, is also its most politically dynamic. The forces contributing to the Roma's political mobilisation pre-date minority rights and the function of Roma politics is to represent the interests of Roma people, reflecting their needs and aspirations. The state's adoption of minority rights imposes an environment to which Roma politics must adapt. The Minorities Law sets the agenda for this politics and the self-government system directs activity towards this agenda. However, as currently constituted, the Minorities Law deals with only some of the Roma population's needs, and excludes others. Moreover, while reducing some obstacles to representation of Roma interests, the self-government system creates new ones. The effect is to distort the development of Roma politics and to perpetuate its weakness. However, the policy offers benefits to the state by enabling Hungary to fulfil (and even exceed) its international obligations while also reducing pressure for a reallocation of resources at home.

References

Ágoston, E. (1994) *The State of Crisis-Management in the Social Stratum of Unemployed Gypsies*, Budapest: Ministry of Labour.
Barbalet, J. (1988) *Citizenship*, Milton Keynes: Open University.
Boda, J., Cseresnyés, J. and Vánkos, T. (1994) *A Kisebbségek Jogai Magyarországon*, Budapest: Közgasdasági és Jogi Könyvkiadó.
Bugajski, J. (1995) *Ethnic Politics in Eastern Europe – a Guide to Nationality Policies, Organisations and Parties*, Armonk: M. E. Sharpe.

156   *Martin Kovats*

Capotorti, F. (1992) 'Are Minorities Entitled to Collective Rights?', in Y. Dinstein and M. Tabory (eds) *The Protection of Minorities and Human Rights*, Dordrecht: Martinus Nijhoff.

Christopulos, D. (1994) 'Minority Protection: Towards a New European Approach', *Balkan Forum* 2 (1): 160–72.

Föglein, G. (1996), 'Közvetíteni a párt és a kormány szavát', *História*18 (9–10): 44–86.

Fóti, K. (1994) 'The Labour Market in Transition: Unemployment in Hungary, *Journal of Communist Studies and Transition Politics* 10 (4): 37–54.

The Guardian 20 July 1996.

Guglielmo, R. and Waters, T. (1996) *Rights Denied – the Roma of Hungary*, New York: Human Rights Watch.

Gyurcsík, I. (1993) 'New Legal Ramifications of the Question of National Minorities', in I. Cuthbertson and J. Liebowitz (eds) *Minorities: the New Europe's Old Problem*, New York: East–West Studies.

Hartney, M. (1995) 'Some Confusions Concerning Collective Rights', in W. Kymlicka (ed.) *The Rights of Minority Cultures*, Oxford: Oxford University Press.

Havas, G., Kertesi, G. and Kemény, I. (1995) 'The Statistics of Deprivation: the Roma in Hungary', *Hungarian Quarterly* 36 (3): 67–80.

Kovats, M. (1997) 'The Good, the Bad and the Ugly: Three Faces of "Dialogue" – the Development of Roma Politics in Hungary', *Contemporary Politics* 3 (1): 55–71.

—— (forthcoming) 'The Roma and Minority Self-Governments in Hungary', in S. Bridger and F. Pine (eds) *Surviving Post-Socialism: Gender, Ethnicity and Underclass in Eastern Europe and the Former USSR*, London: Routledge.

Kymlicka, W. (1995) *Multicultural Citizenship – a Liberal Theory of Minority Rights*, Oxford: Clarendon Press.

Lábody, L. and Íjgyártó, I. (1996) 'Kormánypolitika – pártpolitika – határontüli magyarok', *Magyarország Politkai Évkönyve*, Budapest: Demokrácia Kutatások Magyar Központja.

Lemon, A. (1996) 'Identitás és reprezentáció: Interjü Daróczi Ágnessel és Bársony Jánossal', *Replika* 23–4: 261–74

Lendvay, J. and Szabó, I. (1994) 'Zárt karokkal', *Heti Világgazdaság*, 29 April: 105–6.

Lungo Drom (1997), 5 (7–8): 6–13.

Népszabadság 11 September 1995.

Noszkai, G. (1994) '(T)Örvénybe iktatva', *Respublika* 6: 42.

Szilágy, Z. and Heizer, A. (eds) (1996) *Report on the Situation of the Gypsy Community in Hungary*, Budapest: Office for National and Ethnic Minorities.

Thornberry, P. (1994) 'International European Standards on Minority Rights', in H. Miall (ed.) *Minority Rights in Europe – the Scope for a Transnational Regime*, London: Royal Institute for International Affairs.

Vajda, I. (1995) 'Minket ne válasszanak külön', *Amaro Drom* March: 4–6.

13 Democratisation and division in Czechoslovakia: economics and ethnic politics

Robert Schaeffer

Like many other countries in recent years, Czechoslovakia democratised in the wake of the collapse of authoritarian rule. Yet in Czechoslovakia, democratisation also led to division. The state was divided because democratisation contributed both to economic differentiation, which forced Slovaks and Czechs in opposite political directions, and led to the emergence of 'ethnic' political parties, first in Slovakia and then in Bohemia and Moravia, that demanded the dissolution of the state. Regionally based political parties jointly attacked the state in order to secure different economic and political objectives. Slovak parties wanted to retreat to a reform communist past; Czech parties wanted to advance to a free-market future. Both agreed that these objectives could best be achieved in states of their own. The state succumbed in 1992 because historical and contemporary developments had critically weakened its institutions and undermined its legitimacy and popular support. Fortunately, partition did not lead to conflict within or war between successor states, as it did in parts of Yugoslavia and the Soviet Union during this same period. Czechoslovakia avoided conflict largely because state institutions were weak and incapable of using force to defend the state.

Democratisation in Czechoslovakia

Democratisation in Eastern Europe was a product of crisis originating in the Soviet Union (Schaeffer 1997a). When Mikhail Gorbachev assumed power in 1985, he took steps to solve a series of acute problems, chief among them heavy military spending and declining productivity in agriculture and industry, which had contributed to economic stagnation and decline. Because communist regimes in Eastern Europe were tied to the Soviet Union and each other by common economic, political and military institutions – Council for Mutual Economic Assistance (CMEA) and the Warsaw Pact – Gorbachev's reforms and changed Soviet foreign policy, particularly his decision to rescind the Brezhnev Doctrine and deny Soviet power to allied regimes, created a crisis for the dictatorships of Eastern Europe. These regimes wrestled with economic stagnation and debt and faced growing social movements determined either to topple dictatorship (Solidarity) or flee from it (mass migration from East Germany). Crisis for one became crisis for all. The sudden and simultaneous fall of Eastern European regimes contrasted sharply with events in Latin America. Because regimes in Latin America were not institutionally linked, they faced the debt crisis individually and fell separately, about one each year for more than a decade. By contrast in Eastern Europe, common institutions tied them together like a train. So when the Soviet engine stalled, Eastern European cars jumped track, and the whole train was wrecked.

In Czechoslovakia, the regime faced an economic crisis that had first emerged in the early 1960s. After a post-war economic recovery in the 1950s, which had returned economic output to pre-war levels, agriculture and industry began to stagnate in the early 1960s, and annual growth fell from 7 per cent in 1956–60 to only 1.8 per cent in the years 1961–5 (Stevens 1985: 45). Much of this downturn was caused by the collapse of bilateral trade with China, a casualty of the growing Sino-Soviet split (Shen 1993: 61). Efforts to reform the economy by introducing some market mechanisms and 'submitting [the] economy to the pressure of the world market' under the Dubcek regime's Action Program in 1968 were aborted by Soviet invasion and the reinstallation of a conservative regime under Gustav Husak (Golan 1973: 35, 27). Although the Husak regime scrapped most of the Action Program and reinstated central planning, it adopted one part of the plan: to borrow money from abroad (Golan 1973: 39–40). Like dictatorships throughout Eastern Europe and also Latin America, the Husak regime began borrowing money in the 1970s to cover trade deficits caused by rising oil and food prices, to subsidise domestic food prices as a way to purchase worker loyalty, and to increase productivity in industry (Shen 1993: 74, 107, 160). Czechoslovakia's foreign debt to the West rose from $608 million in 1970 to $6.8 billion in 1980, and then to $7.9 billion in 1989, an 11-fold increase (Prusl *et al.* 1990: 22).

The regime in Czechoslovakia borrowed less and enjoyed more economic success than other regimes in Eastern Europe. Its per capita debt was about half that of Poland, and it used debt to boost economic growth, at least for a time: output grew 5.7 per cent between 1970 and 1975, 3.6 per cent between 1975 and 1980 (Shen 1993: 83–4; Mason 1996: 129). But by the 1980s, economic stagnation had returned (Prusl *et al.* 1990: 76). In Czechoslovakia, indebted development deferred but did not avert economic malaise or arrest the long-term decline in the country's position in the world economy. Before the Second World War, Czechoslovakia was 'one of the ten most industrialised countries in the world', with a GDP per capita comparable to that of Austria (Sujan and Sujanova 1995: 120). But by 1990, 'Czechoslovak GDP per capita...[was] comparable to that of Venezuela and...only...one-fifth that of Austria' (Dybha and Svejnar 1995: 22).

The ongoing economic crisis in Czechoslovakia was exacerbated in 1989 by new international and domestic political crises. The abrupt change in Soviet foreign and military policy, particularly its February 1989 decision to rescind the Brezhnev Doctrine, deprived the regime of Soviet political support and military power, which had installed and maintained the regime since 1968 (Wheaton and

Kavan 1992: 19). The collapse of communist regimes in neighbouring Poland, Hungary and East Germany during the summer and autumn further isolated the regime. Communist leaders in Czechoslovakia recognised that they faced many of the same economic problems that had undermined neighbouring regimes and confronted a domestic opposition movement that could in time become a broad-based, multi-class alliance of intellectuals and workers like Solidarity. The nucleus for such a movement had already been created in 1976, when intellec-tual dissidents based in Prague formed Charter 77 (Bosak 1991: 128–33). But unlike Solidarity, which united intellectuals and workers in a common movement during the 1970s, Charter 77 remained small, without any real ties to the working class (Bosak 1991: 140–2). That changed in November 1989, when Charter 77 members joined first with students to create Civic Forum, forged an alliance with Public Against Violence, and then joined with workers in the 'lunch hour' general strike of 27 November (Wheaton and Kavan 1992: 85–7). Worker participation in the general strike indicated that a Czechoslovak version of Solidarity might soon be forthcoming. Under these conditions, only a gentle push was necessary to force the regime to retire. But while the push from domestic political forces was gentle, the weight behind it was large and growing.

These developments led quickly to democratisation and the transfer of power to the dissident movement led by Vaclav Havel. Yet while economic and political problems led to democratisation in Czechoslovakia, as they did throughout Eastern Europe in 1989, they also led in Czechoslovakia to a division of the state along 'ethnic' lines. As it turned out, economics and politics played important roles in this rather uncommon development.

Economic differentiation

After 1989, economic developments had different consequences in the Czech Lands and Slovakia, forcing them in opposite political directions. As dictator-ships across Eastern Europe fell, the region's economic institutions collapsed, resulting in declining trade and production (Brown 1994: 151, 153). Czechoslovakia's trade with former Council for Mutual Economic Assistance (CMEA) partners dropped from 60 per cent of the total in 1989 to only 20 per cent in 1993 (Dybha and Svejnar 1995: 42). To replace dissolving and discred-ited economic institutions and relations, the government in Czechoslovakia adopted policies designed to open the economy to foreign investment and trade, sell state assets to private entrepreneurs, and demilitarise the economy. But in Czechoslovakia, these policies had different regional consequences.

Efforts to open the economy to foreign investment and trade provided greater benefits to Bohemia than to Slovakia. Bohemia received 80 per cent of new foreign investment, which helped create jobs in the region (Brada 1994: 21). Successive devaluations of the Crown, which fell 70 per cent in 1990, had 'more of a beneficial effect on Czech exports than on Slovak ones' (Shen 1993: 117, 171). The new open border policies made it easier for workers from Bohemia to work in Germany, providing employment and income to workers in that region, and promoted a booming tourist industry in Prague, but not in Slovakia (Urban 1993: 113).

The government's sale of state businesses and public assets also had different regional consequences. Because the government privatised twice as many businesses in the Czech Lands as in Slovakia, and because local entrepreneurs won control of a vast majority of these firms, the benefits of privatisation were unevenly distributed, with the former capturing the lion's share (Shen 1993: 187).

Demilitarisation also had different regional consequences. The government's 1990 decision to end arms exports, and the general collapse of arms markets throughout Eastern Europe and the Soviet Union, devastated the arms industry (Michta 1992: 128). By 1991, the volume of 'arms exports had fallen to one-eighth of their former levels', and the value of trade fell from $8 billion to only $1 billion (Leff 1997: 229). Because Slovakia was more heavily dependent on the arms industry, workers in Slovakia were harder hit by the collapse of trade (Leff 1997: 229). The government's 1991 decision to renew arms exports did not greatly improve matters because the global arms market was saturated, because Eastern European arms were generally uncompetitive with US and West European arms, and because the arms that could be sold on global markets were those made in Bohemia, not Slovakia (Michta 1992: 127). Light aircraft and light firearms made in the former found ready markets, while heavy tanks, which comprised 99 per cent of arms exports for Slovakia, found few buyers (Urban 1993: 117).

As a result of the government's new economic policies, regional disparities quickly became manifest. In 1990–1, employment rates and income levels in the two regions diverged sharply. While the unemployment rate in the Czech Lands 'quadrupled to 4.4 per cent' between 1991 and 1992, 'the Slovak rate quintupled to 12.7 per cent' (Svejnar *et al.* 1995: 286). While the economic downturn adversely affected incomes throughout the country – incomes fell between 20 and 30 per cent in 1990–1 – declining incomes 'created greater hardship in Slovakia, where a higher proportion of households are found in the lowest income group' (Vavrejnova and Moravcikova 1995: 319).

Diverging economic fortunes in the two regions reversed the long, post-war trend towards economic equality (Kucera and Pavlik 1995: 36). During the 1950s and 1960s, the communist regime used tax, price and investment policies to transfer wealth to Slovakia and promote industrialisation there (Sujan and Sujanova 1995: 126). While the value of these transfers is the subject of dispute, the redistributive character of these policies is not (Prucha 1995: 61, 69–70; Dean 1973: 21). Such policies increased Slovakia's share of industrial production from 13.1 per cent of the country's total in 1946 to 25.5 per cent in 1970 (Dean 1973: 22). And rising employment in industry increased income levels in Slovakia, from 70 per cent that of Czechs in 1948 to 92 per cent in 1989 (Prucha 1995: 62, 73–5). In this context, the government's 1990 announcement that it would end redistributive policies, which under communist rule had long bene-fited Slovakia, and henceforth required Slovakia to live 'mainly off the resources generated' in the region, marked the end of post-war economic convergence (Leff 1997: 185).

Those living in the two regions experienced economic change before and after 1989 in different ways. For Czechs, the economic changes associated with the communist regime's 'convergence' policies were bad because they undermined the Czech position in the world economy and improved conditions in Slovakia at their expense. They also saw the new government's free-market policies after 1989 as a positive development that would improve their global position and stop the drain on their resources to Slovakia. For Slovaks, however, communist economic policies had improved their economic circumstances, while the new free-market policies undermined their position and threatened to undo previous gains. Because Czechs and Slovaks drew different lessons from common economic developments, they advanced different solutions to contemporary problems: Czechs supported free-market policies as a solution to the economic legacies of communism; Slovaks wanted to revive communist economic policies as a solution to the problems caused by free-market policies. Implicit in these solutions were different conceptions of the state's role in economic policy. Proponents of free-market policies wanted to reduce the state's role; defenders of revised or 'reform communist' policies wanted to maintain an important role for the state. These divergent views quickly became evident in economic attitudes in the two regions. Public opinion polls simultaneously identified a strong constituency for market policies and a reduced role for the state in Bohemia and Moravia; a strong constituency for reform communist policies and an important role for the state in Slovakia (Millar and Wolchik 1994: 7–15; Wolchik 1996: 76).

Diverging solutions to perceived economic problems were difficult to reconcile because proponents of free-market policies were in a position, as representatives of the Czech majority, to insist on their implementation, while their opponents, representative of the Slovak minority, were not able to prevent the adoption of policies inimical to them. As we will see, the Klaus government's determination to adopt free-market policies, what he called a 'market without adjectives', helped foreclose the development of economic policies that could collectively address the different economic legacies and prospects of people living in different regions (Leff 1997: 180).

Ethnic division

As economic developments pushed people in the two regions in opposite political directions, the unitary state came under attack first from reform-minded communists based in Slovakia, and then from free-market democrats based in Bohemia. And economic differences quickly assumed ethnic features.

In Slovakia, pro-reform communists led by Vladimir Meciar organised the Movement for a Democratic Slovakia (MDS) to defend Slovaks against the problems associated with free-market policies and their status as a political minority (Brown 1994: 60). Meciar organised the movement along ethnic lines for a variety of reasons. First, residual political institutions like the Slovak National

Council and Slovak Assembly, which had been established by the communist regime, provided a political base for politicians unable to compete effectively in country-wide elections against popular Czech dissidents such as Havel and Klaus. These institutions gave the movement a refuge and a bulwark for Meciar, much as they did for Kravchuk and Yeltsin in the Soviet Union, and Tudjman and Milosevic in Yugoslavia (Schaeffer 1997a). Second, appeals to innate ethnicity allowed Meciar to tap into historical and contemporary social affinities. Meciar could argue that Slovaks shared a common history, which included a brief period of 'independence' during the Second World War, and now faced common problems resulting from free-market policies and their status as a minority in a unitary state (Judt 1992: 104). Third, ethnic appeals allowed Meciar to escape the confines of class-based politics and construct a multi-class coalition that could contest effectively for power, at least in Slovakia. By organising along ethnic lines and using residual political institutions in the republic, the movement was able to become the dominant political party in the region (Batt 1991: 98).

Although the MDS, which demanded greater autonomy and possibly independence for Slovakia, was popular in the region, it was not itself strong enough to dissolve the unitary state. It could not secure independence unilaterally because it represented a minority of people in both the country as a whole and in the region (Wolchik 1995: 240; 1996: 80). What is more, prior to the 1992 elections, '81 per cent of the respondents in the Czech Republic and 63 per cent in Slovakia rejected the idea of separation' (Leff 1997: 137–8). As it happened, Slovak nationalists did not have to act alone. They were joined by Czech nationalists in 1992, when Klaus decided that Czech interests were separate from Slovak interests, and together they assaulted the state (Leff 1997: 131).

Scholars have written extensively about the rise of a Slovak ethnic identity, which they trace back to the mid-nineteenth century and finds contemporary expression in Meciar's MDS and other nationalist parties (Brock 1976; Steiner 1973). But they have paid less attention to the emergence of a Czech ethnicity, largely because Czech ethnicity has long had a cosmopolitan, secular and economistic character. It was cosmopolitan because for many people a Czech identity was synonymous with a 'European' identity, an identity that would enable them to 'integrate into Europe' (Leff 1995: 136–7). It was secular insofar as political parties and their supporters did not associate any particular religious belief with Czech identity. And it was economistic because political parties argued that Czechs generated most of the country's economic wealth (Leff 1995: 156–8).

'Ethnicity' need not be understood only as an identity based on parochial, religious or cultural characteristics. What is important is not the particular set of characteristics but the emergence of an identity that distinguishes one group from another. In this case, the cosmopolitan, secular and economic characteristics that comprised a 'Czech' identity helped distinguish 'Czechs' from Slovaks. The emergence of a Czech identity and growing conflict with Slovaks over the distribution of economic wealth and political power in a single state made it possible for Czechs to imagine a state without Slovaks. After the 1992 elections, Klaus joined with Meciar to mount a collective assault on the state. Both evidently decided that the political and economic interests of Czech and Slovak ethnicities could best be pursued separately, in states where each could exercise power on their own terms (Brown 1994: 60–2).

Although Czech and Slovak political parties joined forces to divide the state between them, why were they successful? Generally speaking, the dissolution and division of states is difficult and uncommon, largely because the political, economic and military institutions of states in the twentieth century resist a division of power or a devolution of their authority to others (Schaeffer 1990). In Czechoslovakia, however, historical and contemporary developments critically weakened the institutions of the state, making it relatively easy for Czech and Slovak political leaders to divide it (Musil 1995a: 9–10; 1995b: 77).

Institutional weakness

Political developments before and after 1989 weakened the institutions of the state. Between 1918 and 1989, state institutions were repeatedly compromised by foreign powers and domestic elites. At Munich, the great powers dissolved the state's sovereign authority, allowing principally Germany then to annex and divide it. At Yalta in 1945, the superpowers assigned the state to an expanded Soviet sphere of influence, allowing the Soviet Union and its domestic allies in Czechoslovakia to dissolve the elected government and establish a communist regime in 1948. In 1968, the Soviet Union and its allies invaded Czechoslovakia and dissolved many of the Dubcek government's recently created institutions and reorganised the regime under a new leadership. In 1989, Gorbachev's reform of Soviet military policy fatally undermined the institutions upon which state power in Czechoslovakia was based. Successive interventions by foreign powers created institutions whose sovereignty – the ability to exercise power in Czechoslovakia – was constrained, compromised and impaired in important ways.

Domestic political elites also undermined the strength of state institutions by conceding power in 1938, 1948, 1968 and 1989 without a fight. Because political leaders did not resist foreign intervention and invasion or, in 1989, domestic protest, the state's military and bureaucracy were not tested or tempered as organisations by a concerted effort to defend the state.

Wartime agreements at Pittsburgh in 1918 and at Kosice in 1945 and constitutional provisions in 1948 and 1968 recognised the rights of and provided institutions for Slovaks, as distinct from Czechs, in the state (Dean 1973: 5–6; Bugajski 1995: 67–8). Although the provisions of these agreements and constitutions were frequently ignored, neglected or abrogated, they legitimised demands for greater Slovak autonomy and thereby undermined the constitutional authority of the state, much as the Soviet and Yugoslav constitutions eventually provided a legal basis for self-determination in the constituent republics (Bradley 1991: 78; Schaeffer 1997b).

The Communist Party in Czechoslovakia also helped weaken the state's constitutional position by adopting 'self-determination' as a political principle. In the 1920s and 1930s, the party had argued that Czechoslovakia was a 'jail house of nations' and argued that the state be dissolved, much as the Communist Party in Yugoslavia argued during the same period (Korbel 1977: 73–4, 110). Self-determination was adopted and reiterated as an ideology by successive leaders of communist regimes after 1948. For example, Gustav Husak argued that the 1968 constitution, which made Czechoslovakia a federation, had been adopted to put the right of self-determination into practice (Bosak 1991: 54).

In this context, communist rule legitimised Slovak interests and identity as separate from that of Czechs, without, until 1968, doing the same for Czechs. After the regime fell, Slovak leaders seized on the principles, promises and constitutional provisions articulated and adopted by communist leaders to give their demands greater legitimacy. The Czechoslovak state's organisational, constitutional and ideological institutions were weakened not only by developments before 1989, they were further crippled by events after the communist regime fell.

When that regime collapsed, it devolved political power to a politically weak, geographically narrow social movement. Unlike Poland's Solidarity, the dissident movement represented by Civic Forum and led by Vaclav Havel did not have a wide, multi-class social base (Schaeffer 1997a: 177–81). Instead, it was based in the dissident intellectual and student communities and had few ties with the working and middle classes. While the movement established some ties with Public Against Violence, which was based in Slovakia, Civic Forum drew primarily from a constituency based in Prague. The dissident movement also possessed an ideology that eschewed mass-based politics. Charter 77, which informed the movement's ideas, had declared it was 'not an organisation; it has no rules, permanent bodies or formal membership' and did 'not aim to set out its own programmes of political or social reforms or changes' (Bosak 1991: 133–4). And in 1990, many participants opposed creating a political party, continuing to adhere to the 'anti-politics' of the dissident era (Batt 1991: 62–3). Given its narrow social and geographic base and its self-limiting political perspective, it is not surprising that it did poorly in elections after 1990, almost disappearing as a political entity by 1992. It did however possess a charismatic and popular leader, Vaclav Havel, who as president became the movement's only institutional legacy. The problem was that as the constitutional crisis sharpened, as Meciar and Klaus joined forces against the state, Havel had no mass-based, regionally diverse, politically astute movement or party to rally in defence of union and the state. Because he had no institutional support, only popular sentiment on his side, Havel could only use his office to inveigh against separation or, failing that, to demand that a referendum be held to address the constitutional question (Wheaton and Kavan 1992: 171).

The state had two other institutions that might also have resisted division: the bureaucracy and the army. The bureaucracy did not rally to the defence of the state because it had few political interests of its own separate from those of the political parties who appointed and hired government officials. Democratisation and the passage of the lustration law, which barred former communists from public office, displaced many officials from the previous regime and created an inexperienced bureaucracy. Many of the officials installed by the Klaus government agreed with Klaus that the state's economic role should be extremely limited, making them reluctant to assert a forceful defence of the state's political position. As a result, the bureaucracy was not prepared to defend the state. So when the two leading parties decided to divide the state between them, this new and timid bureaucracy followed their lead.

Much the same was true of the army as an institution. In most countries, the army is organised to defend the state against foreign and domestic opponents. In Yugoslavia and in the Soviet Union, the army intervened forcibly to prevent the division of the state (Schaeffer 1997a, 1997b). Why then didn't the army in Czechoslovakia, like armies in Yugoslavia and the Soviet Union, intervene during the same period? It did not because several developments had weakened its capacity to act. First, the army had no contemporary military experience, either in foreign or civil wars. The brief uprising in Slovakia during the Second World War was the only time domestic forces mobilised to fight, and they did so only with Soviet assistance. The state, in fact, had in 1938, 1948, 1968 and 1989 asked the army *not* to fight, even though the state itself was in jeopardy (Leff 1997: 61; 1995: 139; Rice 1984: 3–4). Second, the Soviet Union in 1948 and again in 1968 had insisted that the army be purged of politically unreliable officers. Recurrent purges and defections of the officer corps weakened the army as an effective military organisation (Rice 1984: 59, 62, 168). Indeed, Soviet policy created an army so weak that it could not even be relied on to fulfil its treaty commitments and assist its nominal allies. Although the Czechoslovak army had been asked by the Soviet Union to assist in the training of its Third World allies before 1968, it did not invite Czechoslovak military participation after 1968: 'When the Soviet role in the Third World was expanding, the Czechoslovaks were not a visible part of that effort' (Rice 1984: 84, 191). Cuban troops were the only forces invited by the Soviet Union to participate in foreign campaigns (Schaeffer 1997a: 130–1). Given these weaknesses, and then the demoralisation of the army following the fall of communism, when the army was reduced in size and its mission was further restricted, it is not surprising that military leaders were unwilling to defend the state, or that the population held the army in low esteem. In 1991, only 43 per cent of Czechs and 47 per cent of Slovaks expressed a 'fair amount' of confidence in the army as an institution (Millar and Wolchik 1994: 20).

Because the legal, political, bureaucratic, military and ideological institutions that might, in other countries, defend the state were weakened by these developments, the state fell when Czech and Slovak leaders combined against it. As in 1989, only a gentle push was necessary to dissolve and divide the state. Elites representing the two largest regional parties simply negotiated a division of state power. The fact that the president was unable to put constitutional questions to a test in a popular referendum – this *despite* widespread support in both regions for maintaining the state – illustrates the fundamental weakness of the state (Bugajski 1995: 304). To their credit, and in contrast to events in Yugoslavia, partition in Czechoslovakia was peacefully accomplished. But that is due primarily to the fact that the two parties *agreed* that the division of the unitary state was in their mutual interest. If they had disagreed about this, events could well have taken a different turn.

Division enabled the dominant parties in each region to move in opposite directions. The Czechs under Klaus advanced towards a free-market, 'European' future. The Slovaks under Meciar retreated to a reformed communist past. The state sheared along 'ethnic' lines, but did so to accommodate separate economic and political interests. Division was a way of accommodating different economic and political objectives: a free-market economy and a weak state for Czechs; a controlled economy and a strong state for Slovaks. As a result, domestic interpretations of the meaning of democracy began to diverge. Because democratisation and division was a product of historical and contemporary developments particular to Czechoslovakia, the 'formula' for a 'Velvet Divorce' probably has little application elsewhere, except, perhaps, where state institutions are weak and willing to surrender power without complaint.

References

Batt, J. (1991) *East-Central Europe: From Reform to Transformation*, London: Pinter.

Bosak, E. (1991) 'Slovaks and Czechs: an Uneasy Coexistence', in H.G. Skilling (ed.) *Czechoslovakia: 1918–88: Seventy Years From Independence*, London: Macmillan.

Brada, J.C. (1994) 'Breaking Up is Hard to Do: the Economics of Creating Independent Czech and Slovak Republics', in J. Krovak (ed.) *Current Economics and Politics of (ex-) Czechoslovakia*, Commack, NY: Nova Science Publishers.

Bradley, J.F.N. (1991) *Politics in Czechoslovakia, 1945–1990*, New York: Columbia University Press.

Brock, P. (1976) *The Slovak National Awakening: an Essay in the Intellectual History of East Central Europe*, Toronto, Ont.: University of Toronto Press.

Brown, J.F. (1994) *Hopes and Shadows: Eastern Europe After Communism*, Durham, NC: Duke University Press.

Bugajski, J. (1995) *Nations in Turmoil: Conflict and Cooperation in Eastern Europe*, Boulder, CO: Westview Press.

Dean, R.W. (1973) *Nationalism and Political Change in Eastern Europe: the Slovak Question and the Czech Reform Movement*, Denver, CO: University of Denver Press.

Dybha, K. and Svejnar, J. (1995) 'A Comparative View of Economic Developments in the Czech Republic', in J. Svejnar (ed.) *The Czech Republic and Economic Transition in Eastern Europe*, San Diego, CA: Academic Press.

Golan, G. (1973) *Reform Rule in Czechoslovakia: the Dubcek Era 1968–1969*, Cambridge: Cambridge University Press.

Judt, T.R. (1992) 'Metamorphosis: the Democratic Revolution in Czechoslovakia', in I. Banac (ed.) *Eastern Europe in Revolution*, Ithaca, NY: Cornell University Press.

Korbel, J. (1977) *Twentieth-Century Czechoslovakia: the Meanings of History*, New York: Columbia University Press.

Kucera, M. and Pavlik, Z. (1995) 'Czech and Slovak Demography', in J. Musil (ed.) *The End of Czechoslovakia*, Budapest: Central European University Press.

Leff, C.S. (1995) 'Czech and Slovak Nationalism in the Twentieth Century', in P.F. Sugar (ed.) *European Nationalism in the Twentieth Century*, Washington DC: The American University Press.

—— (1997)*The Czech and Slovak Republics: Nation Versus State*, Boulder, CO: Westview Press.

Mason, D.S. (1996) *Revolution and Transition in East-Central Europe*, Boulder, CO: Westview Press.

Michta, A.A. (1992) *East Central Europe After the Warsaw Pact: Security Dilemmas in the 1990s*, New York: Greenwood Press.

Millar, J.R. and Wolchik, S.L. (1994) 'Introduction: the Social Legacies and the Aftermath of Communism', in J.R. Millar and S.L. Wolchik (eds) *The Social Legacy of Communism*, Cambridge: Woodrow Wilson Center Press and Cambridge University Press.

Musil, J. (1995a) 'Introduction', in J. Musil (ed.) *The End of Czechoslovakia*, Budapest: Central European University Press.

—— (1995b) 'Czech and Slovak Society', in J. Musil (ed.) *The End of Czechoslovakia*, Budapest: Central European University Press.

Prucha, V. (1995) 'Economic Development and Relations, 1918–89', in J. Musil (ed.) *The End of Czechoslovakia*, Budapest: Central European University Press.

Prusl, J., Carter, J., Cheasty, A., Christensen, B.V., Hansen, L., Haque, N.U. and van der Willigen, T. (1990) *The Czech and Slovak Federal Republic: an Economy in Transition*, Washington DC: International Monetary Fund.

Rice, C. (1984) *The Soviet Army and the Czechoslovak Army, 1948–1983: Uncertain Alliance*, Princeton, NJ: Princeton University Press.

Schaeffer, R. (1990) *Warpaths: the Politics of Partition*, New York: Hill & Wang.

—— (1997a) *Power to the People: Democratization Around the World*, Boulder, CO: Westview Press.

—— (1997b) 'Democratization, Division and War in Yugoslavia: a Comparative Perspective', paper presented for the conference, 'The Lessons of Yugoslavia', Innis College, University of Toronto, 20 March.

Shen, R. (1993) *Economic Reform in Poland and Czechoslovakia: Lessons in Systemic Transformation*, Westport, CT: Praeger.

Steiner, E. (1973) *The Slovak Dilemma*, Cambridge: Cambridge University Press.

Stevens, J.N. (1985) *Czechoslovakia at the Crossroads: the Economic Dilemmas of Communism in Postwar Czechoslovakia*, New York: Columbia University Press.

Sujan, I. and Sujanova, M. (1995) 'The Macroeconomic Situation in the Czech Republic', in J. Svejnar (ed.) *The Czech Republic and Economic Transition in Eastern Europe*, San Diego, CA: Academic Press.

Svejnar, J., Terrell, K. and Munich, D. (1995) 'Unemployment in the Czech and Slovak Republics', in J. Svejnar (ed.) *The Czech Republic and Economic Transition in Eastern Europe*, San Diego, CA: Academic Press.

Urban, J. (1993) 'The Czech and Slovak Republics: Security Consequences of the Breakup of the CSFR', in R.C. Carp (ed.) *Central and Eastern Europe: The Challenge of Transition*, Oxford: Stockholm International Peace Research Institute, Oxford University Press.

Vavrejnova, M. and Moravcikova, I. (1995) 'The Czech Household Sector in Transition', in J. Svejnar (ed.) *The Czech Republic and Economic Transition in Eastern Europe*, San Diego, CA: Academic Press.

Wheaton, B. and Kavan, Z. (1992) *The Velvet Revolution: Czechoslovakia, 1988–1991*, Boulder, CO: Westview Press.

Wolchik, S.L. (1995) 'The Politics of Transition and the Breakup of Czechoslovakia', in J. Musil (ed.) *The End of Czechoslovakia*, Budapest: Central European University Press.

—— (1996) 'The Politics of Ethnicity and the Breakup of the Czechoslovak Federation', in L. Drobizheva, R. Gottemoeller, C.M. Kelleher and L. Walker (eds) *Ethnic Conflict in the Post-Soviet World: Case Studies and Analysis*, Armonk, NY: M.E. Sharpe.

Zacek, J. F. (1969) 'Nationalism in Czechoslovakia', in P.F. Sugar and I.J. Lederer (eds) *Nationalism in Eastern Europe*, Seattle, WA: University of Washington Press.

14 The Germans of Upper Silesia: the struggle for recognition[1]

Tomasz Kamusella and Terry Sullivan

Shifting borders

In 1995 on the fiftieth anniversary of the end of the Second World War numerous celebrations were held in Poland to mark the incorporation of the former *Deutsche Ostgebiete* (eastern territories of Germany). Few of these celebrations consciously alluded to the fact that the incorporation of the *Deutsche Ostgebiete* into post-war Poland had been an unusual compensation for the eastern lands Poland had lost to the Soviet Union in line with the secret Ribbentrop–Molotov Pact of 1939. Having secured the *Deutsche Ostgebiete* for Poland through a policy of *faits accomplis*, Stalin acquired leverage over Warsaw. It was realised that the existence of post-war Poland could be guaranteed only by the Soviet Union because of the virtual impossibility of any rapprochement of the Poles with the Germans. The incorporation of the relatively highly developed *Deutsche Ostgebiete* facilitated the transformation of post-war Poland from an agricultural to agricultural–industrial country. Thus, the 'recovered territories' (christened so by the Polish communist-cum-nationalist propaganda) allowed the communists to attempt to consolidate Polish society around the unpopular goal of 'building socialism' under Soviet supervision, as well as legitimise their seizure of power.

Polish incorporation of the *Deutsche Ostgebiete* was inseparably linked to the question of the German-speaking population who had inhabited the area for about seven centuries. The Polish–German 1939 propaganda war of 'ethnically and historically justified' territorial claims finally brought about on 29 August the official Polish declaration that Warsaw hoped to solve the problem of the Polish minority in Germany and the German minority in Poland through a gradual and peaceful population exchange as had allegedly occurred between Greece and Turkey in 1923. Such ideas had been touted by Czech intellectuals as early as 1937, who argued for the expulsion of part of the *Sudetendeutsche*. After the Munich Agreement of 1938, and the defeat of Poland in 1939 and the resultant expulsions and resettlement of Czechs and Poles, these previously vague proposals were, for the first time, brought before European and world political fora in open discussions between Eduard Benes and his close associate Hubert Ripka (Wiskemann 1956: 47, 62).

The President of the Czechoslovak Government in Exile in London, Benes advocated the ethnic homogenisation of Czechoslovakia through expulsions. Following Hitler's attack on the Soviet Union in June 1941, the Polish Government in Exile in London (under British pressure) concluded the Polish–Soviet mutual assistance Pact of 30 June. The two governments thereby established bilateral relations, and entered into uneasy co-operation with one another. Significantly, the agreement did not guarantee the re-establishment of Poland's pre-war borders, and as such left open the possibility of post-war annexations and population shifts. On 2 December 1942 the Polish Parliament in London resolved that in addition to the restoration of Poland's eastern border as of 31 August 1939, the post-war Polish German border be 'straightened and shortened'. This somewhat unclear declaration was made more specific by Head of the Polish State, General Wladyslaw Sikorski, on 6 December 1942. In the course of his negotiations with President Roosevelt he designated the Oder–Neisse line as Poland's natural security line. Given that all were united in their desire to defeat and punish Germany. Great Britain, the United States and the Soviet Union gradually came to support the idea of post-war 'transfers of population' as the planned expulsions were euphemistically referred to. The expulsion of the German-speaking population from the *Deutsche Ostgebiete* was publicly mentioned for the first time at the Conference in Teheran of 28 November–1 December 1943, when Stalin, supported by Eden, proposed the Oder as Poland's post-war western border (Wiskemann 1956: 63, 66–7, 73–4).

The year 1943 was marked by the severance of already tense relations between the Polish Government in Exile and Moscow. Matters finally came to a head with the discovery of the Katyn massacres, which had involved the mass murder of thousands of Polish army officers by the Soviets. The diplomatic situation became critical. Polish Prime Minister Stanislaw Mikolajczyk did not wish to accept the loss of Poland's eastern territories in exchange for the *Deutsche Ostgebiete*. On 10 October during a meeting at the British embassy in Moscow Mikolajczyk was forced to accede to Soviet demands with regard to Poland's eastern border. Mikolajczyk promised that he would persuade his cabinet to endorse the decision, but failed to do so and, on 24 November, quit the Polish government (Harper and Parlin 1990: 5, 18–20).

The uncompromising stance of the Polish government allowed the Soviets to establish the PKWN (Polish Committee of National Liberation) in the Polish city of Lublin in July 1944. Recognised only by Moscow, the PKWN was to serve as the nucleus of the post-war government in Poland. In an interview for *The Sunday Times* on 17 December 1944, Tomasz Arciszewsk, the new Polish Prime Minister, protested against the possible loss of the Polish eastern territories, but also argued for future Polish incorporation of Upper Silesia and parts of East Prussia, Pomerania and Lower Silesia, but with the exclusion of the cities of Breslau (Wroclaw) and Stettin (Szczecin), in order not to overburden a post-war Poland with a task of assimilating too large a number of Germans. Yet he still was not prepared to take into consideration mass expulsions as a political instrument (Wiskemann 1956: 81–2). An immediate response to this pronouncement was formulated in the 18 December *Pravda* article by Stefan Jedrychowski, head of the PKWN Propaganda Department. For the first time the Oder–Neisse line was officially demanded as the post-war western frontier of Poland. The territorial claims of the Polish communists, together with their acceptance of the loss of pre-war Polish territory to the Soviet Union by the PKWN, augmented Soviet support for its ally and facilitated its transformation into the Provisional Government on 31 December 1944. Hence, at the Yalta Conference of 4–11 February 1945 Stalin could fully support the demands of the Polish communists against the contrary opinions of Roosevelt and Churchill. The concerns of the two Western leaders over the number of Germans who would have to be expelled were dismissed by Stalin. He maintained that a majority of the German population of the *Deutsche Ostgebiete* had already fled before the advancing Red Army. The information was false because 30–60 per cent of the Germans remained in the *Deutsche Ostgebiete*, and many of those who had fled returned (especially to Upper Silesia) after the end of the war (De Zayas 1988: 50, 53).

'Liberation'

In order to analyse the effects of the Red Army's onslaught in Upper Silesia, it is necessary to scrutinise the ethnic make-up of the area at the close of the Second World War. The territory was populated by Germans, Upper Silesians of no clear national affiliation, Poles, Czechs, Moravians and those few Jews who had escaped the Holocaust. During the war some 81,000 Poles had been expelled to the *General Gouvernement*, and subsequently replaced with 36,270 ethnic Germans (*Volksdeutsche*) from territories which lay outside the envisaged Greater German Reich (Anon. 1995: 6). Given that until 1944 Silesia was spared air raids almost 450,000 of the 850,000 people relocated from western and central Germany in order to escape the raids had been moved to this relatively safe part of the Reich, primarily to Lower as opposed to Upper Silesia (Siebel-Achenbach 1994: 23). These frequent and non-supervised population shifts do not allow any exact or reliable estimate of the size and structure of the Upper Silesian population prior to the end of the war.

The relative security of Silesia ceased with the destruction of the *Heersgruppe Mitte* (Army Group Centre), and the invasion of Normandy in 1944. The Soviet armies reached the river Vistula at the turn of June and July 1944. The first Allied bombing raid in Upper Silesia took place on 7 July 1944 (Siebel-Achenbach 1994: 29). By the autumn of 1944 the fear evoked by the Red Army's excesses, combined with misinformation on the part of the Reich authorities, led to the first signs of mass panic on the part of the German population (Wiskemann 1956: 90).

Yet only small sections of the Upper Silesian population had a chance to flee or to be evacuated before the rapidly advancing Red Army, i.e. 20–50 per cent of the rural populace, together with elements of the urban populace from the areas east of the river Oder (Lis 1993: 19). The refugees sought shelter mainly in the *Sudetenland* and in the Protectorate of Bohemia and Moravia (De Zayas 1988:

77). On 12 January 1945 the Soviet armies launched their winter offensive. On 19 January Soviet soldiers burst into Upper Silesia near Herby and Kreuzburg (Siebel-Achenbach 1994: 58). By the end of January almost all the Upper Silesian basin was in Soviet hands. Subsequently, using the Oder bridgeheads in Krappitz and near Cosel, the Red Army commenced the offensive which resulted in the speedy seizure of the rest of Upper Silesia by 26 March.

This offensive had been preceded in November and December 1944 by a wide-scale indoctrination action which incited the Red Army soldiers to perpetrate indiscriminate massacres of and bloody revenge against the Germans (De Zayas 1988: 65). Rape, arson, pillage and murder occurred sporadically after the troops had crossed the wartime borders of the enlarged Reich. The incidence of all these phenomena, however, sky-rocketed when the Red Army reached Germany's pre-war border.[2] Yet the wrongdoings were partially curbed by the widespread though incorrect belief that as far westward as the Oder, Silesia was populated largely by Poles or Polish-speaking people.

When the Soviet occupation of the industrial part of Upper Silesia stabilised in February 1945, what was probably the biggest forced population deportation of all the Reich provinces commenced. Soldiers and civilians alike were transported in unheated freight trains or marched in sub-zero temperatures into the Soviet Union's heartlands. It is estimated that 65,000 were deported in this way to Soviet forced labour/concentration camps (Cholewa 1993). About 50–75 per cent of the Upper Silesian prisoners perished from hunger and disease in these camps (Honka 1993), and many were only freed as late as 1955 (Dobrosielski 1995: 62). Besides those who were deported to the Soviet Union, the Soviet occupation authorities imprisoned several tens of thousands of other Upper Silesians in the so-called DP (Displaced Persons) camps which were in effect forced labour camps (Lis 1993: 20).

The deportations of workers and the despatch of property to the Soviet Union clashed with the interests of the Polish communists, who during the talks between the delegation of the Polish National Council (KRN) and the Soviet government in Moscow, between 14 and 21 February 1945, had obtained the 'right' to establish the Polish administration in the occupied territories of the *Reich* up to the Oder and Neisse line, on the basis of the Soviet–PKWN Agreement of 27 July 1944 (Kowalski 1983: 37). The Polish authorities strove to prevent deportations and the Soviet approved and executed pillage from as early as February 1945, but only at the end of April 1945 did the deportations stop, although the planned seizure of property continued until October 1945 (Lis 1993: 25, 144).

The Polish communists employed the tactics of *faits accomplis* and as early as 5 February 1945 announced that Poland was entitled to administer the *Deutsche Ostgebiete* east of the Oder–Neisse Line (Marzian 1953: 28–9). Earlier, on 28 January, Polish citizens of German descent from the territory of pre-war Poland were deprived of their Polish citizenship, and subsequently expropriated and interned in labour camps (Wiskemann 1956: 96–7). On 29 January the Silesian *Voivod* (regional governor) General Aleksander Zawadzki approved the seizure of all German farms and agricultural machinery (Misztal 1990: 58). A decree of 3 March stated that the property of all Germans living in the 'regained territories' was to be expropriated (Urban 1994: 54). On the same day it was announced that the 'recovered territories' would be populated with Polish settlers from the overpopulated and devastated areas of central Poland. On 5 March the confiscation of the property of Upper Silesians who had fled before the advancing Red Army commenced. On 14 March the Upper Silesian *Voivodeship* was formed and the Dabrowa industrial basin was included inside its boundaries. On 18 March the Oppeln Regency, already controlled by the Polish administration, was added to the *Voivodeship*. The inclusion of the ethnically and historically differentiated territory of the Dabrowa basin inside this 'new Silesian *Voivodeship*' increased the percentage of Poles in the statistics in line with the official policy of creating an ethnically homogenous Polish state.

National verification

The Polish communists proclaimed that indigenous Upper Silesians were in fact Poles. Warsaw was vitally interested in retaining as many of them as possible in order to 'prove' the innate Polishness of the pre-war Oppeln Regency and to justify its incorporation into post-1945 Poland (Strauchold 1995: 8). Moreover, the communists did not want to depopulate the region in its entirety, and thereby further damage the prospects for economic recovery, especially as the number of Poles being re-settled from former eastern Poland was lower than the number of Germans being expelled westward. In addition, the incomers were invariably ill-educated peasants unused to urban industrial environments. Thus, in Cracow on 22 January 1945 General Zawadzki, the Polish Provisional Government's Plenipotentiary for Opole Silesia, oversaw the establishment of the Civic Committee of the Opole Silesia Poles (KOPSO) which was to work out a programme of 'national verification'. KOPSO members arrived in Katowice at the beginning of February. They decided that in order to protect those Upper Silesians who considered themselves or were considered to be Polish from Soviet deportations, it was necessary to 'rid' Upper Silesia and especially Opole Silesia of its 'German element', i.e. of those Upper Silesians who considered themselves or were considered to be German. In a memorandum of 12 February submitted to General Zawadzki, KOPSO proposed the division of the Opole Silesia population into four categories: I Persons with full Polish consciousness; II Persons who know Polish but do not feel any connection with the Polish nation; III Persons who do not know Polish but have Polish surnames or are of Polish ancestry; and IV 'Indubitable Germans'. This division emulated the *Deutsche Volksliste* (DVL) which had been used by the Nazis in its attempts to create an ethnically pure Upper Silesian population during the Second World War (Lis 1993: 25–7). National verification began on 22 March 1945 with a decree of the Silesian *Voivod* (Lis 1993: 28–9). There was no central supervision over the verification process, and as a result appalling irregularities occurred.

The pinnacle of the post-war ethnic cleansing in Upper Silesia was marked by the Potsdam Conference of 17 July–2 August 1945, where the *Deutsche*

Ostgebiete were *de facto* transferred to Poland. On the basis of Article XIII of the Potsdam Agreement Warsaw was allowed to expel the German population of the territories in an 'orderly and humane manner' (De Zayas 1988: 87–8).

The time-consuming process of national verification delayed expulsions from Upper Silesia, which took place later than those from Lower Silesia which was overwhelmingly populated by 'indubitable Germans' whom the Polish communists understandably did not want to nationally verify (Calka 1993: 3). Some Upper Silesians succeeded in returning despite the fortified border controls. If their houses and farms had been already taken over by new Polish owners they were often sent to labour camps which the Soviet administration had earlier transferred to its Polish counterpart. It is estimated that there were twenty-three such camps in Upper Silesia. When the high rates of mortality in these camps are taken into account, some can be considered to have been genuine concentration camps. In the years 1945–7, around 40,000 persons perished in them, including women and children (Anon. 1943). To these camps, the authorities dispatched negatively verified, i.e. Germans or 'inconvenient' Upper Silesians (Nowak 1991: 79), who remained there awaiting either revision of their negative verification, primary verification or expulsion. Moreover, Warsaw did not fully comply with the decisions of the Potsdam Conference and continued to expel certain numbers of Upper Silesians to the Soviet occupation zone until 23 December 1945 when the Soviet Union sealed the border on the Oder–Neisse Line. The subsequent legal mass expulsion lasted intermittently from February 1946 to the end of 1947 (Siebel-Achenbach 1994: 129). The expellees were customarily robbed and intimidated. They were not furnished with appropriate food rations guaranteed by the Potsdam Agreement and were transported in freight trains largely unprepared for humans, which resulted in numerous deaths *en route* (Siebel-Achenbach 1994: 147). The expulsion was revived for a short time during the summer of 1948 (Calka 1993: 5), and afterward the process was continued under the labels of individual departures for Germany, and then under the Family Link Action in the years 1950 and 1951 (Wiskemann 1956: 120).

Prior to this, on 6 April 1946, MZO minister Wladyslaw Gomulka had issued a decree on the procedure of affirming Polish nationality of persons residing in the former *Deutsche Ostgebiete* (Strauchold 1995: 9) which in turn was reflected in the 28 April 1946 Act on Polish Citizenship for the Autochthonous Population (i.e. original inhabitants of the territories who could be potentially Polonised) (Dobrosielski 1995: 61). This act approved the 'broad' approach to the national verification and in many cases was used to stop the expulsion of Upper Silesians. Subsequently, this made it almost impossible for them to leave for Germany.

After the completion of the national verification in 1950, 806,800 Upper Silesians remained in Upper Silesia together with 591,300 Polish expellees and settlers who had moved into the region (Lis 1993: 31), whereas in Germany 800,000 Upper Silesian expellees were now resident (Reichling 1986: 61). The post-war ethnic cleansing in Upper Silesia was in a sense over, but continued in a low-scale manner through individual departures for West Germany until the fall of communism in 1989.

Communism and post-communism

The post-war ethnic cleansing in Upper Silesia had more wide-ranging repercussions for West German–Polish relations than the wider process of expelling Germans from the overall *Deutsche Ostgebiete*. This is due to the fact that 50 per cent of Upper Silesians stayed in their homeland despite the intensified emigration at the turn of the 1980s and 1990s. They still make up nearly a third of the Opole *Voivodehip*'s population of 1.03 million, and as such account for 90 per cent of Poland's German minority. Upper Silesian Germans residing in the *Voivodeship*'s eastern half, on the western border of the Katowice *Voivodeship* and in the north-western corner of the Czestochowa *Voivodeship*, actually constitute the largest compact German group outside the German-speaking states. The situation is starkly different in the other areas of the former *Deutsche Ostgebiete*, where almost all German inhabitants were expelled by the beginning of the 1950s with the exception of a few small pockets.

During the 1950s the German-speaking population of Poland were subjected to a systematic programme of Polonisation. The German language was banned in schools, the media, and religious services, personal and place names were Slavicised, and even the use of German in the home was actively discouraged. What complicated matters for the authorities was that their categorisation of these 'Germans' did not exactly reflect reality. In Upper Silesia especially, where for generations the inhabitants had been subject to both Germanic and Polish influences, blood, language, tradition and culture had been intermingled to create an identity that was uniquely Silesian. These people were not simply German-speaking Slavs, there were many who spoke both Polish and German, and also the indigenous *Wasserpolnisch* dialects. The Polish nationalists faced a formidable task in attempting to unscramble the tangle of ethnic strands that were woven into the identity of an Upper Silesian.

It is difficult to determine how successful this internal homogenisation process would have been in isolation. What facilitated matters for the communist regime, however, was the West German policy towards the German minorities in the east. Wary of pre-war parallels being drawn, the Federal Republic nevertheless undertook to help as many individuals as possible escape the cultural oppression of the regimes of Eastern Europe. Despite Polish claims that in the early 1950s there were only approximately 200,000 Germans living in Germany, an estimated 1,372,188 Germans left Poland between 1950 and 1990 (Marshall 1992: 131). The definition of a German in this context was remarkably generous, the key issue being that of German stock. As far as the application of Article 116 of the Basic Law was concerned, there were two essential elements. The first was the subjective declaration for Germany (*deutsches Volkstum*) in one's *Heimat*, and second, objective attributes to confirm this declaration, such as extraction, language, upbringing and culture. The problem for many Silesians was that they had already declared themselves for their *Heimat* itself. The concept of *Heimat* has been suggested as the most important factor influencing the decision of the Upper Silesians to stay in Poland. This identification with a region is a combination of attachment to place of birth, a sense of collective origins, and an adherence to a particular set of cultural orientations and customs. It could also be argued that this strong attachment to their *Heimat* on the part of the Germans of Upper Silesia was accentuated during the period of German rule. Their Catholicism, Slavic origins and dialect served to distinguish them from other members of the *deutsches Volkstum*. Not even recognised as full Germans under the Nazi *Volksliste*, they were ridiculed for their parochialism by other German speakers. Hence their attachment to their *Heimat* was in many cases stronger than their sense of belonging to the *Reich*.

In the case of Upper Silesia, this area constitutes the largest remaining settlement of Germans in contemporary Poland. Again, estimates vary depending upon the definitions applied, but as many as 600,000 German speakers remain, primarily in the *Voivodships* of Katowice, Opole and Czestochowa. The possible reasons for the existence of this minority have been outlined, but how have they maintained their identity in the presence of the assimilating pressures of the centre? The answer would seem to lie in the fact that their self-perception has undergone a change during the communist period. The virulent nationalism of the PZPR has instilled a greater sense of German identity in a people whose previous national affiliations had been somewhat weak.[3] It has also been suggested that the Soviet system itself was instrumental in fostering national identity. In the context of an all-encompassing, non-reflexive and 'alien' institutional state, the importance of traditionally based cultures is heightened. Essentially, this is because within such a state there are a lack of any other viable options.

The process has also been assisted by the exiles' associations (*Landsmannschaften*) in West Germany. Deemed irredeemably revisionist and revanchist by some, in recent years the practical activities of these groups have centred primarily on maintaining links between themselves and those that remain in Poland.[4] Nevertheless, they continue to fuel Polish fears, particularly when Chancellor Helmut Kohl addressed the Association of Silesian Exiles in 1985, and received tumultuous applause for his statement that the existing Polish–German borders had no legal basis.

It was the border issue that finally forced the Polish government to recognise its German minority. Negotiations between Poland and the FRG had resulted in a Polish 'Information' on the subject in 1970. This allowed the exodus of some 38,500 Germans in return for various economic benefits (Garton Ash 1993: 237). However, it was not until the fall of the communists that any real progress was made. The signing of the Polish–German Treaty on Good-Neighbourliness and Friendly Cooperation on 17 June 1991 finally linked the Polish recognition of the German minority with German ratification of the Polish–German border (recognised under the first Polish–German Treaty of 14 November 1990). Under the terms of the Treaty, members of the German minority have the right to determine their national affiliation according to conscience. The rights of the minority have not only been agreed on the basis of Polish–German relations, but have also been tied to European standards (Gwiazda 1994: 75). Further improvements in the situation of Poland's Germans are not without influence on the situation of other minorities in the country, which in turn elevates the level of minority rights protection to the standards outlined by the Council of Europe. Significantly, the European Union has declared that states which do not meet these standards cannot accede to full membership. Having been invited to membership negotiations in 1998, Poland seems to have passed this part of the test. Many problems pertaining to the rights of Poland's Germans and of Upper Silesian expellees in Germany in relation to their property confiscated in the former *Deutsche Ostgebiete* and dual citizenship, among others, still remain to be solved, but the qualitative improvement in the situation is indicated by the impressive decline in emigration to Germany (to a few hundred per annum) and the recently won freedom of ethnic and national expression.

Prior to any international recognition, the German minority had already set about organising itself. The Social and Cultural Society of the German Minority was registered in the Silesian city of Katowice in January 1990. There is now a proliferation of these organisations within Poland, with a combined membership of over 300,000. The primary task of these societies is to protect and promote the German language and culture in Poland. To this end they publish and distribute German literature, newspapers and magazines. In Upper Silesia they have been particularly successful in gaining access to the broadcast media, and in establishing community centres. The use of the German language in religious services has also been pursued to varying success. Unsurprisingly, the tiny number of Protestants are in a worse position relative to the Catholics. This disparity is not only confined to religious issues, but also extends to employment and educational opportunities.[5]

The Germans have also mobilised themselves politically. The German Minority Organisation (GMO), under the leadership of Heinrich Kroll, contested the 1991, 1993 and 1997 national elections. They are currently represented by two deputies in the *Sejm*, thanks largely to the electoral law that exempts national minorities from the 5 per cent national threshold. The party also has representatives in sixty-three councils in Upper Silesia. With a majority in twenty-eight of those councils there are at present fifteen German-speaking mayors (Bartodziej 1993).

As a recognised minority, the Germans of Upper Silesia now enjoy a certain amount of protection and the financial support of the Federal German government. However, problems still remain. It is becoming obvious that knowledge of the German language is in decline. Banned for decades under the communists, the younger generation tend to have little or no knowledge of German. Many parents, realising the educational disadvantage to their children, even switched to speaking Polish at home. The teaching of German is now allowed in schools, but usually only for two hours a week as a foreign language. In Upper Silesia, where it is supposedly the language of instruction, three hours a week is the norm, although bilingual schools are beginning to appear here and elsewhere in Poland. There is also a lack of German teachers in many areas. In some schools the Russian teachers were simply informed that they were now to teach German instead.[6] However, this is one area where the GMO hopes to achieve some success. German language instruction should be available to school classes where at least seven children want to learn the language. This relatively low threshold has given the German community hope that the issue will be one of resources rather than demand.

However, the presence of a demographic imbalance within the German communities is a further threat to their existence. The policy of the Federal Republic of Germany towards its nationals in other states has altered since the end of the Cold War. Instead of encouraging them to migrate to Germany, the emphasis is now on encouraging the communities to remain where they are. However, due to the increased freedom of travel from the late 1980s, the final great dash for German citizenship consisted mainly of individuals born after 1945. The relatively small size of the younger generation of Germans in Upper Silesia can only facilitate the progressive intermingling and assimilation of the Germans with the majority Polish population. Moreover, the youth organisations of the German minority maintain a separate organisational structure from the wider cultural societies, and the difference is not only technical. Whereas the older generation perceive themselves to be ethnically German, those of the younger generation who have not already migrated to Germany seem perfectly content to identify themselves as Upper Silesians, albeit of German cultural orientation.

At national level, the electoral fortunes of the GMO have been mixed. In the first fully democratic elections held in Poland since the war in 1991, they secured seven seats in the *Sejm* and one in the Senate. Subsequently, changes to the electoral system before the 1993 election saw their representation drop to four parliamentary deputies and one senator. Regardless of the fall in the number of seats, the GMO could still credit itself with a certain amount of success, and even harboured hopes of entering a governmental coalition at some stage, being natural allies of the Freedom Union (UW). Unfortunately, these early successes led to a certain amount of complacency concerning the strength and durability of their electoral support. Whilst the party attempted to gain support outside its natural constituency, amongst members of the other national minorities in Poland, it seems apparent that membership of the cultural societies and the benefits gained did not necessarily preclude ethnic Germans from supporting Polish political parties, given the growing consolidation of the right and increasing dissatisfaction with the Democratic Left Alliance (SLD) in 1997. Consequently, the 1997 election resulted in only two parliamentary seats for the GMO and the loss of the single senate seat. Whether the political wing can recover from this position will rely largely upon their ability to improve their organisational structure, and their ability to mobilise support within a competitive electoral environment.

Operating through the *Landsmannschaften* and the German Embassy in

Warsaw, the cultural associations have been fairly successful in bringing pressure to bear upon Bonn in order to alleviate their position. The response of the Federal government has been to insist that the organisations throughout Poland co-ordinate their requests rather than receive individual support. Needless to say, many ethnic Germans are unhappy with the level of support and with the seeming disinterest of the wider German public. In part, this is because of the years of isolation experienced by the Germans in Poland. An isolation that has resulted in very different orientations and attitudes, particularly with regard to ideas about nation and state, and *Volk* and *Heimat*, amongst the older generation.[7]

The policies of the Bonn government are now directed towards not upsetting the accord it has established with Warsaw. Consequently, the aid it is supplying to the German-inhabited areas of Poland is intended to assist both the Polish and German communities. In this way it is hoped that the two communities will approach some sort of understanding and reconciliation, and ultimately act as a bridge between the two nations. However, certain activities by the German minority have endangered this process. In November 1992, war memorials commemorating the German dead of both World Wars appeared in Silesia. Whether due to arrogance or insensitivity, the memorials caused widespread anger throughout Poland, and even elicited a warning from President Walesa himself.

What must be kept in mind is the ethnic make-up of Upper Silesia. Even if both declared Germans and Silesians are considered together, they are still smaller in number than the Polish population. The Bonn government is aware of the possible tensions between the communities and has endeavoured to tailor its policies accordingly. Any activities of the minorities must, therefore, be directed towards attaining some sort of consensus within the region, rather than fuelling misguided perceptions of the German minority as a 'fifth column' in Polish society

Conclusion

The recently won freedom of national expression for minorities in Poland marks a new era in the conflict between 'objective' and 'subjective' applications of ethnicity. Objective application, or the mandatory attribution of ethnicity, involves the imposition of an ethnic identity upon an individual by the authorities, in line with so-called 'objective' criteria. Subjective application, on the other hand, is the self-declared membership of an ethnic or national group, by an individual, which should be free from any verification (Stourzh 1991: 77).

It is fair to say that since the latter part of the twentieth century, the inhabitants of Upper Silesia have been subjected to the mandatory attribution of ethnicity. This policy is dangerous even when the governing regime has benevolent intentions, and there are a range of institutional safeguards for minority rights. Such an arrangement existed in part during the inter-war period in Poland, but was subverted by the Nationalists after Pilsudski's death in 1935. The horrific ends to which the Nazis utilised objective classification need no further elaboration. Subsequently, the Polish communists instituted their own version in the building of an ethnically homogeneous state. Thus, a large number of people in Silesia and other areas of Poland found themselves being categorised and re-categorised with scant attention paid to how they viewed themselves, unless of course it coincided with the agenda of the governing power of the time.

Following the war most Upper Silesians who remained in their homeland remained entrenched in their traditional identity marked by more or less full bilingualism in the Upper Silesian dialects of Polish and German. Atrocities, *szaber*, mass expulsion, the influx of eastern Poles, verification, discrimination, forced Polonisation and the destruction of their traditional way of life convinced indigenous Upper Silesians that culturally and ethnically they were closer to Germans than to Poles. They could not express this stance openly on pain of reprisals, but 'voted with their feet' by emigrating to West Germany. Subsequently, the average Polish neighbour came to equate them with Germans. The authorities tacitly agreed with this opinion and barred Upper Silesians from any meaningful careers available in the 'People's Republic', fearing their disloyalty. As second-class citizens, Upper Silesians wrapped themselves in the haven of their traditions largely impervious to various events of significance to Poles. After the fall of communism it seems that most Upper Silesians declared themselves as Germans (although members of their families living in Germany were often perceived as Poles), and Warsaw officially recognised the existence of a German minority as part of its endeavour to create good relations with Bonn, which in turn became the main advocate of Poland's accession to West European structures.

At last Upper Silesians may openly identify themselves as Upper Silesians, Germans or Poles without fear of reprisals or persecution. Admittedly, there are still areas in which relations between German and Polish communities could be improved. However, it is apparent that for the first time since the advent of nationalism in this Germanic/Slavic borderland the cycle of violence has been broken. Recent studies have shown that relations between German and Pole in Upper Silesia are viewed more positively within the region than media reports would have the wider Polish public believe (Ostrowska and Bochenska 1996: 112). The turbulent history of the region has at various times seen either Slav or German in the ascendancy. Both groups have suffered at one time or another at the hands of the other. If there is to be any meaningful reconciliation, then it is in the borderlands where it will be tested on a daily basis.

Notes

1 This work was supported by the Research Support Scheme of the Polish Higher Education Support Programme, grant no.: 11/1995.
2 The assaults against the civilian population were designed not only to unleash a vast refugee movement that would impede the military operations of the Wehrmacht, but

also as an introduction to and the first stage of the subsequent ethnic cleansing (Hubatsch *et al.* 1967: 313).

3 Interview with Dr Dieter Bingen of the *Bundesinstitut für ostwissenschaftliche und internationale Studien*, 8 November 1994.

4 Interview with Tadeusz Willan, Chairman of Mazurian Society, in Allenstein, 14 November 1994.

5 Interview with Tadeusz Willan, Chairman of Mazurian Society, in Allenstein, 14 November 1994.

6 Interview with Heinrich Kroll, Member of the Polish *Sejm*, 16 November 1994.

7 Interview with Dr Dieter Bingen of the *Bundesinstitut für ostwissenschaftliche und internationale Studien*, 8 November 1994.

References

Anon. (1943) *The German New Order in Poland*, London: Hutchinson.

—— (1995) *Deutscher Ostdienst* 'Zwangsumsiedlung Deutscher im Krieg', 2: 6.

Bartodziej, G. (1993) *Die Lage der deutschen Minderheit in Polen*.

Brehmer, D. (1994) 'Mniejszosc niemiecka w Polsce jako most miedzy narodami', in F. Pflüger and W. Lipscher (eds) *O problemach polsko-niemieckiego sasiedztwa*, Warszawa: ISP PAN.

Calka, M. (1993) 'Exodus: Wysiedlenia ludnosci niemieckiej z Polski po II wojnie swiatowej', *Mowia Wieki* 2: 3–10.

Cholewa, K. (1993) 'Slazy w ruskich lagrach', *Gazeta Gornoslaska/Oberschlesische Zeitung* 20: 1, 4.

Davies, N. (1981) *God's Playground: A History of Poland, Vol. II: 1795 to the Present*, Oxford: Clarendon Press.

De Zayas, A.M. (1988) *Nemesis at Potsdam: the Expulsions of the Germans from the East*, Lincoln, NB and London: University of Nebraska Press.

Dobrosielski, M. (1995) 'Mniejszosc niemiecka w Polsce – historia i wspolczesnosc', in Anon. (ed.) *Mniejszosc niemiecka w Polsce – historia i terazniejszosc*, Warsaw: Elipsa.

Garton Ash, T. (1993) *In Europe's Name*, London: Jonathan Cape.

Gwiazda, A. (1994) 'National Minorities in Poland and the Baltic States', *International Relations* 12 (1): 75.

Harper, J.L. and Parlin, A. (1990) *The Polish Question During World War II*, Washington DC: The Johns Hopkins Foreign Policy Institute.

Honka, N. (1993) 'Ofiary nieludzkiej ziemi', *Gazeta Gornoslaska/Oberschlesische Zeitung* 23.

Hubatsch, W. *et al.* (eds) (1967) *The German Question*, New York: Herder Book Center.

Karwat, K. (1995) 'Slaskie drogi: Wojna zaczela sie po wyzwoleniu', *Dziennik Zachodni* 111: 8.

Kowalski, Z. (1983) *Powrot Slaska Opolskiego do Polski*, Opole: Instytut Slaski.

Lis, M. (1993) *Ludnosc rodzima na Slasku Opolskim po II wojnie swiatowej (1945–1993)*, Opole: Instytut Slaski.

Magocsi, P.R. (1993) *Historical Atlas of East Central Europe*, Seattle, WA and London: University of Washington Press.

Marshall, B. (1992) 'Migration into Germany: Asylum Seekers and Ethnic Germans', *German Politics* 1 (1): 131

Marzian, H. (1953) *Zeittafel und Dokumente zur Oder–Neisse Linie, 1939–1952/53*, Kitzingen: Holzner Verlag.

Misztal, J. (1990) *Weryfikacja narodowosciowa na ziemiach odzyskanych*, Opole: Instytut Slaski.

Nowak, E. (1991) *Cien Lambinowic: Proba rekonstrukcji dziejow obozu pracy w Lambinowicach 1945–1956*, Opole: Centralne Muzeum Jencow Wojennych w Lambinowicach-Opolu.

Ostrowska, A. and Bochenska, D. (1996) 'Ethnic Stereotypes among Polish and German Silesians', in H. Grad, A. Blanco and J. Georgas (eds) *Key Issues in Cross-Cultural Psychology*, Lisse, Netherlands: Swets & Zeitlinger.

Reichling, G. (1986) *Die deutsche Vertriebenen in Zahlen. Teil 1: Umsiedler, Verschleppte, Vertriebene, Aussiedler 1940–1985*, Bonn: Kulturstiftung der deutschen Vertriebenen.

Siebel-Achenbach, S. (1994) *Lower Silesia from Nazi Germany to Communist Poland, 1942–1949*, New York: St Martin's Press.

Stourzh, G. (1991) 'Problems of Conflict Resolution in a Multi-ethnic State', in U. Ra'anan *et al.* (eds) *State and Nation in Multi-ethnic Societies*, Manchester: Manchester University Press.

Strauchold, G. (1995) 'II wojna swiatowa i jej konsekwencje. Weryfikacja i (re)polonizacja', *Hoffnung* 18/19: 8–9.

Urban, T. (1994) *Deutsche in Polen: Geschichte und Gegenwart einer Minderheit*, Munich: C.H. Beck.

Wiskemann, E. (1956) *Germany's Neighbours: Problems Relating to the Oder–Neisse Line and the Czech Frontier Regions*, London: Oxford University Press.

15 Official and academic discourse on ethnicity and nationalism in post-Soviet Russia

Alexander Ossipov

The process of democratisation in the USSR and the newly independent states has turned out to be indivisible from the rapid rise of ethnic movements and inter-ethnic conflict. Thus issues related to ethnicity and nationalism have been some of the core elements of public debates on society's current and future development before as well as after the break-up of the Soviet Union. Post-Soviet Russia is not only facing the problems of disintegrative political trends, but is also passing through an intensive quest for new forms of non-Soviet legitimisation of the state. This quest provokes discussions on this new country's ethnopolitical configuration including basic principles concerning the relations between the state and minorities. It is not an easy task to grasp the logic of action in this process without first analysing the corresponding normative vocabulary, ways of perception and evaluation used by the political elite.

Discourse in the policy-making community

The term 'discourse on ethnic issues' in contemporary Russia is appropriate to the problem under consideration, since the ongoing debates encompass more than the area of ethnicity and nationalism, and embrace a wider circle of mutually bound subjects, views and concepts. These are expressed by an enormous variety of agents, including journalists, spokesmen from political parties and movements, academics and officials. Nevertheless, one is able to select a less or more distinct community of persons which regularly produces and expresses views and evaluations in the area, who are recognised as experts by the official power or who come out as spokesmen of the legislative power and government in the corresponding area and who serve the state power at the federal as well as regional levels in the field or analysis and ideology. It should be stressed beforehand that it is not possible to separate official and academic discourses or even to draw a distinct boundary between them for several reasons. First, a number of academics or persons coming from the academic community play a significant role in decision-making. Second, many politicians try to represent themselves as specialists in social science disciplines. Third, generally speaking social sciences were traditionally used in the Soviet society as a tool for legitimisation of political goals, and this tradition has not changed since the USSR's dissolution.

The continuation of this state of affairs is further explained by reference to some structural peculiarities of the Russian government. The federal power structure itself is a large-scale consumer of ideas and plans related to the nationalities issue. Organisational ties between the state power and science are traditional since universities and dozens of research institutes within the Academy of Sciences are run by the state. Major political decisions are approved by the president and his close advisors, and the relevant information and draft decrees are obtained from different sources and competitive groups. This scenario not only secures a stable demand for the production of ideas, but also engenders complete irresponsibility on the part of its producers (Tishkov 1997b: 498).

There are a number of official bodies in charge of nationalities policies within the legislative as well as executive branches of power. The highest legislative body – until October 1993 the Supreme Soviet, formed by the Congress of People's Deputies, and since December 1993 the State Duma – both developed structures directly responsible for ethnic problems and for preparation of draft laws on the corresponding subjects. Within the federal government there is also an office which has to pursue nationalities policies. In 1992–3 it had the rank of State Committee and in 1993 it became a Ministry, with, as of the end of 1997, the title of Ministry of Federative Relations and Nationalities Affairs (MINNATS). Formally it is responsible for the production of analyses, the early warning and prevention of conflicts, the preparation of draft laws, the implementation of the federal programmes and maintaining co-ordination between the different arms of the executive power which operate within the field.

Both the State Duma and MINNATS recruit persons from academic institutes or with an academic background as experts or staff members, and many people use this channel to enter the political/governmental realm. Some scholars such as the ethnologist Galina Starovoitova, the philosopher Ramazan Abdulatipov, and the historian Vladimir Lysenko became MPs in 1990. Abdulatipov managed to attract a number of scholars from the Academy of Sciences to serve as experts on the relevant parliamentary committees. More or less this same group of persons was later co-opted on to the working groups of the Committees of the State Duma. In 1992 Valery Tishkov, the director of the Institute of Ethnology and Anthropology, became head of the State Committee/Ministry of Nationalities Affairs, with Lysenko becoming his deputy.

A considerable number of the MINNATS employees are former members of academic institutes. One in fact could speak of a continuous circulation of key persons within the sphere of nationalities policies, in other words, a specific *nomenklatura* has been created. Many politicians have an academic background and vice-versa. Some retired politicians have headed independent research institutes, and others such as Abdulatipov have shifted from the legislative to the executive branch. In addition, some academics do not participate directly in the expert groups, but do have regular access to the mass media and can influence the situation by publishing their opinions and comments. However, it would not be completely true to say that individuals who originate from the academic community dominate among views-makers in the area. The most influential section is represented by former Communist Party functionaries or specialists in 'ideological disciplines'. For example, since 1995, the Minister of Nationalities affairs has been Vyacheslav Mihailov, who during the Gorbachev period was a head of a department of the Central Committee of the Communist Party of the Soviet Union (CPSU). Vladimir Zorin, the chairman of the Committee on Nationalities Affairs in the State Duma, was also a party functionary. Correspondingly, this group of people and their cohorts have attempted to institutionalise themselves and their ideas within the new Russia.

The Soviet theoretical heritage

Debate on the nationalities question in the Soviet period was a core element of Marxist–Leninist theory. Officially sanctioned theoretical thinking on nationalities affairs in Soviet society was not only a product of fixed ideological dogmas, but also the result of rather changeable interpretations of the previous theoretical baggage, which were dependent on specific political conjunctures (Connor 1984; Szporluk 1988: 214–24; Young 1992). The logic of the Soviet theoretical thinking in the field of the nationalities question was affected by Marxist positivism, materialism and evolutionism. Until the 1960s, the approaches towards nations and nationalism in the Soviet Union were monopolised by the 'ideological disciplines' of 'Marxist–Leninist philosophy', the 'History of the Communist Party'. Nations and pre-national formations ('peoples' and 'tribes') were perceived as changeable and developing; linguistically and culturally distinct collectivities with a unity of social and economic life.

From the 1960s the so-called 'theory of *ethnos*' was elaborated within the Institute of Ethnography (Bromley and Kozlov 1989; Kozlov 1988). This approach basically meant the continuation of the same 'organistic' paradigm with some additions to the old Marxist–Leninist 'theory of nation'. 'Ethnies' have been described as historically developing social entities with specific cultural features. In other words, cultural boundaries are equated with ethnic boundaries and cultures are interpreted as products of the historical experiences of the given ethnic collectivities, which in turn represent social systems with an inherent capability of adaptation. It is important to stress that an ethnic group is described as, first, a sort of social organism, and second, as a 'collective personality', possessing interests, freedom of will, and endowed with the ability for reflection and rational decision-making.

Theoretical research in the field of the nationalities question was strongly influenced by the needs of the ruling party. After 1917 the Bolsheviks faced a contradictory task: they sought to establish the Soviet Union as a natural model for the revolutionary movements of other countries, whilst simultaneously creating a centralised state subject to a given totalitarian ideology which would secure the allegiance of peripheral ethnic elites. As a result, the Communist Party elaborated rather a complicated and contradictory approach. On the one hand, it supported 'national liberation' or 'anti-imperialist' movements and the principle of 'national self-determination' was enshrined as an integral part of the

Soviet ideological arsenal. On the other, the Bolsheviks proclaimed themselves rigid enemies of nationalism and fighters for 'internationalism', peaceful coexistence and mutual co-operation between peoples as dictated by the needs of the socialist revolution. Notions of ethnic nationalism were incorporated into official ideology and the state maintained 'institutionalised multi-nationality' (Brubaker 1994: 49).

In Soviet parlance, personal ethnic self-classification was a concept quite separate from that of citizenship, and in many cases determined a person's social opportunities and status. The major ethnic communities ('nations' and 'peoples') possessed officially recognised territories. In addition, the state pursued policies of nation-building in the social and cultural spheres towards the peripheral nationalities (Simon 1991; Tishkov 1997a: 24–35, 228–33). The communists did not perceive the country as a bourgeois nation-state (Brubaker 1994: 51–2). Yet, they strove for societal integration by different political, social and cultural means (including the population's total subjugation to a given ideology) and those attempts were reflected by the slogans of 'proletarian internationalism', 'peoples' friendship', 'the flourishing and rapprochement of nations' (Young 1992: 86–7). In general, the communists in Russia till the early 1990s simultaneously remained consumers of ethnonationalist vocabulary and fierce enemies of nationalism, evaluating class loyalty and class goals as superior to ethnonational ones.

The heritage of perestroika

It would not be true to say that democratisation in the Soviet Union provoked public debate on ethnic issues. On the contrary, discussions about the nationalities question began at least eighteen months before the first essential shifts towards democratisation were initiated by the leaders of the CPSU. After mass inter-ethnic disturbances in Alma-Ata, the capital of Kazakhstan, in December 1986, the Plenum of the Central Committee of the CPSU decided in January 1987 to pay much more attention to inter-ethnic relations and to work for their 'further perfection'. A number of dedicated offices were formed within the party apparatus and within the Academy of Sciences a series of specialised publications, discussions and conferences commenced immediately after the January Plenum (Cheshko 1996: 241–5). Demonstrations of the Crimean Tatars in 1987, growing political unrest in the Baltic Republics and the (ethnic) movement in Armenia and Nagorno-Karabakh demanding the transfer of the latter from Azerbaijan to the former demonstrated the relevance of ethnic issues to the actual life of the country.

During the following two years the number of people involved in such discussions grew rapidly, especially after the first competitive elections of 1989 and the appearance of independent political movements. A number of new agents – high officials of the Communist Party and of the republican authorities, ideologists of the new movements, and members of the academic institutes – joined the debate and started to set the agenda. It should be stressed that the main protagonists shared a common language and in general common slogans. Party ideologists viewed inter-ethnic relations as relations between territories (national-territorial units) or between the central government and the 'ethnic territories', with the same approach being evident among their opponents. Except in a few cases, neither communist nor oppositional ideologists challenged the official status quo. Official spokesmen advocated the 'improvement' or 'perfection' of the 'national-state system', implying decentralisation, whilst the opposition's proposals differed from official ones only in terms of nuance. Official theorists, intellectuals from the academic community, together with ethnic activists did not hesitate in claiming that ethnic groups were the only possible bearers of sovereignty. Discussions either came out in favour of 'renewing the socialist federation', or for establishing confederative ties. The demand for full independence arrived later. All factions tried to rationalise ethnic movements and their goals: the conservatives treated them either as an embodiment of the peoples' interests, needs and desires or, when they were thought to be too radical, as examples of 'false consciousness'.

Since defenders and opponents of the old regime used the same notions and vocabulary (even implying in many cases different things) and since the ideological initiative belonged to the radicals, the latter turned out to be the winners in the propaganda battlefield and managed to impose their vision of the problems and the perspective on the active part of the society. The discourse and the main slogans gradually became more radical, and the views of 'peripheral' ethno-nationalists came to be accepted by the radical opposition (the democrats) in Russia itself together with demands for 'ethnic revival', 'dismantling of the empire', 'national self-determination', 'equality of nations', and 'freedom of national development'. The old system was criticised as an overcentralised 'empire', which suppressed its 'peoples'. The goals of 'self-determination' and decentralisation were equated with democracy and 'progressive reforms'. Freedom of political expression and political action for the 'suppressed' ethnic groups and ethnic movements were perceived as a necessary prerequisite of democratisation, market economy and creation of a 'civilised' society (Robinson 1995; Smith 1995).

The political context

In June 1990 the Supreme Soviet of the Russian Soviet Federative Socialist Republic (RSFSR) became an alternative centre of power within the Soviet Union. Previously the RSFSR had possessed only a decorative statehood, and the new Russian authorities tried not only to breathe life into its political institutions, but rather sought to use the wider process of administrative reform in order to restrict the power of the central government. Boris Yeltsin, newly elected chairman of the Russian Supreme Soviet and since, June 1991, as President of RSFSR, the main opponent to Gorbachev's Presidency and the CPSU, exploited the slogans of 'democratic' and 'anti-totalitarian' reforms. The new national movements, which came out for full independence of their union republics, combined with the new *nomenklatura* of the republican Communist parties, which wanted more freedom and more concessions from Moscow, became the natural allies of Yeltsin's team. Yeltsin supported the Soviet Union's decentralisation, but refrained from exploiting Russian nationalism and restricted himself to calling for 'sovereignty' of the RSFSR within the Soviet Union. The central government tried to utilise minorities within each of the union republics as a counterbalance to the authorities of the union republics and as a tool of pressure against them, since the representatives of minorities with the union republics opposed plans to grant them sovereignty. In 1990–1, the government of the USSR put forward the idea of either inviting the representatives of republican minority nations also to be signatories of the new Union Treaty or of raising the status of their administrative units to that of constituent union republics.

Yeltsin's team, unlike the authorities of the other constituent republics, decided to make deep concessions in the political and economic spheres. Promising the leaders of the Russian autonomous republics 'as much sovereignty as they can carry' within the Russian Federation, he became a hostage of this slogan and had to face mounting demands not only from the ethnic periphery, but also from within the entire RSFSR. Bargaining between Moscow and the 'ethnic' republics within Russia, when combined with the continual stream of concessions from the central government, had rather a chaotic character until the signing of the Federative Treaty in March 1992.

Non-governmental ethnic movements in general have not been a real threat to the central authorities. In general, they have always been at the periphery of political struggles both in the centre and in the regions. The space for such struggles has been limited by the administrative structures. Under the terms of the treaty, republics and autonomous districts, together with other administrative units, provinces and federal cities, were proclaimed to be 'subjects of the federation', and became signatories of the Federative Treaty. In so doing they raised their status and real political capacities to the level close to that possessed by the republics themselves. Yeltsin's manoeuvres in general were successful as far as that republican leaders avoided direct control of the central government and that separatist trends in Tatarstan were neutralised by the signing of a separate treaty in 1994. However, one side-effect was that the federal authorities became dependent upon regional governors. Hence the issues of federalism including its 'ethnic component' became crucial elements of state-building and the debates around it irrespective of what the governments wanted (Teague 1994). Proponents of the democratic reforms in Russia clearly understood the weakness of their social base and the risk of social unrest, connected with the transition to a market economy. Yet they also viewed the Communist Party, the old repressive machine, and even the 'conservative minded' part of the population as a real threat to 'reforms' and to the regime. Thus, the activity of Yeltsin, his team and supporters was geared to producing irreversible changes. This explains the reformists' radicalism, why they did not pay much attention to the social cost of their actions and why they did not neglect any potential allies including peripheral nationalists or regional *nomenklatura*. Only later, after adoption of the new constitution and elections to the new parliament in 1993, was this logic substituted for consolidation of the new ruling elite, concern about political stability and search for a wider formula of legitimacy.

Nationalities policies

In Russia, traditionally expressed views on ethnic issues mostly concern ethnic management, i.e. they are devoted to analysing and designing possible forms of inter-ethnic group co-existence. Nationalities policies are viewed as a specific branch of official management, which is to be conceptualised, brought into a system and subjected to the certain requirements of science. These views are not challenged and are shared by almost all of the experts, even those who support competing views in some particular areas. It is not surprising that the government's undertakings in the field of minority protection or conflict prevention have been criticised for a lack of a single 'scientific and systematic' concept of nationalities policies (Abdulatipov 1995: 4–11; Lysenko 1995: 84–5; Tishkov 1997b: 275–6). It is also quite natural that when they got the opportunity, persons who pretended to be the ideologists of a given area concentrated efforts on elaboration of a draft official concept. Thus after being appointed a minister of nationalities affairs in 1992, the initial step of Tishkov was to form a working group for the preparation of government policy (Tishkov 1997b: 149–53). Whilst being occupied as the chairman of the chamber of the Supreme Soviet, Tishkov's rival, Abdulatipov, who also pretended to be the chief ideologist in nationalities affairs, engaged in similar activity. Neither produced anything that was ever implemented, but in 1994 one such proposal was adopted as a 'Programme' by the non-governmental 'Senezhskii Forum', which in turn was supported by the Cabinet of Ministers (*Gosudarstvennaia* 1994). Finally, the official concept of nationalities policies was elaborated by the MINNATS and adopted by the government in May 1996 and signed by the President that June.

Despite the fact that these and other proposals were prepared by rival groups which to a certain extent pretend to follow different approaches, they had much in common. Nationalities policies are not primarily equated with the prevention of discrimination and protection of minorities. Rather, they are perceived as a complicated system of strategies, measures and instruments in the fields of administrative management, legislation, party politics, economics and social, demographic, cultural and educational undertakings. Neither is this policy aimed at minor or non-dominant groups, its object is usually defined as all the 'peoples' of the country. The basic goals include 'creating conditions for the peoples' 'free development' and 'regulation of inter-ethnic relations'. Russians as the major and numerically dominant community in the three cases have been selected as the object of special measures in the spheres of economic, demographic and cultural policies. Mind you, the authors did not explain what the differences between plain economic, social and cultural policies, on the one hand, and policies towards a people, which constituted 82 per cent of the entire population, on the other, actually are.

The most interesting element of such proposals is their ideas and goals, which are declared but not defined. The first goal to be mentioned is that of non-discrimination. The slogans of the citizens' equality before the law and ban of any restrictions on ethnic grounds abound, but this problem is absolutely absent in subsequent publications and discussions. There have been no attempts to analyse what actually constitutes discrimination against minorities or 'non-titular' populations or to elaborate and put forward any preventive mechanisms. Similar evaluations could be made over such notions as 'peoples' development', 'peoples' rights', 'prevention of ethnic conflicts', and 'national (vernacular) education'. Ethnic conflicts, being one of the most popular subjects for the Russian scholars and politicians, are usually perceived as clashes between ethnic collectivities and as such are explained by a positivist approach which asserts they have been caused by some 'objective' political and social contradictions. The role of the state and of 'symbolic elites' in constructing conflicting agencies is usually neglected and there are few concrete suggestions on how to confront ethnic tension. The creation of 'national schools' is usually cited as a core element of 'ethnic revival' and re-creation of ethnic cultures, but it was not made clear until recently who should be responsible for organising and main-taining such schools. The same approach was demonstrated in some draft laws related to the nationalities affairs. There is a rather radical rhetoric based on the notions of 'group rights' and 'group development' combined with generous promises to create the conditions for nationalities' 'free development'. Yet there is an almost complete lack of any definite tools and mechanisms of implementa-tion for such policies. Thus the mainstream conceptual approach could be characterised as one of romantic social engineering based on the perception of society as a community of ethnic communities and of these ethnic groups as 'social organisms'.

Federalism, national statehood and self-determination

Since the advent of Gorbachev's perestroika, federalism has been regarded by reformist intellectuals as an integral and inescapable element in the development of Russian democracy. For Russia, federalism is a basic principle of the self-organisation of public life, the lack of which signifies the failure of all the changes and reforms (Lysenko 1995: 243). Federalism is often equated with decentralisation and democratic rule, with all other forms of administrative-political organisation consequently becoming equated with centralised authoritarianism (Abdulatipov 1995; *Gosudarstvennaia* 1994). The Russian reformists have also proclaimed their desire to establish a 'real' fedaralism as opposed to the 'decorative' federalism of the Soviet period and actually have done much to raise the status of the regions and widen the scope of their authority. In Soviet times, official ideology regarded federalism as a tool for 'resolving' the nationalities question. By the late 1980s, national statehood, i.e.

the idea that an administrative unit belonged to a certain 'titular' ethnic group, had become widely accepted. Moreover, some persons looked to the 'revival' of ethnic nations as a basic and prerequisite for the creation of civil society (Starovoitova 1989: 91).

It is also significant that federalism is still perceived as a form of 'peoples' self-determination' and 'sovereignty'. Already in the late 1980s there were some voices which criticised the notion of an ethnic 'ownership' of a given territory as a principle contradictory to the goals of non-discrimination and democracy. These views, combined with a generally negative attitude towards ethnonation-alism, have become very popular and even predominant among the mainstream scholars and politicians, especially following the escalation of ethnic conflicts within the former Soviet Union as well as the growth of separatist trends in Russia itself. Criticism of 'ethnic federalism' in favour of the idea of a unitary state and of abolishing the 'national' administrative units, as promoted by the Russian nationalist opposition, has also played a considerable role. Nevertheless, this turn has not led to any radical practical prescriptions against ethnic feder-alism. Those who support 'ethnic statehood' within a federal state as a mode of 'peoples' sovereignty', and those who express negative attitudes towards the status of a given ethnic group within the power structure, together oppose any suggestion of changing the status of any of the constituent elements of Russia, or any encroachment upon their 'ethnic' character. In both cases the arguments are similar. Each group claims that any attempt to revise the status quo will necessarily provoke ethnic unrest and strong opposition from both the republican authorities and the grassroots and thereby threaten the federation's territorial integrity. These debates also display the basic similarity of the two groups. Opponents of 'ethnic federalism' insist on the civic equality of each of the republics' inhabitants irrespective of ethnic identity and on recognising the whole population of a given territory as citizens. Leaders of the republics usually make the same claim, and republican constitutions proclaim priority of their 'titular' groups only indirectly and contain anti-discriminatory reservations. Yet, neither the federal constitution nor the constitutions of the republics within Russia determine the republics as 'national states' of their 'titular' groups.

The protected groups: minorities, repressed peoples, indigenous populations

Although Russia has signed international conventions concerning the prevention of discrimination and protection of non-dominant groups, these issues either occupy a marginal position in the debates or acquire a specific interpretation. In accordance with the Soviet terminological tradition, the meaning of 'national minority' turns out to be close to 'non-indigenous', 'non-native' or 'migrant' population. A draft law on minorities' rights was elaborated within the Council of Nationalities of Russia's Supreme Soviet in 1992–3, but was not adopted prior to the parliament's dissolution. The draft's basic approach and terminology were inherited by the working group of the Committee on Nationalities Affairs within the State Duma, but still had not been adopted as of the end of 1997. The bill incorporates the notion of 'ethnic entities' and the legislative body and its experts perceive minorities as 'non-indigenous' groups, a part of an ethnos living outside its 'historical boundaries'. Significantly, this approach has not been challenged during the debates. 'Titular' as well as 'indigenous small-in-number' peoples are not considered to constitute a minority irrespective of their share of the population.

The draft has some interesting features. It declares the rights of persons belonging to a minority to be equal to those enjoyed by all other citizens of Russia. It forbids all forms of discrimination, and proclaims ethnic self-identification as a matter of free personal choice. It also utilises the language of group rights and proclaims a number of rights to be simultaneously individual and collective. These include the right to preserve a given identity and language, the right to found public organisations and mass media, participation in political life, reception of information, and the right to maintain ties with compatriots abroad. However, it could be argued that the politicians and academic circles who drafted the bill paid much more attention to other problems, which may also be considered as issues related to minorities.

Since 1989 the mass media together with some radical political activists have raised the problems of those communities who were subject to deportation *en masse* during the Stalin period, and have demanded their rehabilitation. In April 1991 'The Law on Rehabilitation of the Repressed Peoples' was adopted by the Supreme Soviet of the RSFSR. The law was based on two concepts: compensation for a historical injustice and group rights. The law envisaged 'rehabilitation' not only of individual members of 'repressed' communities, but also of the entire 'repressed people' as a group. It recognised the right of restoration of the predeportational 'national-territorial units' and their boundaries, but did not offer any mechanisms for the realisation of such schemes. According to the opinion of many observers, the law itself was a strong provocative factor leading to the Ingush–Ossetian conflict of 1992. Articles 3 and 6 which deal with 'territorial rehabilitation' were suspended by presidential decree, but the issue remained on the agenda. In October 1992 the Commonwealth of Independent States (CIS) signed the Bishkek agreement on the restoration of the rights of the deported peoples and ethnic groups, and since 1997 the State Duma has been preparing the draft law on rehabilitation concerning particular peoples, such as the Balkars and Volga Germans. One of the most discussed ideas has been that of 'national-cultural autonomy', or the extra-territorial autonomy of ethnic groups. This idea is descended from the project put forward at the beginning of the twentieth century by Karl Renner and later criticised and banned by the Bolsheviks. In post-Soviet Russia it is usually perceived as either a substitution for ethnoterritorial division or as a supplement to the existing system.

Returning to the draft law, we find that finally, after two years of debate, the State Duma adopted The Law on National-Cultural Autonomy in June 1996. The principle that any particular group had a monopoly of representation for any given ethnic group was rejected. According to the Law, the government may grant funds for educational and cultural activities in the frame of special federal and regional programmes, and distribute some part of them via 'national-cultural autonomies'. Despite these changes, the problem of identity was still on the agenda at the end of 1997. This was because although the relevant federal laws had been adopted by the Supreme Soviet in 1993, and three times between 1995 and 1997 by the State Duma, they have not been signed by the president on the grounds they contradicted the constitution. The ongoing debates demonstrate two approaches. One, shared by a number of scholars mostly from the Academy of Sciences, is based on determining 'indigenous peoples' as groups maintaining a traditional mode of living based on hunting, gathering and reindeer breeding and on emphasising two crucial problems of indigenous groups: the nature of local self-government and the ultimate ownership of territories and their natural resources. The other approach is based on the notion of the 'small-in-number' ethnic groups which live on their 'own' territories and which may be distinguished by the fact that they are fewer than fifty thousand in number. This concept does not employ such criteria as the traditional mode of life, but does envisage preferential treatment, aimed at creating conditions for a group's 'free development'. What is significant is that both approaches use the language of 'group rights' or 'rights of a group'. Within the Supreme Soviet and as well as later within the State Duma the second approach has been absolutely dominant, although some elements of the first have been employed in the legislation of some regions.

What is the Russian/Rossian nation?

This issue is being discussed more frequently in geopolitical and philosophical contexts, rather than in connection with the country's ethnic composition. The overwhelming majority of scholars or official spokesmen do not challenge the term 'multinational people' inserted into the Constitution and Declaration of the Sovereignty of the RSFSR, i.e. Russia's citizens are perceived as a combination of ethnonations. Subsequently the authorities need an integrative formula and since 1991 have used the word 'Rossians' which signifies membership of Russian society irrespective of ethnicity. Simultaneously Russian ethnic nationalism as a systematic or even clearly expressed concept is barely articulated within the state's ideological mainstream. Yet some of its constituent elements such as preferential treatment of the Orthodox Church appear more and more frequently. There have been several initiatives aimed at promoting an inclusive nationalism, based on the idea of a nation as a community bound by a single culture, but not by ethnicity or ethnic origin, but so far these undertakings have remained marginal.

One of the few persons to try and promote the notion of a civic multi-ethnic nation has been Tishkov. He develops the idea of nation-building to include multicultural policies and the cultivation of a common civic identity. One can hardly say that his views are completely free of the Soviet heritage, which he himself criticises. Double-thinking may be predetermined, however, by the positivist language shared by the academic community. Tishkov opposes the approaches based on the 'organistic' paradigm and on the perception of ethnic groups as a species of 'super individual'. Yet at the same time he uses terms such as the 'interests of ethnic groups or peoples' and talks about the groups' representation in the state apparatus, economy or mass media (Tishkov 1997a: 272–93). Coming out in favour of the creation of a civic nation within the federation, he admits that the republics have and must continue to have 'specific characters' and 'ethnocultural features', as determined by their 'titular' groups (Tishkov 1997b: 275–300).

His main problem has turned out to be a lack of adequate opponents. He was criticised both by the admirers of the Soviet theory and by the spokesmen of the regional leaders. The arguments used by both categories are similar: the cultivation of a civic identity will be rejected by 'the peoples'. They argue that such a notion signifies an unjustified rupture with well-established political and academic tradition, a super-ethnic identity is a threat to their 'sovereignty' and 'rights', a first step towards assimilationist policies, and that the application of the idea of a civic nation to Russia undermines the possibility of protecting 'compatriots abroad' (Bagramov 1994). It is possible to conclude that discussions of this type, as well as the numeric weakness of the proponents of Russian civic nationhood, reflect the lack of demand within the state apparatus and society for such ideas. Besides, some trends within contemporary politics reduce the scope for any form of civic nationalism. The goal of supporting 'compatriots abroad' is of particular importance here. When referring to the Russian diaspora, the authorities and mass media use terms such as 'compatriots abroad', 'the Russian-speaking population' and 'ethnic Rossians abroad'. Though the last has been used in some governmental documents and is a working term within MINNATS, its meaning has never been made clear. Yet it can be interpreted as referring to persons belonging to ethnic groups which have their historic 'homelands' within Russia. Despite the ideas of those such as Tishkov, it is fair to say that the main trend still represents the creation of new identities on the basis of ethnonationalist thought and language.

Conclusion

In general the new regime in Russia faces problems similar to those which the Bolsheviks faced after 1917. During any period of radical transition the ruling elite has to find a new formula of state legitimacy, curb disruptive and centrifugal tendencies, and integrate society within the political system. The differences lie in the fact that contemporary Russia has a different ethnic composition to that of the Soviet Union, and that the Russian government treats grassroots initiatives in politics and economics as an inalienable element of the new system. Nevertheless, one can justifiably refer to a continuation of previous traditions in the area of nationalities policies rather than there having been a radical break. As before, the discourse on ethnic issues contains two main elements: radical rhetoric, based on the notion of 'group rights' and 'group development', and the social engineering approach, which views society as being comprised of ethnic communities. Ideological discourse of this type can be very flexible. The government can use three 'ideal' strategies of 'nationalities policies': 'ethnocratic', where a certain ethno-nation is proclaimed the subject of a particular state, but in which a system of minority protection also exists; 'liberal', or 'civic', where ethnicity is considered to be of secondary importance; and 'pluralist', where society and state are constituted as a community of institutionalised ethnic groups.

The Russian authorities and affiliated academic experts manage to combine elements of all three approaches in their rhetoric. However, practice constitutes a separate domain, and the question of to what extent the given discourse can affect official political practice requires a special analysis. The supposition that the given discourse determines to a significant extent virtual reality for the officials dealing with nationalities policies seems valid. One may assume that in Russia during the period of transition, discourse and social perception of that type have led to the following practical policies: a strategy of concessions in cases of ethnically motivated political pressure and unequal treatment of different ethnic groups under the guise of administrative expediency in cases when officials do not face pressure of this type. Examples in favour of this assumption can be found in the current Russian reality.

References

Abdulatipov, R. (1995) *O federativnoi i natsionalnoi politike Rossiyskogo gosudarstva*, unpublished discussion paper.

Bagramov, E. (1994) 'Natsiya kak sograzhdanstvo?', *Nezavisimaya Gazeta*, 15 March.

Bromley, Y. and Kozlov, V. (1989) 'The Theory of Ethnos and Ethnic Processes in Soviet Social Sciences', *Comparative Studies in Society and History* 31 (3): 425–38.

Brubaker, R. (1994) 'Nationhood and the National Question in the Soviet Union and post-Soviet Eurasia: an Instititionalist Account', *Theory and Society* 23 (1): 47–78.

Cheshko, S.V. (1996) *Raspad Sovetskogo Soyuza*, Moscow: IEA RAN.

Connor, W. (1984) *The National Question in Marxist–Leninist Theory and Strategy*, Princeton, NJ: Princeton University Press.

Drobizheva, L. *et al.* (1996) *Demokratizatsiya i obrazy natsionalisma v Rossiyskoi Federatsii 90-h godov*, Moscow: Mysl.

Gosudarstvennaia programma natsionalnogo vozrozhdeniya i mezhnatsionalnogo sotrudnichestva narodov Rossii (1994) Moscow: Senezhskii Forum.

Kozlov, V. (1988) *The Peoples of the Soviet Union*, Bloomington, IN: Indiana University Press.

Lysenko, V. (1995) *Ot Tatarstana do Chechni (stanovleniye novogo rossiiskogo federalisma)*, Moscow: Institut Sovremennoi Politiki.

Millar, J. and Wolchik, S. (eds) (1994) *The Social Legacy of Communism*, Cambridge: Cambridge University Press.

Robinson, N. (1995) *Ideology and the Collapse of the Soviet System: a Critical History of Soviet Ideological Discourse*, Aldershot: Edward Elgar.

Simon, G. (1991) *Nationalism and Policy Towards the Nationalities in the Soviet Union*, Boulder, CO: Westview Press.

Smith, G. (ed.) (1995) *Nationality and Ethnic Relations in the Post-Soviet States*, Cambridge: Cambridge University Press.

Starovoitova, G. (1989) 'E pluribus unum', in *V chelovecheskom izmerenii. Perestroika: glasnost, demokratiya, sotsialism*, Moscow: Progress.

Szporluk, R. (1988) *Communism and Nationalism*, New York: Oxford University Press.

Teague, E. (1994) 'Center–Periphery Relations in the Russian Federation', in R. Szporluk (ed.) *National Identity and Ethnicity in Russia and the New States of Eurasia*, London: M.E. Sharpe.

Tishkov, V. (1997a) *Ethnicity, Nationalism and Conflict in and after the Soviet Union. The Mind Aflame*, London: Sage.

—— (1997b) *Ocherki teorii i politiki etnichnosti v Rossii*, Moscow: Russkii mir.

Young, M.C. (1992) 'The National and Colonial Question and Marxism: a View From the South', in A.J. Motyl (ed.) *Thinking Theoretically about Soviet Nationalities. History and Comparison in the Study of the USSR*, New York: Columbia University Press.

16 The Tajik minority in contemporary Uzbekistani politics

Stuart Horsman

Introduction

Beyond charges of ancient and intractable ethnic enmities, Uzbek chauvinism and Tajik irredentism, discussions on Tajik–Uzbek relations in Uzbekistan have been limited. This chapter aims to examine this neglected area of post-Soviet inter-ethnic relations in its political context. The principal focus will be upon the activities of the Samarkand Movement, comprising the Social-Cultural Association (SCA) and National Cultural Centre of Tajiks and Tajik-speaking Peoples (NCC), and its relationship with the government of President Islam Karimov.

An historical section will illustrate the manner in which physical and cultural assimilation have been a continuum in Uzbekistan's politics, influencing the contemporary situation. The latter section will place the Tajik minority in the broader context of the republic's politics. It will examine how democratisation and cultural pluralism have been discredited and suppressed by the government's application of an ideology of stability. It will analyse the manner in which ethnic collective aspirations have been used as a pretext for maintaining authoritarianism; and demonstrate that this discrimination is symptomatic of wider undemocratic trends within the republic.

Tajik–Uzbek relations in historical context

Two core historical processes are crucial in understanding contemporary Tajik–Uzbek relations. These are 'the millennium-long relationship between the Turkic and Iranian peoples in Central Asia and…Soviet nationalities policies' (Subtelny 1994: 45).

The origins of the Tajiks are to be found in the ancient Iranian sedentary civilisations of Transoxiania, the inter-riverine lands between the Amu Darya and Syr Darya. The term *Tajik* was initially applied by Turkic groups to all Central Asian sedentary Muslims. By the eleventh century, the term was used to define the region's Iranian population (Subtelny 1994: 48). They are the region's only non-Turkic indigenous group. The Tajiks are predominately Sunni Muslims and Farsi-speakers, although the Pamirs of the former Gorno-Badakhshan autonomous oblast are Ismaili, with a distinct eastern Iranian language (Porkhomovsky 1994: 11).

In turn the Uzbeks emerged from the Turco-Mongolian nomads that migrated across the Kipchak Steppe, in the fifteenth century (Olcott 1987: 7). Their language is Turkic of the Chagatai group, with other Turkic and some Persian influences. Increased Uzbek involvement in Transoxianian affairs resulted in their conquest of the region between 1507 and 1510. Their arrival introduced a 'critical mass of Turkic and Turkicised Mongolian nomads into Central Asia', resulting in the *Turkification* of the Iranian population (Subtelny 1994: 50). Traditional Uzbek nomadic political and social structures were ill-suited to administrating sedentary territories. Local customs were therefore adopted. This process aided the evolution of an Uzbek identity distinct from the nomadic core, with greater centralised authority, acceptance of sedentarism, and adherence to Islam.

Within the khanates of Bukhara, Khorezm and Kok, ethnicity was amorphous and of little significance to those unaffected by politics, although Uzbek identity was closely associated to political authority (Manz 1994: 48). The two groups' territorial and cultural proximity, and the political and demographic supremacy of the Uzbeks, appeared to be resulting in an irreversible assimilation of the Tajiks and the growth of a hybrid Uzbek–Tajik population, known as *Sarts* (Carlisle 1995: 75).

The Soviet period

Soviet control accentuated the Uzbeks' and later Uzbekistan's regional stature. The most significant influence for this process was the Soviet national-territorial delimitation of Tajik–Uzbek lands between 1924 and 1929. An Uzbek Soviet Socialist Republic (Uzbek SSR) was created in 1925. Subordinate to it was a Tajik Autonomous Soviet Socialist Republic until 1929, when the latter also received Union republic status. The Uzbek SSR received the bulk of the Bukharan SSR, the Samarkand region of former Soviet Turkestan, the Tashkent area, and most of the Fergana Valley and Khiva. The most controversial aspects for Tajik–Uzbek relations was the allocation of the Tajik-dominated cities of Samarkand and Bukhara to the Uzbek SSR; and the Khojent region, with a large Uzbek population, to Tajikistan in 1929 (Carlisle 1994: 117).

A required accompaniment of delimitation was the creation of national groups to be identified with the territories. 'Nation-building from above' transformed previously amorphous ethnic groups into titular nations with eponymous republics, official histories and distinct languages (Carlisle 1995: 73). This was problematic for three reasons. First, national histories had to be invented where none existed, and within the confines of Marxist–Leninist historiography at that. Second, there was in fact a shared Tajik–Uzbek heritage. Third, in order to get the new message across, the trappings of a modern administration, bureaucracy and education system had also to be created. The Uzbeks' nomadic heritage meant they were difficult with regard to incorporation into Marxist nationalities and economic theories, and was downplayed by Soviet historians (Subtelny 1994: 52–3). The Uzbeks became direct descendants of the ancient Transoxianian civilisations and, with the Tajiks, were disingenuously referred to as 'two great branches emerging from the trunk of a single [Indo-European] tree' (*Istoriia Uzbekskoi SSR* 1967: 501 and *Istoriia tadzhikskogo naroda* 1963: 3 in Subtelny 1994: 48). This re-interpretation of their cultural and geographical roots and signifi-cance has proved advantageous for Uzbekistan's contemporary elites' construction of an inclusive and expansive Uzbek national concept.

Uzbek regional political dominance increased within the limits that Moscow allowed. Early Soviet directives criticising 'Great Power chauvinism' within the region may have been directed towards Uzbek high-handedness towards the Uzbek SSR's minorities, especially the Tajiks and Turkmens, as well as local Russian behaviour (Carlisle 1994: 120). Despite such criticisms, Tashkent's rela-tionship with Moscow was beneficial for both elites and helped legitimate Uzbekistan's dominance *vis-à-vis* Tajikistan. Tashkent supported the political elevation of the Khojent clan of the Leninabad oblast, who in return recognised Uzbekistan's regional position and 'made Tajikistan faithfully follow Uzbekistan's policies' (Gretsky 1995: 223).

The establishment of a separate Tajik SSR, with the creation of associated cultural and political structures, 'undercut the ongoing assimilation process' (Carlisle 1994: 117). Outside of their eponymous republic this counterpoise was limited. Tajiks remaining in Uzbek SSR complained of official assimilatory pres-sures (Haghayeghi 1995: 195). That the problem of shifting identities was not unknown in Soviet East Asia can be witnessed by statements such as: '(w)e are Tajiks but our children will be Uzbeks' (Rakhimov 1989: 119 in Subtelny 1994: 54). Duress was placed on them to register as Uzbeks in the 1926 census, which was reportedly falsified. The official number of Tajiks in Uzbekistan dramati-cally declined. The recorded Tajik population of Samarkand fell from 95 per cent in 1872 to 10 per cent in 1926, whilst Uzbeks increased from below 1 per cent to 41 per cent (Zarubin 1926 and 1975 in Schoeberlein-Engel 1996: 18).

Soviet internal passports, introduced in 1932, further affirmed assimilatory trends. By the end of the 1930s, the nationality entered had to correspond with that of one's parents (Kozlov 1988: 36). Soviet authors have since accepted that this ran counter to the usual understanding of nationality as a social rather than biological category (Kozlov 1975: 256 in Kozlov 1988: 34).

The exploration of these historical trends has enabled us to illustrate two major points of contemporary relevance. These are the close and amorphous Tajik–Uzbek interaction and the incremental regional pre-eminence of the Uzbeks. Their relationship has been fashioned by shared cultural, linguistic and territorial experiences, and complicated by Soviet manipulation of these. With independence, these legacies are subject to re-definition and incorporation by new political demands.

The Tajik community in contemporary Uzbekistan

The most decisive element in the appearance of Uzbekistan as an independent state was of course the failed reform programme of Mikhail Gorbachev. However, despite promises and rhetoric, major political reforms have not followed in the wake of independence, which was achieved on 31 August 1991. Karimov, previously the First Secretary of the Central Committee of the Communist Party of Uzbekistan (CPUz), became president in March 1991, and has continued to maintain a centralised system. Diverse political figures and movements from Shukurulla Mirsaidov, the former Vice President and presidential ally, to opposition groups, including Birlik and the Islamic Renaissance Party (IRP), have been subject to harassment and repression. The numerous registered parties, including the People's Democratic Party of Uzbekistan (PDPU) and Progress of the Homeland Party (*Vatan Tariqqieti*), provide a superficial sense of democracy. They are, however, government created and/or sponsored (Dailey 1996: 43). Serious political diversity is lacking. In the December 1994 Oli Majlis (Supreme Assembly) elections, all the deputies elected were members of either the PDPU or the Progress of the Homeland Party (*Narodnoye slovo* 1995; *Interfax* 1995). All ethnic- and religious-based parties have been banned because, the government argues, their objectives are divisive and destabilising (*OMRI* 1997). Registration for other parties has been difficult or impossible. Birlik and Erk were unable to re-register in 1993 because they lacked headquarters. Previously, the authorities had confiscated the former's base, and declared the latter's a fire hazard and closed it (Bichel 1997: 6).

The government has periodically indicated it is planning political liberalisation. These improvements have been limited and directed more to the international community than domestic activists. Human Rights Watch/Helsinki (HRW/H), whilst recognising a political 'thaw', notes that there has been 'no tangible improvement in [the regime's] abusive practices' and 'pervasive, repressive tactics used to maintain strict control on all citizens' (HRW/H 1996a: 2). It is unclear whether this change demonstrates the government's commitment to cautious reform or whether it is engaging in the contemporary international aid-rights discourse as a means of gaining international political and economic assistance. It is in this political climate that Tajik cultural and political demands have been articulated.

Post-Soviet Tajik demography and identity

Before discussing the minority–government relationship, it is expedient to examine two key and interconnected background factors: demography and identity. Inconsistencies between territorial and group boundaries have resulted in the creation of ethnically heterogeneous states, with substantial Uzbek and Tajik minorities in Tajikistan and Uzbekistan respectively. The Uzbeks make up 70 per cent of Uzbekistan's population, itself the most populous state in Central Asia, and are the region's largest ethnic group with a diaspora in all four other republics (1989 Soviet census in Bremmer and Taras 1993: 555–9). Prior to the Tajik civil war, up to 25 per cent of Tajikistan's population was ethnic Uzbek.

The number of ethnic Tajiks in Uzbekistan has always been contentious. According to the 1989 Soviet census, of the 4.6 million Tajiks recorded, 933,560 resided in Uzbekistan (Gleason 1993: 388). It is argued that the Uzbek SSR figure was an underestimate due to official assimilatory practices and individual Tajiks perceiving it advantageous to assume a public Uzbek identity (Carlisle 1995: 88; Foltz 1996: 213, 215). There appears to have been no re-assessment of the Tajik population in independent Uzbekistan. Consequently the number of citizens who regard themselves as Tajiks is difficult to determine. Tajiks within and outside of the republic, Samarkand State University (SamGU) academics and international commentators suggest that there may be between six and seven million Tajiks in Uzbekistan, constituting 30 per cent of the republic's twenty-two million population, rather than the official figure of 4.7 per cent (Foltz 1996: 213; Carlisle 1995: 88). Tajik-dominated regions include the cities of Bukhara and Samarkand, the Chorvok area, parts of the Fergana Valley; Jizzakh province, Surkhan Darya and Kasha Darya (Foltz 1996: 213).

The discrepancies between the official and actual number and the Tajik community's ambiguous sense of national identification are a consequence of several factors. The historical Tajik–Uzbek relationship has blurred the distinction between the groups. The weakness of a Tajik identity is also a result of official attempts to assimilate the minority and discourage minority members from taking an interest in their Persian background. Although Articles 4 and 18 of Uzbekistan's Constitution guarantee respect of and equal right to all citizens, there are claims that Tajiks have been dissuaded from identifying themselves as Tajiks in independent Uzbekistan, as was the case in Soviet Uzbekistan, for fear of incurring official displeasure and possibly discrimination (Republic of Uzbekistan 1993; Foltz 1996: 213–15). Foltz believes that 'many Tajik-speakers sense advantages in claiming Uzbek identity and perhaps fear anti-Tajik prejudice if they don't' (1996: 215).

Equally important for this weakness and the contemporary Tajik–government scenario has been Tajikistan's recent history. The Soviet Tajik identity was a construction for disparate groups in the Tajik SSR. Cultural, political and territorial cohesion within Tajikistan are weak. Clan networks have reinforced intra-Tajik divisions. The Khojent clan dominated the republic's politics and economy throughout the Soviet period, whilst the democratic–Islamic movements which emerged in the late-Soviet period obtained the majority of their support from the under-represented Garm and Pamir regions. In other words it could be deduced from this evidence, that despite over eighty years of nation-building, there is still no widely shared perception of a shared Tajik consciousness.

Since independence, Tajikistan has been beset by political instability and conflict. The civil war rooted in unequal regional political access further accentuated intra-Tajik fractures. Regional divisions became politically divisive in the conflict. Although an agreement between the now Kulyabi-dominated government and the secular and Muslim United Tajik Opposition was concluded in December 1996, low-level violence remains endemic and local militias relatively autonomous (Pannier 1997: 97). However, the prospects for reconciliation between regional groups and the creation of a national identity, appear negligible in the near term.

The impact of the war on domestic Uzbekistani affairs is considerable. One NCC member has declared that 'the internal conflict in Tajikistan [is] the main cause of cultural problems for Uzbekistan's Tajiks' (Author's interview 6 November 1996). The Uzbekistani Tajik community has a vague notion of its nationality, to the extent that many have assumed a 'superficial Uzbek identity' (Schoeberlein-Engel 1996: 19). Tajik activists have complained about their co-national's lack of knowledge of their own heritage and the broader Persian culture. As Foltz notes, this indicates the partial success of the Soviet objective of separating the Soviet Tajiks from the broader Persian world (1996: 214–15).

The growth of Tajik activism in Uzbekistan

Glasnost allowed for a renaissance in political debate. Tashkent acknowledged past discriminatory practices, and Tajik–Uzbek issues and communal conflict were reported in the media (Roi 1991: 24–5). The establishment of the SCA in March 1989, under Uktum Bekmuhammadov, was followed by the foundation of the NCC, in 1990. The joint movement is commonly referred to as Samarkand. It is difficult to gauge the level of public support the movement commands, although according to Jamol Mirsaidov, Samarkand's co-chair, 60,000 Tajiks signed an open letter presented to Karimov in 1991 (Mirsaidov 1995: 8).[1]

Samarkand, although primarily concerned with promotion of national aspirations, is in its platform and political methods compatible to the numerous moderate nationalist movements that emerged in the glasnost period. Its core aims, educational and cultural improvements for the minority, have been accompanied by democratic objectives. The movement sought to provide

> constructive proposals about how to resolve ethnic problems and to meet the lawful demands of our ethnic group...[and] facilitate the provision of real equality of all the citizens of the Republic of Uzbekistan, regardless of their nationality, social status, position, political views or faith.
>
> (Mirsaidov 1993: 1)

The communist government, aware of the movement's increasing grassroots support, met members of Samarkand in early 1989. At this meeting three demands were listed: the ability for Tajiks to choose their nationality on official documentation; Tajik to become the republic's second language; and the freedom to undertake legally recognised educational and cultural activities (Haghayeghi 1995: 96). The movement's core objectives were expanded in a subsequent letter to the president, published in *Ovozi Tadzhik*, 17 March 1991.

These were: national education; the use of Tajik language in politics and mass communication; culture and heritage; and political and legal rights.

In terms of national education, the movement proposed a comprehensive use of Tajik language in pre-school to university education. Attempts to revive links with the broader Persian culture were to be aided by the establishment of Persian and Farsi studies at SamGU. External co-operation, which would hopefully reaffirm the republic's Tajiks' position in the wider Persian community, was sought through the training of scholars in foreign universities. Other proposed means of reviving the fortunes of Tajik scholarship and ultimately those of the whole community included an independent Tajik-language publishing house for educational material.

Linguistic demands included the greater use of Tajik in mass and specialist communications. Daily and weekly Tajik-language television programmes, joint Tajikistan–Uzbekistan programme production and transmission and a two-fold increase in Tajik-language radio broadcasting were proposed. The political reforms that the SCA–NCC's letter focused upon were the establishment of anti-discrimination practices in state employment, an institutional framework to counter ethnic discrimination and the introduction of a commission to monitor Tajik minority-related problems. The commission would provide the president with relevant information, and establish dialogue and confidence between the minority and the authorities.

Further SCA–NCC material continually stresses the constitutional demands for the recognition and equality of their culture and language in a multi-ethnic Uzbekistan, which respects and guarantees the rights of all its citizens (Mirsaidov 1993: 1). The movement supports the territorial integrity of Uzbekistan, discrediting the oft-cited charge both in Uzbekistan official and some secondary sources material of Tajik ambitions of integrating Tajik-dominated areas into Tajikistan. Mirsaidov informed the then UN secretary-general, Boutros Boutros-Ghali, that 'the national-cultural development of this ancient ethnic group on the territory of the contemporary sovereign Republic of Uzbekistan' does not require any 'revision of the Tajikistan–Uzbekistan border or the formation of a Tajik national-territorial autonomy for the age-old Tajik communities in Uzbekistan, even though all the pre-conditions for this are present' (Mirsaidov 1993: 1).

Obviously, irredentism would not be treated lightly in Uzbekistan, whose constitution declares that the frontiers and the territory of the Republic 'are inviolable and indivisible' (Art. 3). This in itself does not suggest that the movement has a covert secessionist agenda. In the brief period of open debate, 1988–91, other groups proposed serious challenges to the status quo. The People's Party of Turkestan advocated a single Central Asian state (Bichel 1997: 7–8). It is important to illustrate that radical alternatives were briefly discussed in Uzbekistan but the SCA–NCC did not advocate such programmes. This is of significance in reference to the official response towards the minority's demands.

Government responses to Tajik demands

After the brief period of governmental dialogue with the Tajik movement there has been a dramatic reversal in relations (Haghayeghi 1995: 196). It is, however, difficult to determine both the true degree of the early improvements and later retrenchments given the paucity and unreliability of much of the relevant material and the restricted nature of political debate in Uzbekistan. Authoritarianism and censorship, as well as more indirect forms of control including the reliance on patronage systems, all have contributed to this situation. The Tajik case is no exception.

The 1989–92 period saw limited improvements especially in terms of culture and education for the minority. Tajik-language education benefited during this period (Author's interviews November 1996). The expansion of Tajik-language education, including the opening of new higher education courses teaching in Tajik in Bukhara, Samarkand and Termez, has been described as the 'fruit of independence' (Author's interview 12 November 1996). According to Tojiboy Ikromov, of Tashkent Tajik Cultural Centre, approximately two hundred schools in Uzbekistan provide Tajik-language education (Author's interview 6 November 1996).

The reversal in the republic's political direction may be alluded to by the declining fortunes of Tajik-language education since 1992. Reportedly, the late-Soviet era increase in the number of Tajik-language schools has since halted. Mirsaidov has stated that there has been a substantial drop in the number of Tajik-language classes in Samarkand oblast. According to Mirsaidov, the 1996–7 academic year saw a two- to three-fold increase in the number of classes being transferred from Tajik language to Uzbek (Author's interview 18 November 1996).[2] There have also been criticisms at the lack of Tajik-language educational material, although this may be a consequence of financial constraints rather than deliberate discrimination (Mirsaidov 1995: 2).[3]

Tajik national education in Uzbekistan has been further complicated by relations between Uzbekistan and Tajikistan, and the war in the latter. Unconfirmed reports noted that numerous Tajik-language schools in Samarkand oblast were closed in July 1992 as the political situation in Tajikistan deteriorated (Nissman 1995). The war provided an ideal pretext to act against internal dissent. Entry examinations for universities are still not conducted in Tajik, although Russian is permitted (Author's interviews November 1996). Whilst the majority of the state's Tajik population is bi-lingual there is an element of discrimination, given the fact that university courses are taught in Tajik but entry to these requires knowledge of a second language, i.e. Uzbek.

Both Tajiks and government officials are keen to highlight the existence of a Tajik-language publishing house, newspapers, and television and radio services. These advances are rather superficial. The Samarkand-based publisher *Sughdion* and the Tajik-language department of *Uzbekiston* publishing house have only produced limited material (Foltz 1996: 215). Expansion of Tajik-language media, a key SCA–NCC objective, has been circumscribed and has been criticised for its brevity and failure to meet the community's educational and cultural needs (Mirsaidov 1995: 8). Censorship, endemic in independent Uzbekistan, has resulted in the publication of appeals for humanitarian aid to Tajikistan and historical treatises on good government being labelled seditious and prohibited (Mirsaidov 1995: 8). Understandably, discussion on the Tajik issue is lacking.

The Tajik civil war has also had a detrimental impact, preventing the possibility of inter-republican media and educational co-operation. The importation of books from Tajikistan has also been curtailed (Author's interview 6 November 1996). Least progress has been made in the field of political rights. The early modest advances were soon lost by the restoration of repression. By 1991, the authorities were accusing SCA–NCC of assuming political aspirations (Haghayeghi 1995: 196–7). Politics became further curtailed in the aftermath of a series of political events during 1992: the Shukurulla Mirsaidov–Karimov power struggle, demonstrations in Tashkent and Tajikistan's descent into civil war.[4]

Apprehensive at the movement's expanding popular base, the government began to move against Samarkand. The organisation fell foul of the 1993 law forcing all political movements to apply for re-registration. A pro-government Tajik association using the designation the *Tajik Cultural Association-Samarkand* was established and registered. The independent movement was thus prevented from registering, even after the Samarkand oblast court ruled against the Justice Department's decision (HRW/H 1996a: 18).

Bureaucratic harassment was accompanied by frequent gross violations of SCA–NCC activists' rights. From June 1991, leading members of the movement have been arbitrarily arrested, beaten or forced to leave Samarkand city. Bekmuhammadov has been subjected to considerable government attention. In 1991, he was initially jailed for four months (Polat 1995: 197). In December of the same year, he was involved in probably the most notorious of Uzbekistan's anti-opposition actions. Uzbekistani security service agents kidnapped Bekmuhammadov, along with Abddumannob Polat, the founder of Birlik, and another Birlik member, Takhir Bakaev, who were attending a human rights conference in Bishkek, Kygyzstan. Although Polat's argument that Bekmuhammadov and Bakaev were arrested to prevent them from reporting Polat's abduction is probably correct, the case illustrates the extent to which the regime is prepared to go in order to silence opposition figures. Bekmuhammadov, who received a ten-day jail sentence, has since been accused of being a Russian spy and emigrated (Mirsaidov 1995: 4).

Tajik activists have also been prevented from meeting with international organisations. Since 1992, the authorities have prevented Tajiks from attending the Annual World Congress of Tajiks, in Dushanbe, even though the Constitution guarantees that '(a)ny citizen...shall have the right to...free entry to and exit from [the republic] except in the events specified by law' (Article 28). A meeting between a US State Department delegation and Samarkand members resulted in the 'preventative' detention of thirty-six individuals. Mirsaidov was the only activist able to meet the delegation (HRW/H 1996a: 18).

Independent figures have also been the victims of more indirect forms of control. A common ploy is the threat of dismissal from employment. Given the republic's present economic hardships and the patronage of the social-economic life this is an effective method of stifling dissent. Several Samarkand figures, mostly academics, have been removed from their positions (Mirsaidov 1993: 2). Other reports suggest that ethnic Tajik candidates were prevented from standing in the December 1994 Oli Majilis elections, although Tajik candidates from approved and registered parties were elected (Gibova 1995: 4; Usmanov 1995 cited in *Khalq Suzi* 1995: 2).

This study's focus upon politically active Tajiks is not meant to imply that other Uzbekistani citizens, Tajik and non-Tajik, are unaffected by discrimination. It is difficult to determine the level of government and police discrimination and harassment of individual Tajiks, as reports are anecdotal.[5] Evidence suggests, however, that there is no significant communal enmity between the two groups (Novak 1994).

The harassment that Tajik activists face is no greater nor more specific than that encountered by other opponents of the regime, whether secular, Muslim, nationalist, or democratic. The government's treatment of the minority is politically motivated and indicative of the systematic abuse of power.[6] Accepting this interpretation therefore requires further discussion of the case in relation to the wider political life of the republic.

Security and stability[7]

The main thrust of Uzbekistan's authoritarianism has been 'stability at all costs'. This is justified as a temporary measure which will provide a basis for gradual political and economic reforms. Karimov has described the present system as expedient: 'during historic periods when a country gains its own statehood, the more so, during a transition period from one system to another [in order] to prevent bloodshed and confrontation and to preserve ethnic and civil accord, peace and stability' (*ITAR-TASS* 1993).

The call for stability does have an objective political rationale. Inter-ethnic violence in Osh, Kyrgyzstan, in 1989, the temporary breakdown of central authority in Namangan and Andijan and conflicts in Afghanistan and Tajikistan, all illustrate the unstable regional environment in which Tashkent has had to formulate domestic and foreign policies. Although there appears to be popular acceptance of the present political system, the government's repression is, however, arguably more an attempt by the ex-communist elite to retain personal power than provide a secure base for subsequent cautious reform (Lubin 1995: 59; Haghayeghi 1995: 134).

Neighbouring wars have serious implications for Uzbekistan's security and inter-ethnic relations. Tashkent's manipulation of these situations for domestic objectives has, however, been noted by several commentators, who question Uzbekistan's perceived fear of violence, nationalism and political Islam emanating from the Tajik conflict and its much professed role as guarantor of regional stability (Akiner 1996: 13; Clark 1993: 22; Polat 1994: 36).

Uzbekistan's involvement in the Tajik war has aided the republic's elite construction of post-Soviet nation and state identities. By associating the threat of regional instability with the events in Tajikistan, Tashkent has created a discourse of stability in which Uzbekistani pluralism, including Tajik demands, has been marginalised (Horsman forthcoming).

As Tajikistan descended into violence through 1992 and an Islamic–democratic government briefly existed in Dushanbe, Uzbekistan intervened in the conflict. Brown closely associates the removal of Rahmon Nabiev as President of Tajikistan in May 1992 with the onset of political oppression in Uzbekistan. Karimov immediately condemned the Islamic–democratic government as 'tantamount to a Muslim fundamentalist take-over', and used the situation to launch a counter-offensive on Uzbekistan's nascent pluralist political culture (Brown 1993: 3). In December 1992, an Uzbekistani-trained and -supported force had helped remove the opposition from Dushanbe (Orr 1996: 3). Since this action, Uzbekistan's involvement has been regularly reported, including air strikes on opposition camps and military assistance for Ibudollo Boimatov's uprising in January 1996 (Olcott 1996: 128; *Labyrinth* 1996: 8).

Uzbekistan has sought to portray Tajikistan's democratic and Islamic movements as radical, inherently unstable and ill-suited for contemporary Central Asia. In the Uzbekistani conservative analysis of Tajikistani events, the proliferation of political movements and demands for 'radical' political reforms are responsible for the civil war. Domestic groups were to be associated with external enemies attempting to destabilise Uzbekistan. As the war escalated, Uzbekistan's opposition movements faced increased harassment (Brown 1993: 3–4). The ability to associate Uzbekistan's Tajik community with instability in the neighbouring republic was emphasised by the regime. The 1992 crackdown on SCA–NCC was partially justified by accusations of Samarkand harbouring irredentist objectives. Official media reports frequently comment upon the potential import of violent Tajik nationalism and Islamic fundamentalism from the adjoining republic. One report claimed Tajikistani Islamic agents had attempted to ferment Tajik–Uzbek enmities in Surkhan Darya and Kasha Darya provinces (Usmanov 1994). There is, however, no evidence to suggest that Uzbekistan's Tajik community has given any assistance to the belligerents in Tajikistan, beyond humanitarian assistance (Mirsaidov 1993: 1; Rotar 1992: 7).

Had the Islamic–democratic movement been successful in Tajikistan, the Karimov regime may have been vulnerable to similar pressures. It was, therefore, in the *nomenklatura*'s interests to respond to this potential challenge at its source, Tajikistan. One international observer, sceptical of Uzbekistan's motives for intervention, has stated that 'Karimov was not too worried about the Islamic–communist conflict but he objected to the IRP being incorporated into a coalition government' (Author's interview November 1996). The IRP's presence in the Tajikistani government highlighted Karimov's greatest fear. Political Islam was, and remains, the only viable challenge to the existing government, and could not be allowed to succeed in a neighbouring state. The level of militant Tajik nationalism in Uzbekistan and its relationship with political Islam is difficult to determine and is probably exaggerated (Foltz 1996: 215). This has not prevented Tashkent attempting to gain political benefits by upgrading the issue of Uzbekistan's Tajiks from a mildly disaffected but peaceful minority to an internal subversive group linked to neighbouring violence.

One commentator has noted that, due to the success of prior assertive domestic and foreign policies, the authorities are now able to ease the level of repression, because there no longer exists any effective political opposition, at least in the open, that could benefit from the modestly improved situation (Author's interview November 1996). Birlik's membership dropped from approximately 500,000 to 1,000, with a similar decline noted by Erk (*Wall Street Journal* 1992; cited in Brown 1993: 4). HRW/H has reported that open 'peaceful political opposition within Uzbekistan [has been] virtually liquidated' (HRW/H 1996b: 5). How effective Karimov's actions have been in eliminating potential sources of opposition, and the implications the cessation of constitutional opposition has had on driving the opposition underground, are as yet unclear.

State and nation building

Accompanying the physical establishment of an independent Uzbekistan has been a re-examination of the Uzbek national identity which is far more political in character than is usually recognised. Writing on post-Soviet Uzbekistan, Schoeberlein-Engel declares that

> the most common way of establishing a state's identity is through asserting that the identity of the state represents the identity of its population....New states are keen [to] promote themselves as having a deep history and important presence in the world....The Government of Uzbekistan seems to partake of the notion that Uzbekistan can achieve the stature of a great nation if the number of Uzbeks is large and if they have a strong sense of their identity.
>
> (Schoeberlein-Engel 1996: 12)

A constant theme in the construction of this identity has been the emphasis upon authority and stability. This form of post-communist nation building seeks to combine elements of both the recent and distant past. The official revival of Timur, the fifteenth-century empire-builder and Sharaf Rashidov, the influential CPUz First Secretary 1959–83, have focused upon the benefits of authoritarianism. As Kangas notes, Timur's rehabilitation 'is no accident [for] he unified the peoples of the region [and] instilled a sense of order during a time of chaos' (Schoeberlein-Engel 1996: 26).

Tajik cultural expression within Uzbekistan has been hindered by this assertive Uzbek identity. The state-sponsored revival in Uzbek identity has caused concern amongst the republic's other nationalities and marginalised other interpretations of history. This failure to recognise the diversity of Uzbekistan's heritage, in which Persian–Tajik culture is significant, and may result in the creation of a strategic *ethnie*, suggests that 'Uzbekistan is allowing a very rich part of its heritage to remain unacknowledged and largely untapped' (Foltz 1996: 214).

This re-evaluation of history, as well as being an understandable response to Soviet historiography, has a distinct political dimension, attempting to assert the Uzbeks' historical significance. Other Central Asian nations and governments, especially the Kyrgyzs and Tajiks, have charged the Uzbeks and Uzbekistan with chauvinism. Such criticism has often noted an implicit connection between Uzbekistan's attitudes towards other Central Asian states and nations with attempts to foster Uzbek cohesion (Nissman 1995).

Conclusion

The existence of regional divisions, economic and social dislocation resulting from the collapse of the USSR, the presence of sizeable minority communities, together with the instability of neighbouring Afghanistan and Tajikistan, all present Uzbekistan with serious political challenges. These problems cannot be ignored but as this chapter has demonstrated these have been manipulated in order to legitimate the continuation of authoritarianism and discredit and check potential adversaries.

A specific Uzbekistani identity has been promoted, which emphasises stability, respect for authority and the Uzbeks' position in Central Asian cultural history and contemporary politics. A core objective of this is to confirm the regime's legitimacy and use of authoritarianism. Internal challenges to the regime, including any by Tajiks, have been stifled. Authoritarianism is portrayed as expedient in this period of transition, and political debate must therefore remain within the narrow confines of 'constructive opposition'. Politics outside of these parameters is seen as un-Uzbek, extremist and liable to result in instability and conflict. This specific interpretation of regional history and politics has denied essentially modest Tajik cultural and political aspirations.

The externally imposed politicisation of the Tajik identity in Uzbekistan may ultimately be counter-productive. Constitutional methods have failed to provide benefits for the Tajiks. The lack of political alternatives, a consequence of government actions, may lessen the possibility for future compromise between the incumbent and its rivals.

Conversely, one must acknowledge the weaknesses of the Tajik identity and at least tacit public support for authoritarianism, an understandable attitude in response to the instability in neighbouring states. It is evident that this suits Tashkent's objectives but to what extent the official linkage between non-state nationalism, democracy and instability has influenced public opinion, and in what direction, is unclear, as is the degree of any deep-seated identification within the Uzbekistani Tajik minority or Uzbekistan in general with political reform and democratisation.

Notes

1 This figure is not excessive. Birlik's membership was approximately 1 million in 1991–2 (*The Wall Street Journal* (1992); cited in Brown (1993: 4)).
2 Other material produced by Mirsaidov, however, does not substantiate these claims. See Mirsaidov (1996).
3 The financial argument may have a discriminatory aspect, with the politically weaker minority being the first to face these economic cuts.
4 See Carlisle, D. (1995) 'Geopolitics and Ethnic Problems of Uzbekistan', in Y. Roi (ed.) *Muslim Eurasia: Conflicting Legacies*, London: Frank Cass, for greater discussion on political events during this period.
5 Discrimination has also been noted in the legal system. Uzbek defendants have received more lenient sentences than non-titular defendants accused of the same crimes. In one murder case, the two Tajik defendants, Bahodir Sharipov and Sukhrob Sobirov, found guilty, were executed whilst their Uzbek co-defendants received lighter sentences. One human rights observer commenting on this case stated that 'there are strong suspicions that the difference was due to ethnicity not the level of guilt'. Police searches of Tajiks on public transport, for narcotics, are also commonly reported. (Author's correspondence with Uzbekistani citizens and representatives of international organisations.)
6 See Human Rights Watch/Helsinki (1996a) *Uzbekistan: Persistent Human Rights Violations and Prospects for Improvements*, 8 (5D), for the widespread nature of repression.
7 See Horsman, S. (forthcoming) 'Creating a Regional Role for Domestic Consumption: Uzbekistan's Involvement in the Tajik Civil War', *War Studies Journal*, for greater discussion on internal and external security issues in Uzbekistan.

References

Akiner, S. (1996) 'Conflict, Stability and Development in Central Asia', in C.J. Dick (ed.) *Instabilities in Post-Communist Europe*, Portsmouth: Carmicheal & Sweet.

Bichel, A.A. (1997) 'Political Parties in Turkestan Republics', *BITIG* 12: 6–11.

Bremmer, I. and Taras, R. (eds) (1993) *Nations and Politics in the Soviet Successor States*, Cambridge: Cambridge University Press.

Brown, B. (1993) 'Tajik Civil War Prompts Crackdown in Uzbekistan', *RFE/RL* 2 (11): 1–6.

Carlisle, D. (1994) 'Soviet Uzbekistan: State and Nation in Historical Perspective', in B.E. Manz (ed.) *Central Asia in Historical Perspective*, Boulder, CO: Westview Press.

—— (1995) 'Geopolitics and Ethnic Problems of Uzbekistan', in Y. Roi (ed.) *Muslim Eurasia: Conflicting Legacies*, London: Frank Cass.

Clark, S.L. (1993) *The Central Asian States: Defining Security Priorities and Developing Military Forces*, Alexandra: Institute for Defense Analyses.

Dailey, E. (1996) 'Uzbekistan: the Human Rights Implications of an Abuser Government's Improving Relations with the International Community', *Helsinki Monitor* 7 (2): 40–51.

Foltz, R. (1996) 'The Tajiks of Uzbekistan', *Central Asian Survey* 15 (2): 213–16.

Gibova, I. (1995) 'One Party Parliament in Uzbekistan', *Sevodnya*, 11 January; reprinted in *Current Digest of Post-Soviet Press* XLVII (2): 29.

Gleason, G. (1993) 'Uzbekistan: From Statehood to Nationhood', in I. Bremmer and R. Taras (eds) *Nations and Politics in the Soviet Successor States*, Cambridge: Cambridge University Press.

Gretsky, S. (1995) 'Civil War in Tajikistan: Causes, Development and Prospects for Peace', in R. Sagdeev and S. Eisenhower (eds) *Central Asia: Conflict, Resolution, and Change*, Chevy Chase, MD: CPSS Press.

Haghayeghi, M. (1995) *Islam and Politics in Central Asia*, Basingstoke: Macmillan.

Horsman, S. (forthcoming) 'Creating a Regional Role for Domestic Consumption: Uzbekistan's Involvement in the Tajik Civil War', *War Studies Journal.*

Human Rights Watch/Helsinki (HRW/H) (1996a) *Uzbekistan: Persistent Human Rights Violations and Prospects for Improvements* 8 (5D).

—— (1996b) *Tajikistan: Tajik Refugees in Northern Afghanistan* 8 (6D).

Interfax News Agency (1995) Moscow, 16:44 gmt, 18 January. *SWB* SU 2010 G 5–6.

Istoriia tadzhikskogo naroda (1963) Vol. 1, Moscow: Izdatel'stvo vostochnoi literatary.

Istoriia Uzbekskoi SSR (1967) Vol. 1, Tashkent: Fan.

ITAR-TASS (1993) World Service 11:31 gmt, 12 February. *SWB* SU 1616 B 4.

Kangas, R. (1996) 'Imposing Order on Uzbekistan', *Transitions* 2 (18): 26–9.

Kozlov, V.I. (1975) *Natsionalnosti SSSR: Ethnodemgraficheskij obzor*, Moscow: Statisikia.

—— (1988) *The Peoples of the Soviet Union*, London: Hutchinson.

Labyrinth (1996) 3 (1): 8.

Lubin, N. (1995) 'Islam and Ethnic Identity in Central Asia: A View From Below', in Y. Roi (ed.) *Muslim Eurasia: Conflicting Legacies*, London: Frank Cass.

Manz, B.E. (1994) 'Historical Background', in B.E. Manz (ed.) *Central Asia in Historical Perspective*, Boulder, CO: Westview Press.

Mirsaidov, J. (1993) *Open Letter to Boutros Ghali*, 2 October.

—— (1995) *Perechen' Faktov Politisheskoi Diskriminatsii Demokraticheskikh Organanizatsii Tadzhikov i ikh Aktivistov*, 26 March.

—— (1996) *Predsedateliu HRW/H Gospodinu Dzonatanu Fentonu*, 9 November.

Narodnoye slovo (1995) 20 January *SWB* SU 2010 G 5–6.

Nissman, D. (1995) 'The Ethnic Factor in Central Asia', *Prism*, Part C, 11 July.

Novak, Y. (1994) 'Mezdethicheskie Otnosheniya v Uzbekistane', *Sotsiologicheskie Issledovaniya* 4: 49–51.

Olcott, M.B. (1987) *The Kazakhs*, Stanford, CA: Hoover Institute Press, Stanford University.

—— (1996) *Central Asia's New States: Independence, Foreign Policy, and Regional Security*, Washington DC: US Institute of Peace.

OMRI Daily Digest (8 January 1997) 1 (5).

Orr, M. (1996) 'The Russian Army and the War in Tajikistan', *Conflict Studies Research Centre Paper*, K21.

Pannier, B. (1997) 'A Year of Violence', *Transitions* 3 (2): 96–7.

Polat, A. (1994) 'Political Prisoners in Uzbekistan: Five Pardoned Eight on Trial', *Central Asian Monitor* 6: 31–8.

—— (1995) 'Central Asian Security Forces Against Their Own Dissidents in Exile' in R. Sagdeev and S. Eisenhower (eds) *Central Asia: Conflict, Resolution, and Change*, Chevy Chase, MD: CPSS.

Porkhomovsky, V.V. (1994) 'Historical Origins of Interethnic Conflicts in Central Asia and Transcaucasia', in V.V. Naumkin (ed.) *Central Asia and Transcaucasia: Ethnicity and Conflict*, Westport: Greenwood Press.

Rakhimov, R.R. (1989) 'Ivan Ivanovich Zarubin (1887–1964)', *Sovetskaia ethnografia* 1: 119.

Republic of Uzbekistan (1993) *Constitution of the Republic of Uzbekistan*, Uzbekistan: Tashkent.

Roi, Y. (1991) 'Central Asian Riots and Disturbances 1989–90: Causes and Context', *Central Asian Survey* 10 (3): 21–54.

Rotar, I. (1992) 'A Mine Laid by the Kremlin Mapmakers', *Nezavisimaya gazeta*, 25 December; reprinted in *Current Digest of Post-Soviet Press* XLV (1): 7.

Samarkand (1991) 'Otkrytoe Pis'mo Prezidentu Uzbekskoi Sovetskoi Sotsialisticheskoi respubliki Karimovu, I.A. ot obshestvenno-kul'turnogo ob'edineniia (OKO) i natsional'nogo kul'turnogo tsentra tadzhikov i tadzhikoiazychnyich narodov (NKTsT) Samarkand', letter published in *Ovozi Tadzhik* 17 March, No.4: 4.

Schoeberlein-Engel, J. (1996) 'The Prospects for Uzbek National Identity', *Central Asian Monitor* 2: 12–20.

Subtelny, M.E. (1994) 'The Symbiosis of Turk and Tajik', in B.F. Manz (ed.) *Central Asia in Historical Perspective*, Boulder, CO: Westview Press.

Usmanov, L. (1994) 'Will the Islamic Factor Determine the Country's Future', *Nezavisimaya gazeta*, 6 January; reprinted in *Current Digest of Post-Soviet Press* XLV (1): 17.

—— (1995) *Radio Liberty*, 14 January; cited in *Khalq Suzi*, 2 February 1995, *SWB* SU 2225 G 6–7, 11 February.

Zarubin, I.I. (1926) *Naselenie Samarkandskoi*, Leningrad.

—— (1975) *Vsesoiuznaia perepis' naselnii 1926 goda*, vol. 15, Moscow: Uzbekskaia SSR.

17 Conclusion: whither Europe?

Karl Cordell

The collection of essays in this volume has hopefully served to highlight a number of issues which are of interest to students of political science from different branches of the discipline, but most of all to those who study the politics of ethnicity. Both the diverse nature of the chapters together with the corresponding diversity of the conclusions drawn illustrate the variety inherent within the field itself. That no collective overall conclusion has been drawn should come as no surprise. This to one side, there are a number of common threads which have been highlighted throughout the narrative, and this concluding piece represents an attempt to focus upon the more pertinent of such threads.

If the contributors have achieved one single thing it is hopefully to drive another nail into the coffin of the notion that ethnicity and race are identical concepts. As Sandra Schmidt points out, there is an overlap in the sense that *volkish* notions of race can be employed in the construction of an ethnically based sense of identity. However, the fact remains that in essence, race is a biological construct, which shares with ethnicity a common heritage of intellectual abuse. As has been demonstrated in this volume, as elsewhere, ethnicity is a social construct, and as such it is fluid and even more amenable to change than is any idea of race. Indeed, ethnicity, as Agneza Bozic among others made clear, signals difference, as opposed to uniformity, that such difference is a normal state of affairs and one which does not automatically lead to conflict.

Rather it is the case that ethnic difference invariably becomes a source of conflict only when other specific factors come into play. In general we can say that ethnic conflict erupts only when a society becomes dysfunctional or enters a state of crisis. As Robert Schaeffer indicates with the example of Czechoslovakia, such dysfunctionality is more often than not spurred by economic dislocation. Even then, there is no inevitability in ethnicity becoming a mobilisational base let alone a cause of fundamental conflict. In order for individuals to adopt a collective badge of ethnicity, there has, among other things, to be an absence of other collective social bonds, such as those based around class. Although by implication this volume has sought to demonstrate why class has become a secondary source of collective action, additional factors conducive to the mobilisation of ethnicity will also have to be present.

Such factors may include a paucity of institutions which are ready and able to defend the status quo. The role of the media may also be of importance in this context especially in terms of how it portrays the nature of any crisis. The media is not however an agency independent of human hand. As the case of Yugoslavia demonstrates, if highly motivated, well-placed groups and individuals are in such a position, they can choose to utilise the media in order to magnify difference and mobilise their chosen audience against supposedly alien elements within society. This of course does not necessarily mean that those who engage in such activities are themselves 'true believers'. Indeed, the examples of Yugoslavia, Czechoslovakia, Russia and Uzbekistan (which is in addition caught between two continents) all illustrate the extent to which naked ambition and sheer opportunism are masked by appeals to 'the people', on the supposition that the ethnic identity and way of life is under threat from 'The Other'.

Given that for better or worse the ethnic genie is out of the bottle, another question that arises is one over the way in which inter-group relations are regulated. As the contributions of Dave Chandler, Martin Kovats and Adam Burgess all illustrate, this is a particularly delicate matter. In theory it is no bad thing to establish an international regime which monitors the conduct of inter-ethnic relations and seeks to ensure that acts of discrimination are not executed with impunity. However, the existence of such a regime immediately poses a number of questions. These revolve around such matters as just who exactly is responsible for establishing a set of standards? How are such standards to be guaranteed? Should such standards be applied equally to all countries in all cases? Lastly, there is the thorny issue of rational self-interest. Despite protestations to the contrary, it would be somewhat naive to believe that states act out of anything other than rational self-interest, even if that interest seems at times to be rather obscure. There is then inevitably the issue of the extent to which an issue may be raised in order to manipulate a situation towards a desired end. In addition, Chris Gilligan makes the point that the elevation of collective rights (based around the idea of ethnicity) may actually serve to fracture society and impinge upon the exercise of individual civil liberties.

With regard to the arena of inter-state relations, as Martin Kovats makes clear, the attitude of the Hungarian government towards the Roma of Hungary is in part governed by foreign policy considerations. Hungary is seen as being something of a role model in the area, but domestic minority rights legislation has been devised from a mix of motives. That is not to deny that successive post-communist governments in Hungary have not been concerned about the plight of the Roma. However, it is beyond question that Hungary aspires not only to membership of the European Union and NATO, but also that it keeps a weather eye on the fate of the Hungarian diaspora. In effect Hungary sets an example, quite obviously in the hope that its neighbours emulate it in order that the Hungarian diaspora is better protected.

The case of Hungary, together with that of the Slovene minority in Austria, illustrates the age-old problem of the implementation gap. Legislation on its own, no matter how well intended and drafted, is never enough. Put simply, governments have to prioritise the allocation of finite resources. It may well be the case that a government simply does not necessarily possess either the political or economic capital to implement (minority rights) legislation. Indeed, it could be argued that on occasion, given the scarcity of resources at the disposal of some states, it would be better not to pass such legislation and create unrealisable aspirations on the part of minorities. Poland presents an interesting case in point, whereby the German minority all too often cries foul when either the German or the Polish government fails to deliver on promises.

We have also seen how in newly democratised countries the issue of what form the state should take also arises. The question of territorial-political organisation is an obvious one within this context. As Hugh Miall warns, we should not assume that what is good for Western Europe, is necessarily good for the eastern part of the continent. Sasha Ossipov's piece on Russia illustrates how old ways of thinking do not disappear as quickly as the regimes which spawned them, and how in some states solution to the issue of accommodation is badly defined and lacking in an overall strategy. The example of Spain on the other hand, illustrates that the Russian case is by no means universal. Spain, was the first multi-ethnic state in post-1945 Europe to complete the transition from dictatorship to democracy. The skill with which a potentially deadly situation was dealt with shows that the process of democratisation can proceed alongside the recognition of diversity, that existing nation-states need not collapse under such pressures, and that they may even emerge enhanced.

In Europe, as we move into a new millennium the nation-state as conceived in the wake of the French Revolution is facing ever greater challenges. In essence it is faced with the age-old problem of adapt or die. As Philip Payton indicates, thirty years ago the issues with which this volume concerns itself were deemed (in Western Europe at least) to have been solved through the creation of the modern welfare state and the standardisation of language and culture of which Britain was the prime example. The experience of Britain in particular since the late 1960s gives the lie to such wishful thinking. Indeed all the chapters have either implicitly or explicitly acknowledged that we are now faced with the countervailing pressures of globalisation, demands for an ever-closer political union in Europe and pressure from below to reconstruct both nation and state.

As these phenomena work their way through the political system so the meaning of the word nation will change yet again. Countries such as Germany will eventually have to make decisions on how to include 'immigrants' who were overwhelmingly born in Germany itself within society as citizens. What may be novel for Germany in this context simply serves to re-enforce the point made by Jeff Richards early on in the volume that the meaning and application of the word nation has changed constantly for over two millennia, as indeed have the nature and meaning of the word democracy and the nature of the *demos* itself. In the light of the above observations, it is to be hoped that this volume has made a positive contribution to the contemporary debate on the issues it has sought to address.

Index